FINDING
GRANDDAD'S
WAR

FINDING
GRANDDAD'S

Jeffrey Badger

WAR

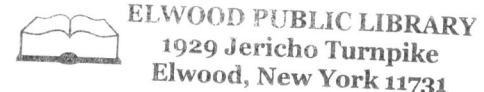

❧ancestrypublishing

Library of Congress Cataloging-in-Publication Data

Badger, Jeffrey A.
 Finding granddad's war / Jeffrey A. Badger.
     p. cm.
 Includes bibliographical references.
 ISBN 978-1-59331-321-0
 1. United States. Army. Engineer Maintenance Company, 978th. 2. World War,
1939–1945—Regimental histories—United States. 3. World War, 1939–1945—Personal
narratives, American. 4. World War, 1939–1945—Europe, Western. 5. History—
Research. 6. Kavanaugh, Leo, 1919–1970. I. Title.

 D769.335978th .B33 2008
 940.54'1273092—dc22
 [B]
                                        2008026469

Published by
Ancestry Publishing, a division of
The Generations Network, Inc.
360 West 4800 North
Provo, UT 84604

First printing 2008
Printed in the United States of America

10 9 8 7 6 5 4 3 2 1

DEDICATION

DEDICATED TO MY GRANDFATHER, who wasn't around to tell me about it personally, and to all the men of the 978th who opened up to me about this important time in their lives. As they leave us, may their stories and their priceless contribution to our world never be forgotten.

CONTENTS

PART TWO

FOREWORD

MOST MILITARY HISTORIES CONCENTRATE ON the big picture—such-and-such army, division, regiment, or battalion went here, did this, moved on to the next battle, etc. Jeff Badger's *Finding Granddad's War* does something different, something special, that makes it stand out and keeps it from being just another rehash of history.

Finding Granddad's War is a very personal account of the Second World War centered around one soldier—Leo Kavanaugh—one of over 14,000 cogs in the very large wheel that was the Ninth Army—and the efforts of that deceased soldier's grandson to piece together his ancestor's past in an effort to better know the man behind the photos in the family album.

So intrigued did Jeff Badger become with the grandfather he never knew (Leo Kavanaugh died when Jeff was only two months old) that he devoted many years to researching his grandfather's personal history, the history of the unit to which he was assigned, interviewing his old buddies, and even visiting the towns and villages of France, the Netherlands and Germany through which his grandfather's unit passed. Much of this book is about Jeff Badger's search—a fascinating tale in itself.

Make no mistake—the Ninth was a genuine combat outfit, filled with young men caught up in a war not of their making but who were willing to fight for their country and, if the fates were willing, live long enough to restore the world to a state of peace. Leo Kavanaugh's unit within the Ninth—the 978th Engineer Maintenance Company—was not what one might call a front-line combat outfit, but it nevertheless was always close to the front lines and saw its share of what war does to people, equipment and countries. You might say that Leo Kavanaugh and his buddies had a ringside seat for the war going on all around them—and occasionally had to get into the ring itself.

You come away from this book with the feeling that you, like the author, know the men of Leo Kavanaugh's unit. They become flesh and blood, as real as your own family members. You also come away feeling like you know a little more about war—the mundane, the sometimes humorous details that make up the bulk of what military service is all about, as well as the frightening, blood-chilling moments. Finally, you come away with a sense of reverence and awe—that you have been made privy to the past and have gotten to know some of the magnificent men who were part of what Tom Brokaw labeled "The Greatest Generation."

Told in direct, guileless, poignant prose, *Finding Granddad's War* is a remarkable document of men's odyssey through a world at war—and a loving grandson's untiring efforts to follow in the footsteps of that odyssey.

And, if Leo Kavanaugh were alive to read his grandson's tribute to him, he would no doubt be a little embarrassed at the attention being lavished upon him and his buddies. Chances are good, however, that he would no doubt tousle his grandson's hair, blink back a tear, and say, "Nice work, kid."

Flint Whitlock
Author of *The Fighting First*
November 2006

PREFACE

MY GRANDFATHER, LEO KAVANAUGH, a World War II veteran, died in 1970, at 51, two months after I was born. When I was twenty-seven years old, I decided to search the Internet for information about his military unit, the 978th Engineer Maintenance Company. I quickly found a person who sent me a brief history of the unit, written shortly after the war, that included a roster of the 377 men who had served in it. Motivated by my newly acquired information, I started trying to track down anybody who had served in the 978th and perhaps somebody who had known my grandfather, all the while wondering if any of those men were still alive.

Many, indeed, were still alive, and I found several of them. In fact, I located thirty-two men from my grandfather's company (see Table 1), including my grandfather's four best buddies. Flattered by my interest, these men confided in me, shared their experiences, and sent me hundreds of original photos taken during the war in England, France, Belgium, Holland, Germany, the Philippines, and Japan; a few even sent souvenir guns and swords. I corresponded with some of these men by letters, while others I e-mailed, talked to on the telephone, or visited in their homes. Most of them had never talked about the war to anyone. But now, in the twilight of their lives, they opened up to me in a way I never could have imagined—and told me their stories. In many cases their recollections dredged up painful memories that, although repressed, were always near the surface. Many broke down and cried during our conversations. Sometimes this was cathartic. Sometimes it was not—it just opened up old wounds. But whatever their reaction, they almost always insisted on continuing.

Built on those early successes, my search expanded and eventually took me to Europe, where I traveled to the places the 978th had passed through and tracked down people who had befriended my grandfather's buddies during the war. Visiting the places that were important in the history of the 978th gave me an appreciation of both scale and detail that I could not otherwise have realized. What's more, the people of France,

Table 1:   Veterans and veterans' family members with whom I corresponded. Dates of birth and death given when known; residences at the time I was in contact with them.

1.	Linwood B. Anderson (b. 1920)	Richmond, Virginia	Letters
2.	Sylvester S. Augustynek	Calumet City, Illinois	Phone
3.	James L. Bjorgen	Seabeck, Washington	Letters
4.	Maxwell Burford	Russell, Pennsylvania	Phone
5.	Austin Jack Cable	Mount Dora, Florida	Letters
6.	Merlin Clark (1914–2006)	San Jacinto, Texas	Letters, phone, one visit in 2001
7.	Herschel E. Clawson (b. 1925)	Clariton, Pennsylvania	Letters, phone.
8.	Howard E. Cushing	Wilmington, Delaware	Letters
9.	Farran V. Helmick	Lake Havasu, Arizona	Letters, phone, e-mail
10.	Joseph H. Humphrey	Waco, Texas	Deceased; letter from wife
11.	Stephen F. Kalman	Levittown, New York	Letters
12.	Elmer J. Kulback (1919–2005)	Carnegie, Pennsylvania	Phone
13.	Chester J. Lesneski (b. 1915)	Deerfield, Massachusetts	Letters
14.	Shearl Lomax	Washington State	Brief phone conversation in early 2008
15.	Marvin Mangham (b. 1923)	Waco, Texas	Letter, two visits in 1999 and 2007
16.	Donald G. Mazzera (b. 1923)	San Mateo, California	Phone, e-mail via daughter
17.	Lewis P. McLarty (b. 1922)	Sergeant Bluff, Iowa	Letter
18.	Francis Mulderrig. (b. 1922)	Ocean City, New Jersey	Phone
19.	William Musiker (1915–2005)	Deerfield Beach, Florida	Letters, phone, e-mail
20.	Warren K. Neaderhiser		Deceased, corresponded with daughter via e-mail
21.	Elroy E. Nowitzke	Ft. Lauderdale, Florida	Letters
22.	Thomas Orton (1922-2005)	Chicago, Illinois	Phone, four visits from 2001 to 2004
23.	Leo Packer (b. 1920)	Cambridge, Massachusetts	Letters, phone, e-mail, two visits in 2004 and 2006
24.	William P. Pappan	Norman, Oklahoma	Letters, phone
25.	Carlyle H. Parsons	North Liberty, Iowa	Letters, phone
26.	John Powasnik (b. 1915)	Bayonne, New Jersey	Letters, phone, two visits in 1999 and 2002
27.	George Patrias (1918–2004)	Detroit, Michigan	Phone, one visit in 2004
28.	Francis V. Recktenwald	Seattle, Washington	Letters
29.	Clifford E. Siebold (b. 1919)	Cleveland, Ohio	Letters
30.	Russell J. Thayer (b. 1921)	Fort Meyers, Florida	Letters
31.	Max Voron (b. 1923)	Philadelphia, Pennsylvania	Letters, phone, one visit in 2000
32.	Charles Wojcik (1918–2003)	Montello, Wisconsin	One visit in 2001
33.	Edward M. Zewicke (b. 1924)	Dearborn, Michigan	E-mail via daughter

Holland, and Germany who were part of the story of the 978th provided fascinating information from perspectives that were very different from those of the ex-GIs.

A few years into my search, while bored at work one afternoon, I designed and put on the Internet a Web page describing my quest and the men I had met. Over the next few weeks search engines found my page and it started to receive visitors. The "counter" on my site quickly exceeded its ten-thousand-visitor limit. I received hundreds of e-mails from people who wanted to hear more about my search and how they could find information about their own family members' service during WWII, Korea, or Vietnam. Numerous newspapers, magazines, and Internet sites in the U.S. and Europe did stories on my search. Many people even suggested that I should write a book about my quest, and, after thinking about the idea for a year or so, I decided to do just that.

This book chronicles my journey to learn not just about my grandfather, Leo Kavanaugh, and his experiences during WWII but also the type of work the 978th did, the places my grandfather and his unit served, the now-elderly GIs who shared this journey with him, and the other people and places I encountered in my ever-expanding quest to reconstruct two years of my grandfather's life.

Most of my information about my grandfather's life as a soldier came directly from the men who served with him. Several of my "war buddies," as I came to refer to them, or "sources," as historians call them, knew my grandfather—some well, some less so. Others did not know him at all, but provided valuable information about the 978th. Individually, their stories are a mishmash of recollections and feelings tempered by time and were nothing like accounts I had read in popular histories, seen in movies, or come to expect from soldiers. They offered few tales of harrowing battles or superhuman bravery. Rather, theirs were stories of the everyday life of young men, many still teenagers, in a war zone trying to do their jobs—as well as have some fun, find some liquor, and pick up girls—all while trying not to get killed. Some of their stories were painful and gut-wrenching—getting strafed by German airplanes; repairing damaged equipment under enemy fire; witnessing the death of a best friend; and, for a Jewish GI, coping with anti-Semitism, not from the Germans but from his fellow GIs. Other stories told of humor and mischief—tales of bank robberies and drinking runs, visits to brothels, and drunken barroom brawls. Taken as a whole, all of the information provided by my sources contributed to the development of a sense of the time, the places, and the events—the mundane and spectacular, the memorable and not—that unified their experiences as soldiers in the 978th.

In my interviews, I could never predict how the men might behave or react. One GI might break down crying; the next would say that he "had a good time" and that the war was "the great adventure" of his life. But even the men who broke into tears went on, wanting finally to make peace with the war and to tell their stories before they passed into history. Without exception, the war was still very much alive in every one of these men.

In writing this book I've focused mostly on first-person accounts and have let the GIs tell their stories in their own words. Since the original goal of my interviews was to satisfy personal curiosity rather than to meet some academic or historical objective, my approach was informal, flexible, and variable. I did not approach my subjects as a historian or a social scientist, but rather as a curious individual with a passionate interest in learning more about his grandfather's experiences in WWII. I did not have a predetermined agenda or rigid methodology. Instead, I sought information as effort, opportunity, and circumstance allowed. Generally, I gave my sources considerable freedom to tell me what they thought was important. As I developed closer relationships with some of the men, however, I pursued some issues—including those that were more sensitive—more systematically.

My interviews raised a number of additional questions of broader scope. How could two GIs recount the same event in such different ways? Why did the war leave such permanent scars on some men, while others appeared to be able to forget about the experience, and some even seemed nostalgic about it? Why are so many young people, particularly young men, so obsessed with WWII or war in general? What is the collective American memory of WWII, and how closely does it reflect reality? What does it really mean to call the WWII veterans "The Greatest Generation," and what do younger generations need to learn from these passing veterans before they are all gone?

Finding Granddad's War is divided into two sections. The first is the story of my quest for information on my grandfather and his unit; the second gives suggestions to help others conduct their own search, offering some

Figure 1. William Musiker (left), Valkenburg, the Netherlands. Musiker, at age eighty-two, sent me about two hundred original photos from the war. He wrote, "You can keep them. When I die they'll just get thrown out." (Photo courtesy of William Musiker)

straightforward instructions on how to use the Internet to locate information about a family member's war story, along with a few case studies of people who have done just that.

Discovering a loved-one's war story and history is fascinating and rewarding. You do not have to go to the lengths to which I have gone to get meaningful and satisfying results. Simply tracking down the unit history of your father's company or finding out the details of the action that resulted in your great-uncle's death in Vietnam can be a rewarding experience. Taking the time to learn more about a loved-one's time in war is enlightening, pays tribute to his or her sacrifice, and shows respect for the great contributions made by these legions of ordinary men and women who have served in our armed forces.

ACKNOWLEDGMENTS

FIRST AND FOREMOST, I'D LIKE to thank all of my "war buddies" for making this book and project possible. They opened up their hearts to me and I will always be grateful.

I would also like to thank all the people in France, the Netherlands, and Germany who told me their stories, contributed to my project, or just assisted me in some way: Louis Palmen in Heerlen; Leon in Spek; Francis, Maryvonne, and Sophie Renard in Bricquebec; Sjef and Maria (Merx) Mommertz, and the Walters sisters in Spekholzerheide; Pierre Schlangen in Limburg; the Meisenburgs, Albert Esten, Toni Andre, and Ingo and Frank Schönhold in Mariadorf; the van Zandvoort family in Simpelveld; John Borghouts in Landgraaf; Michel Laurent in La Belle Etoile; and Uwe Bergheimer in Gedern.

I'm also grateful to everybody who cheered me and kept me going during the long years of researching and writing this book. Sometimes it was a word of encouragement, sometimes it was just showing an interest and expressing enthusiasm in my project. The Badger family in Texas; Eric and Aileen Constans in Pitman; Erica Runyon in Morristown; Mara Ceirule in Riga; Anton and Ingrid Van Weert in Alphen aan den Rijn; Genevieve Cron in Paris; Tracy (Sawyers) Mazloum in Uvalde; Doreen in Morristown; Karin Lundgren and Henrik Zuback in Halmstad; Linda in Heerlen; Tuija Tiittanen in Dublin; Virginia Walker in Austin; Theresia (Tessie) Rensen-Brouns and family in California and Spekholzerheide; Thea Dropuljic-Hermans in Kerkrade; Erwin van de Wiel in the Netherlands; Louis Palmen in Limburg; Rosemary and Emmanuel Benard in Belfast; John Paul Attwood in Imatra; Conor MacCormack in Ardee; Theron Snell in Racine; John Roberts in Chicago; Angelo Germidis in Paris; Lizzy Wilkes in Mansfield; Barry Eggleston in Dallas; Brian Kueker in Dallas; Pete Ward in Sheffield; Jan Tiberg in Söderfors; Chris Andlauer in Paris; Julia Collins in Somerville; Stacy Ware in Ohio; Susan Griffith in Austin; James Megellas in Colleyville; and Flint Whitlock, Kurt Stauffer, and Dana Michel. Also, Dr.

Jerry McDonald for his valuable contributions in editing and Frank Towers, president and historian of the 30th Infantry Division Veterans of WWII. And all the other people with whom encounters were brief, but whose encouragement and interest kept me going: Rose-marie in Paris; Marc Van Rompay in Arromanches; Beatrice in Paris; the waitress at the Italian restaurant in Greenwich Village; the guy at the Lion Hotel in Worksop. I would like to thank my editor, Paul Rawlins. Finally, I would like to thank Mr. Chaney for teaching me the "rudiments of writing."

PART ONE

Figure 2. Leo Kavanaugh and his daughter Judith, my mother.

Jeff, you ask about your grandfather's time during the war. Well, I don't really know much. My dad didn't talk much about the war, and when he did he sometimes got choked up. So I just don't know a lot about it. He talked about Ski, his best friend, who I guess got his nickname because of his Polish background. And there was another guy from Detroit and a guy from Chicago. But I have no idea who they were. He mentioned the looting and the raping, by both the Americans and the Germans. He sometimes talked about "the bodies in the water," how the water was red from the blood of the soldiers. But I was too young to appreciate these things and ask him more questions. And then he died, so young and unexpectedly. And it was too late.

My mom, Judith Kavanaugh Badger,
speaking about her father, Leo Kavanaugh

PLANTING THE SEED

DURING MY CHILDHOOD, MY MOM told me and my two older brothers wonderful stories about her dad, a tough, no-nonsense guy with a gentle nature and a big heart. Through these stories, he became something of a hero to me. My mom told us:

> He was a prince of a guy. Big and handsome. He was tough, didn't take any guff off of anybody. But he was the gentlest father in the world. When my little sisters would cry in the middle of the night, he was the one who would wake up and change their diapers. Then he'd wake up at five o'clock in the morning to go drive the crane in downtown Chicago, in the bitter cold. I used to wake up and have coffee with him. And I hated coffee, so I had to put gobs of milk and sugar in it just to tolerate it. But this was my time with my dad. He was always interested in what I was doing with my friends and activities. I still miss him.

My mom talked about her dad often, and it was obvious she missed him. I imagined a tall, emotionally strong, no-nonsense, straight-talking guy who was also a soft-hearted father, and would have been a soft-hearted grandfather. My mom said we would have gotten along great, and I felt cheated that I never got to know him.

Leo Kavanaugh was born on the south side of Chicago in 1919. During the Depression, he was forced to drop out of high school to help support his family. Later, he married my grandmother and they had a baby girl, my mother. During World War II, he was drafted into the Army and sent overseas. He survived the war and returned home to have two more daughters. He worked in the construction business in Chicago as a heavy-equipment operator until 1970, when he died suddenly of a stroke. I was two months old.

The old black-and-white photos he brought home from the war, taken of him in his uniform in Europe in 1944 and 1945, only added to his mystique. They were stored with hundreds of other old family photos in a cardboard box in the closet. As a child, these wartime photos—pictures of a tall, handsome, confident-looking soldier in his uniform, taken in what were to me exotic, far-away lands—made a strong impression on me. I would stare at them for hours, absorbing every detail and wondering all sorts of things. What were these GIs thinking? What had they seen? Where did they fight?

One photo in particular stuck in my mind throughout my childhood. It was a yellowing picture of my grandfather and another GI walking self-assuredly down a city street in France, looking as if they knew where they were going and were hustling to get there. I used to think that if I could stare

Figure 3. Leo Kavanaugh and "Ski."

at that photo hard enough, they would turn to me and speak, telling me where they were off to and why they seemed to be in such a hurry. The caption on the back read "Ski & I with Mac & Davis in background. Marseille, France." According to my mom's memories, Ski was my grandfather's best friend during the war, and he got his nickname because of his Polish origins. Other than that, she did not know much about him. I found myself especially wanting to know, Who was Ski?

———

In addition to the photos, the box also contained a small serviceman's notebook. In the back was a list of names, each with an amount in dollars or francs next to it: Powasnik — $1, Silverman — $10, Voron — $10, Orton — $10, Wojcik — $4, Ski — 25 Francs, etc. Having heard about my grandfather's fondness for gambling, I figured this was some sort of debtors list from a card game. I wanted to know, Who were these guys?

I had so many questions. But there were no answers to be had.

My grandfather was dead.

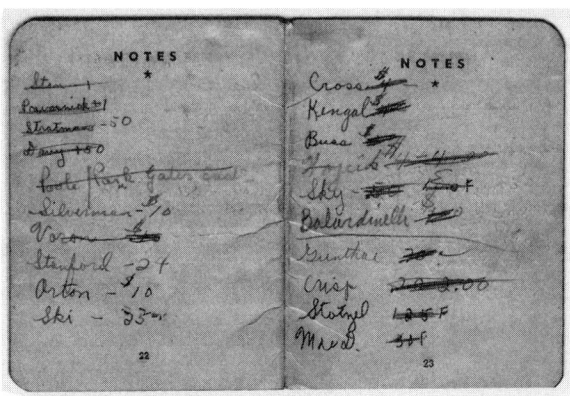

Figure 4. Page in my grandfather's notebook.

A HISTORY
OF THE 978TH

I STARTED MY SEARCH FOR MY grandfather's war in 1998 when I was twenty-seven years old and attending Trinity College in Dublin, Ireland, where I was working on a Ph.D. in mechanical engineering. I had recently read several books on World War I, and that had started me wondering about my grandfather's service in World War II. My mom told me that the name of his unit was inscribed on his tombstone in Chicago, so I e-mailed my aunt, who lives close to the cemetery where he is buried, and asked if she would send me a copy of the inscription. She sent what I assumed was what I needed: 978TH ENG MAINT CO — WWII.

Unsure of what the cryptic nomenclature meant, I posted a query on a veterans site on the Internet. The next day I received an e-mail from someone who directed me to another site. One thing led to another, and I soon found Theron Snell, whose father had served in the unit, the 978th

Figure 5. Leo Kavanaugh in Nice, France.

Engineer Maintenance Company. In the late 1970s and early 1980s, Theron, who now works as an academic counselor at the University of Wisconsin at Parkside and teaches a course in international studies, had interviewed and corresponded with many of the men from the 978th. He later used these interviews as the basis for his Ph.D. dissertation, "Orphans in the Storm: A Collective Experience of War. The 978th Engineer Maintenance Company in World War II."

During the next few weeks, Theron provided me with much information about the 978th. The unit's role in the war had been to maintain and repair equipment—jeeps, trucks, tanks, artillery, tractors, motors, weapons, and so on—and to machine spare parts for this equipment. The war had taken them to Wales, England, France, Belgium, the Netherlands, Germany, the Philippines, and Japan. In 1946, when the unit was in Japan, one of the company officers, 1st Lieutenant Leo Pecker, had written a forty-page history of the unit titled *The Long Way Home*. Theron kindly sent me a copy. The opening paragraph reads:

> This is the story of an engineer maintenance company. It does not tell of exceptional bravery or superhuman self-sacrifice, yet the story has a claim to existence. It is intended as a tribute to the men of the 978th Engineer Maintenance Company, wherever they may be, for their ability to do a skilled, resourceful job under the hazards and pressure of modern war. In another sense, the story outlines the little known achievements of this independent type of combat zone service unit.

From Theron's e-mails and Pecker's history, I was able to put together a picture of the unit's activities during the war.

————

The 978th came into existence on November 5, 1943, at Camp McCoy, Wisconsin. The initial cadre of men consisted of 1 officer and 10 enlisted men who came from the 472nd Engineer Maintenance Company, which was stationed in Iceland. During the next few months men were brought in from all across the U.S. Many were transferred from other units. Forty-eight were brought in from tank divisions, while 144 were ex-antiaircraft artillerymen shipped in from California. The rest came from other units or were recent draftees, some of whom had prior experience in machinery and repair. The

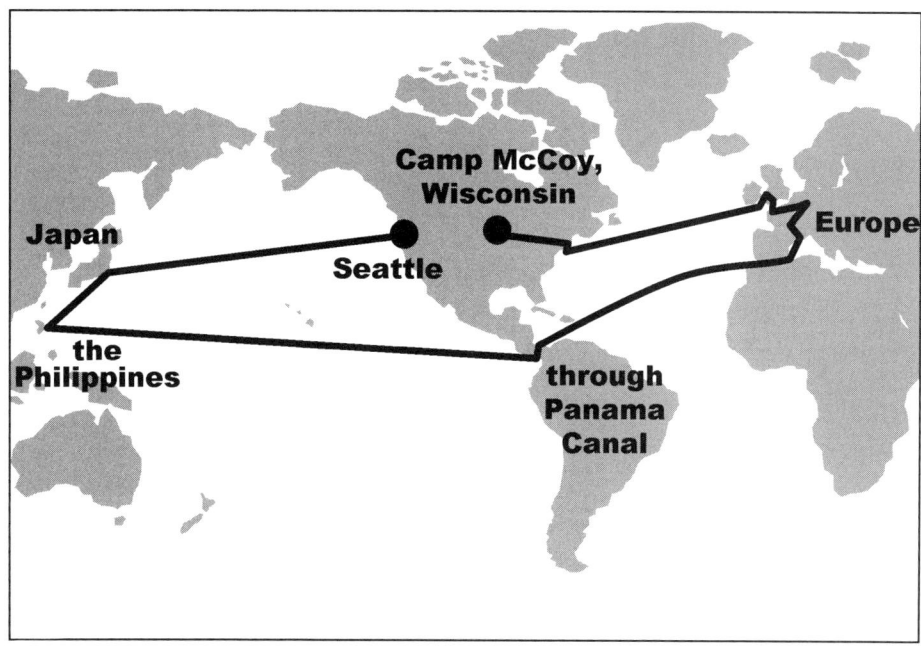

Figure 6. Map of the 978th's travels.

unit reached full strength with 189 men and 6 officers and was organized into a headquarters platoon, a contact platoon, and two maintenance platoons, each with about 44 men.

The 978th received its training at Camp McCoy, Wisconsin, in the bitter winter of 1943–44, "brisk, cold and clear, ideal for basic engineer training," according to Pecker. "The job consisted of transforming a machine gunner into a welder, a platoon sergeant into a shop foreman, and a basic soldier into a tractor mechanic." The men received instruction in automotive repair, welding, mechanics, and other skills, along with training in weapons, combat principles, demolitions, map reading, and military protocol.

My grandfather's discharge papers say he entered the service on March 2, 1944, and list his civilian occupation as "operating engineering" and his military occupation as "construction equipment mech 319."

On August 11, 1944, the 978th traveled by train to Camp Myles Standish, in Massachusetts. Five days later they boarded the SS *Margarita* in Boston. They sailed to New York Harbor and dropped anchor in the lower bay, off Brooklyn, where the men could see Coney Island, the Statue

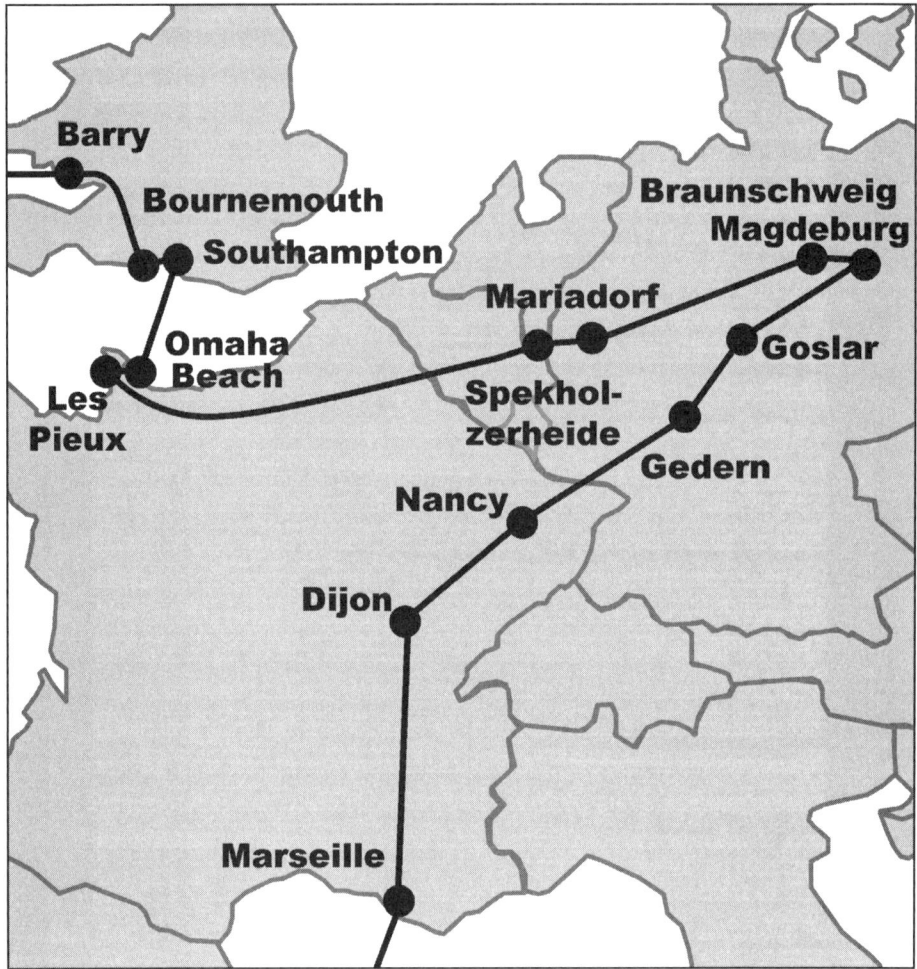

Figure 7. Map of the 978th's travels in Europe.

of Liberty, and the skyscrapers of lower Manhattan—quite an experience, according to Pecker, considering that many of the men had never ventured far from their hometowns. Here the unit joined its assigned convoy and, on August 19, began the two-week trip across the Atlantic.[1] The *Margarita* docked in Barry, Wales, and the men traveled by train to Bournemouth, England, where they spent several weeks.[2]

On September 29, after waiting on the dock for seventeen hours, the 978th boarded the SS *Omar E. Chapman* and sailed to Omaha Beach on the coast of France, three and a half months after the initial Allied landings on D-Day. They set up camp in a field near the town of Les Pieux, on the northwest side of the Normandy Peninsula, and spent a month there.[3] Pecker commented that the undernourished children, deprived conditions, shattered houses, burnt-out vehicles and tanks, and disordered appearance of the countryside made a strong impression on the men. Although the 978th would later encounter far worse devastation in the Netherlands and Germany, Pecker wrote that the strongest impression was still the first one.

On November 3, the 978th left Les Pieux and traveled in convoy through France and Belgium to Spekholzerheide, the Netherlands, a journey of five hundred miles. The trip took three days, an "ambitious undertaking" according to Pecker, as the convoy consisted of many slow and heavy vehicles that had to travel on secondary roads since the primary roads were reserved for the Red Ball Express.[4]

The unit spent three weeks in the coal-mining town of Spekholzerheide. The people of "Spek," who had been liberated from the Germans only weeks earlier, welcomed the Americans warmly. Friendships and romances developed between the GIs and the local people. The Americans also saw the effects of the German occupation on the Dutch people. Pecker wrote:

> The men of the 978th soon witnessed at first hand the effects of German occupation. Coming out of the mess hall to wash mess gear, the men were crushed by a clamoring mob of hungry, under-nourished children carrying little pails and cans begging for the scraps of left over food. After several days, it became a serious problem, because the violence of the desperate kids dismayed the soldiers. Then a system was evolved whereby all the remaining food was put into one container and a volunteer Dutch policeman distributed it to the kids in an orderly manner.

It was also at this time that the 978th, a year after its formation, started doing the work for which it had been created. The 978th, part of the XIXth Corps of Engineers, which was part of the 9th Army, was now attached to the 1104th Engineer Combat Group, a veteran of the Normandy Campaign. Repair crews from the 978th were traveling to the front in Germany to provide maintenance and repair service.

During this time the 29th and 30th Infantry Divisions and the 2nd Armored Division were fighting the Germans near Aachen. The Germans had been pushed back to the Roer River, but were dug in, and a river crossing by the American forces was imminent. On November 29, the 978th was ordered to move closer to the front and prepare to provide support for the crossing of the Roer River. The unit moved to the abandoned ruins of the Mariagrube coal mine, where it remained for almost a month.

The Mariagrube coal mine, adjacent to the town of Mariadorf, was situated in the shadow of a slag pile so large that it could be seen for miles. According the Pecker, this was "the most depressing place the 978th ever occupied." The 978th arrived shortly after a battle between the Germans and the Americans. The Germans had been defeated; the Americans had moved deeper into Germany; and left behind were abandoned supplies of ammunition, minefields, and the dead bodies of German and American soldiers. The 978th was responsible for picking up the bodies of the dead American soldiers that were scattered about one of the minefields, a process that required the men to "painstakingly" probe the minefield with their bayonets, dismantle the mines, clear a path to the bodies of the American soldiers, and retrieve the corpses. Meanwhile, emergency crews were sent day and night to repair equipment damaged by enemy action, mines, or accidents and to evacuate damaged vehicles with tow trucks. In addition, at the mine they repaired equipment that had been brought back from the front.[5] During this time, the men could hear the constant artillery fire at the front and were regularly strafed by German planes.

In late February, the anticipated attack and crossing of the Roer River finally took place. The Germans, who held the dams upstream, released a flood that made the river much wider and swifter than usual. Under German machine-gun, artillery, and mortar fire, the engineers built a total of fifteen foot and pontoon bridges across the racing river for foot soldiers and later tanks and jeeps to cross deeper into Germany. The 978th's role was to repair bridge-building machinery damaged by German fire, either at the bridge site or after evacuating it and taking it behind the front. One bridge was built, destroyed by the Germans, and rebuilt a total of nine times.

On March 1, the 978th crossed the Roer River and moved deeper into Germany, to Wickrath, where they set up their operations in an abandoned leather factory. The first task was to place guards around the plant to keep away scavenging Germans who were "trying to carry away anything they could find." It was also here that the 978th encountered hordes of recently liberated Russian and Polish slave workers used by the Germans. Some were malnourished and were vacated to the rear for medical attention; others were "celebrating their new freedom by looting and beating up their former masters" and "taking over their homes." As a result, the 978th also had to contend with frightened German civilians begging for protection from these Poles and Russians, along with surrendering German soldiers, who became something of a "nuisance."

Other tasks included working with the bomb-disposal unit to dig up and evacuate aircraft bombs that the Germans had buried and booby-trapped before retreating, assembling eight "sea mule" river barges, and overhauling outboard motors that would be used in the upcoming crossing of the Rhine River.

On March 29, the 978th crossed the Rhine River at Wallach. At this point, wrote Pecker, the company began to work under unstable conditions with frequent moves and new jobs. The four platoons and small groups of soldiers were scattered about, and the men often operated independent of any direct command. Following behind the advancing front, the 978th made eight moves in three weeks and never remained in one place more than ten days. The unit usually traveled at night under blackout conditions and quickly moved through Spellen, Gartrop, Asheberg, Verl, Hovelhof, Blomberg, Gronau, Braunschweig, Magdeburg, and Goslar—some of which had been demolished or were still aflame. Pecker wrote, "Drivers were so exhausted that they fell asleep at the wheel of their trucks. When the convoy stopped for a few minutes, in order to proceed it was necessary to wake many drivers who had fallen asleep instantly." Guides who were supposed to direct traffic were absent, road signs were incorrect or nonexistent, and it sometimes took hours to find the assigned bivouac areas. After driving all night, the 978th often arrived at the break of dawn, only to begin work again.

On May 12, four days after V-E Day, the unit left Goslar for Gedern, where it set up camp in an open field. While driving through the woods at night the 978th experienced its only fatality of the entire war. PFC Thomas E. Kulick fell from a truck and sustained a fatal injury. The unit held a memorial service in Gedern in his honor.

Table 2: # THE 978TH'S TRAVELS

	Arrive	Depart
Camp McCoy, Wisconsin		August 11, 1944
Camp Myles Standish, Massachusetts	August 13, 1944	August 16, 1944
Boston Port of Embarkation	August 16, 1944	August 17, 1944
New York Harbor	August 18, 1944	August 19, 1944
Atlantic voyage on SS *Margarita*	August 19, 1944	September 1, 1945
Barry, Wales	September 1, 1944	September 1, 1944
Bournemouth, England	September 2, 1944	September 23, 1944
Marshalling Area C-12, England	September 23, 1944	September 26, 1944
Southampton England	26 September, 1944	September 27, 1944
Channel voyage on SS *Omar E Chapman*		
Omaha Beach, France	September 29, 1944	
Transient Camp 2, Insigny, France		September 30, 1944
Les Pieux, France	September 30, 1944	November 3, 1944
St. Anne, France	November 3, 1944	November 6, 1944
Soissons, France	November 6, 1944	November 7, 1944
Spekholzerheide, the Netherlands	November 7, 1944	November 29, 1944
Mariadorf, Germany	November 29, 1944	December 24, 1944
Walheim, Germany	December 24, 1944	January 25, 1945
Stolberg, Germany	January 25, 1945	February 5, 1945
Mariadorf, Germany	February 5, 1945	March 1, 1945
Crossed Roer River	March 1, 1945	
Wickrath, Germany	March 1, 1945	March 29, 1945
Crossed Rhine River	March 29, 1945, 2:00 p.m.	
Spellen, Germany	March 29, 1945	March 30, 1945
Gartrop, Germany	March 30, 1945	April 1, 1945
Asheberg, Germany	April 1, 1945	April 2, 1945
Verl, Germany	April 2, 1945	April 4, 1945
Hovelhof, Germany	April 4, 1945	April 5, 1945
Blomberg, Germany	April 5, 1945	April 9, 1945
Crossed Weser River at Hameln	April 9, 1945	
Gronau, Germany	April 9, 1945	April 13, 1945
Braunschweig, Germany	April 13, 1945	April 19, 1945
Magdeburg, Germany	April 19, 1945	April 29, 1945
Goslar, Germany	April 29, 1945	May 11, 1945
Gedern, Germany	May 12, 1945	June 7, 1945
Nancy, France	June 7, 1945	June 8, 1945
Dijon, France	June 8, 1945	June 9, 1945
St. Rambert, France	June 9, 1945	June 10, 1945
Calas Staging Area, Marseille, France	June 10, 1945	July 16, 1945
Atlantic Voyage on USS *Admiral Benson*	July 16, 1945	July 27, 1945
Panama Canal	July 27, 1945	July 29, 1945
Pacific Voyage on USS *Admiral Benson*	July 29, 1945	August 20, 1945
San Fernando, Luzon, the Philippines	August 20, 1945	August 20, 1945
Manila, the Philippines	August 21, 1945	October 28, 1945
Voyage on LSM crafts	October 28, 1945	November 7, 1945
Yokohama, Japan	November 7, 1945	January 1946
Voyage across Pacific, arriving in Seattle		different for each GI

Total distance traveled as a unit, from training camp in Wisconsin to Europe, the Philippines, Japan, and Seattle: 29,800 miles.

The 978th spent three weeks fishing, swimming, and boating in Gedern. The war in the Pacific was still raging, but, according the Pecker, few men suspected that the 978th would be one of the units chosen to go directly to the Pacific. The redeployment policy was clarified, however, and engineer maintenance companies were given highest priority for direct transfer to the Pacific Theater. On July 16, 1945, the 978th shipped out on the USS *Admiral Benson*, bound for the Pacific.

The *Admiral Benson* arrived in Manila five weeks later. While the 978th had been en route, the Americans dropped the atomic bombs on Nagasaki and Hiroshima, and the war in the Pacific ended. Nevertheless, the unit spent two months in Manila. According to Pecker, "In that time, not a single piece of equipment was repaired by the unit. No operational mission was ever assigned the outfit. A few men worked on a driving detail down by the docks, but otherwise no work was done aside from housekeeping and routine tasks. The heat and humidity were depressing and discouraging."

Several men were released from the 978th while it was in Manila and went home. The unit dwindled to 109 enlisted men and 4 officers. On October 28, the remaining men boarded flat-bellied amphibious crafts for a ten-day voyage to Japan. Pecker wrote that almost everyone on this journey was seasick at least half the time. The company arrived in Yokohama on November 7 and set up at the Tachikawa airfield. In the weeks that followed, more men went home. The unit was finally deactivated in early 1946. After two years, thirty thousand miles, and eight countries, the men of the 978th returned home to their parents, wives, children, and friends.

---

1. When the convoy was just off the coast of Ireland, the lead boat, a tanker filled with gasoline, exploded and sank. The men on deck of the *Margarita* could see a huge cloud of smoke where the ship had been, with millions of gallons of gasoline still burning. The convoy continued on, uncertain whether the explosion was caused by a torpedo, a mine, or an accident It was later determined that the convoy was attacked by a German U-boat, *U-482*, which was commissioned December 1, 1943, and sank four ships and one warship before being sunk on November 25, 1944, by depth charges from the British frigate HMS *Ascension*. (Source: <uboat.net/boats/ u482.htm>) The tanker that was sunk was the SS *Jacksonville*. According to one Internet source, <www.armed-guard.com/ag2a.html>, of the forty-nine merchant crew and twenty-nine naval armed guards, only two survived.

2. Bournemouth is a resort city on the southern coast of England. The 978th spent three weeks there, billeted at the Royal Exeter Hotel. Some of the men were sent to other parts of England to procure equipment, while others spent their time on the veranda of the hotel. The Royal Exeter Hotel is still a functioning hotel.

3. I later learned that the one-month stay was due to a clerical error, and the only reason they were given orders to leave Les Pieux was because someone became curious and asked the high command why they were still there.

4. The Red Ball Express was the term for the massive convoy system of trucks that supplied the Allied forces in Europe after D-Day. Most drivers in the Red Ball Express were African American. For more information, see <en.wikipedia.org/wiki/Red_Ball_Express>.

5. In early February, when Germany was covered in snow, eleven American tractors and dozers were put out of commission by landmines in just two days. The 978th worked around the clock to repair them and had several back in operation within twenty-four hours and the rest repaired and back in service on an average of two days. This work earned the 978th the Meritorious Service Unit Plaque.

FIRST STEPS

PECKER'S HISTORY, ALTHOUGH INTERESTING AND informative, was official and somewhat impersonal. It described the unit's actions, but it did not comment on the personal feelings and experiences of the men. It was hard to get a feel for the place and time. And there were no names mentioned in the history, perhaps reflecting the nature of a military unit where no one person is considered more important than any other. Did this history accurately reflect what *my grandfather* experienced?

Theron told me in an e-mail that the men he talked to respected Pecker's history in that it gave a fairly complete outline of the unit's record but that it left "out the bad feelings, cold, fear, etc." and did "gloss over most of the daily history and some of the less favorable incidents."

Theron went through his notes and photos and found only one reference to my grandfather. A 978ther, Joseph Dinkelman, had given Theron his address book, and written in it were my grandfather's name and address: "Leo Kavanaugh / 425 W. 74th St. / Chicago, IL." This address was the small apartment complex where my mother lived until she was ten years old. Although this connection was a distant one, it was important to me because it tied the present to my grandfather via one of his buddies from the war. Unfortunately, Theron told me, Dinkelman was dead. Regarding the other men in the unit, he said, "As far as the number of 978thers I know who are still alive … I am not sure anymore. I had contacted quite a few, but a great many of them have died since." It was 1998; the war had been over for fifty-three years.

At the back of Pecker's history was a roster with the names of the 377 men who had served in the company. I looked through the list and wondered if any of these guys might be the men in my grandfather's photos and if any of them were still alive. Most of all, I noticed the Polish names ending in "ski": Lesneski, Nowitzke, Jankowski. Could one of these be my grandfather's close friend Ski?

I asked Theron about addresses for the men, but he said he could not help me. He no longer had many of them, and many men had moved since the 1970s. On top of that, he was not allowed to give out any individual details about the men because of a confidentiality agreement with the university.

My first break came when I found Switchboard.com, a phone directory on the Internet with residential listings for the entire U.S. I entered some of the more unique-sounding names from the roster in Pecker's history. A few matches came up. There was a Max Voron in Pennsylvania, a Thomas Orton in Chicago, and a William Pappan in Oklahoma. Of course, I paid special attention to the Polish-sounding names and found a few matches, including an Elroy Nowitzke in Florida and a Chester Lesneski in Massachusetts. Were these the same guys whose names were in my grandfather's notebook? Would they remember my grandfather? Could one of them be Ski?

For the next few days I could not get the names out of my head. Certainly at least a few of the phone numbers I had found must belong to men who had served in my grandfather's unit. Some of the men in the photos could still be alive, and the possibility of speaking with someone who had served in the same unit as my grandfather—or who actually knew him—was overwhelming. Ski might be just a phone call away.

It was all I could do to keep from calling. But I resisted. More than fifty years had passed since the war. Even if some of the telephone numbers were correct, and if the men were still alive, would they really want to hear from some stranger asking questions about a long-past time that they might rather forget?

A few more days went by, and I mulled the idea over again and again. But I finally conceded that I could not hold back. If I was going to find somebody from my grandfather's unit, it would have to be now. In another fifty years—in another ten years—it would be too late.

I took forty or so of the less common names from the roster and looked them up on Switchboard.com. After an hour's work I had a list of twenty names and addresses. I wrote a letter introducing myself, asking the men if they had served in the 978th, and, if so, could they tell me a little about their time in the unit—memories, anecdotes, anything at all. I also included copies of my grandfather's photos from the war.

Thinking myself half crazy, I dropped the letters in the mail, not expecting much of a response, if any.

And then I waited.

A RESPONSE

A FEW WEEKS WENT BY. I did not receive a single response to my letters. I started to think that the entire venture might have been futile. Finally, after about a month, I received a small envelope with a return address of an Elroy Nowitzke of Florida. I tore into it eagerly.

> Hello Jeffrey:
>
> In as much as you took a lot of time doing research on your grandfather, Leo, I figure you should at least receive a letter in return.[*]
>
> I will say this I AM NOT the 'Ski' he referred to. Even thou I will say this, the photo of him does have a lot of similarity. But I was taller than him and thou I knew of your grandfather, I was in a different "Squad" and didn't get the chance to chum around with him. Then too: I was with many companies and 978th was the last. I was with Special command and was transferred where ever help was needed. I was in England a year before that Big Day "D" Day, and went in D Day with a different outfit, went up thru France and two different companies before getting tied with the 978, and then up thru Battle of the Bulge and then in Germany and then tied up with 978 after the war ended in Europe and then we went down to Mar. France and shipped out thru the Panama Canal to Leyte and then up to Manila and then Up to Japan. I should have gone home, but they decided to keep me going and I shipped out of Japan Dec 24 Christmas Eve for home at last.

---

[*] I have left the spelling and grammar in the correspondence as they were in the originals.

I never smoked cig. Always got my rations and then gave them to someone that smoked cig. I was always a cigar smoker myself, still am. I'll be eighty in June.

I am sorry I can't help you much. I looked thru 1000s of pictures. I thought I had a picture of the tent camp in the Manila area + also on in Japan. Sorry no luck.

Good luck searching.

Elroy Nowitzke

P.S. I am sending the photos back, you might be able to use them. Sorry no "Ski."

I sent a thank-you letter to Nowitzke and asked if he could provide me with any more information. A few weeks later I received another letter with a few more details about the 978th, along with a photo of the 978th when the unit was in Japan.

Figure 8. "Jeff, I found this photo, taken in Japan. Maybe you can find Leo in there." (Photo and caption courtesy of Elroy Nowitzke)

———

After Nowitzke's letter, I received a letter from Max Voron in Philadelphia, and then an e-mail from William Musiker in Florida. Musiker later sent me hundreds of original photos that he took in Europe and the Pacific. "You can keep them," he wrote. "When I die they'll just get thrown out."

This comment was unsettling. Didn't these veterans' family members care about their photos? I treasured them, not only because they were from my grandfather's unit but also because they were a part of history. Were there other bunches of photos that were going to get thrown out when these veterans died? If so, I had to find these guys soon.

And so began my years of correspondence with the men of the 978th. The more I learned about the unit and the experiences of its men, the more I wanted to continue. I wanted to find somebody who might have known my grandfather. And, of course, I wanted to find Ski—if he was still alive.

I was hooked.

WHAT'S WORTH REMEMBERING

I STARTED MY SEARCH WHILE I was in graduate school in Dublin, Ireland. At the end of the workday, we usually went to the local pub for a Guinness. Before heading to the pub, however, I often stayed at the office for another hour or two, collecting more unusual names from the roster of the 978th and searching for their addresses in the Internet telephone book. Once I had found ten or twenty names and addresses that looked promising, I would print a copy of my letter and a set of photographs, stick them in envelopes, and drop them off at the post office on my way to the pub.

The highlight of any day came when I received a response in the mail from a GI . Typically, he would write a few paragraphs about his experiences while in the 978th, and the letter often included photographs of the unit in Europe or the Pacific. At first I did not share my project with my friends. But when I read a letter or looked at some old black-and-white photographs in the pub, they could not help but notice and ask what I was doing. Their reactions were interesting. Some just didn't get it and looked at me like I was crazy. Others found it fascinating and couldn't hear enough about it.

The GIs I contacted varied in their interest in communicating with me as well. Francis V. Recktenwald, age eighty-eight and living in Seattle, Washington, sent a very short reply to my letter. He gave only a few details about the 978th and its responsibilities, and closed with an apology.

Jeff, I know you would like to hear more than I have written, but what is, to me, such a waste, and my memories are of destroyed buildings, dead men and people hoping to survive. Good luck in your search.

I interpreted Recktenwald's letter the same way I would come to interpret letters from other GIs who sent similar short, polite replies—he appreciated my interest and felt I merited a response, but believed that he did not have much to say or, more likely, simply preferred not to get into it. I sent him a thank-you letter but did not expect to hear from him again. A few weeks later, however, he wrote again:

I am going to try and tell you two events which, to me, mean something.

The 978th had a company blacksmith who was a burly fellow named Sgt. Elmer Lickey. At one place we bivouacked near a minefield and Lickey decided he wanted to test his courage and cross it. This meant taking his bayonet and probing each footstep. In making the crossing, he encountered two US corpses. He later notified "Graves Registration." He was then ordered to lead a squad into the minefield to retrieve the bodies.

At another time we were in a town whose name I believe is Wickrath [Germany]. We had just been served chow, outdoors, and I was sitting on a bulkhead considering the meal when a very mangy looking dog approached me with a forlorn look. I looked at him and looked at my mess kit, thinking to myself, he needs this more than I do, and gave him my dinner. We were sleeping in an empty building. The Germans use latches on the doors instead of knobs. We had settled down to fix our beds and I happened to look at the door and saw the latch handle move. The door opened and in came the mangy dog. He became a part of the company from then on. It turned out he was not much more than a pup, but very bright. He had regular meals from our mess and became healthy and active. There were several times when it seemed he understood what we were telling him. Eventually we wound up in Marseilles and some of us were designated to go to the Philippines. As I went up the gangplank he followed me and reached the top where he was stopped. I had arranged with my best friend, Gordon Mathews, who was staying behind, to try and take care of the dog. He wrote me later that the dog disappeared and was not seen again.

I am enclosing the negative of the photograph. The dog, I named Mutt, is with me and my buddy, Gordon Mathews is on my left. You may keep the negative. The equipment is a mobile crane under repair by the 1st and 2nd platoon.

—Have Fun

—Francis V. Recktenwald

I sent Recktenwald a second thank-you note, along with a few more questions, but I never heard back from him. Perhaps his other memories were too painful to share. Perhaps his friendship with Mutt the dog was one of his few positive experiences in the war.

Figure 9. Gordon Mathews (left), Francis Recktenwald, and Mutt the dog (fate unknown).
(Photo courtesy of Francis Recktenwald)

Figure 10. Another photo of Mutt the dog (fate still unknown).
(Photo courtesy of Herschel Clawson)

Three years after I received the photo of Mutt from Recktenwald, Herschel Clawson of Clairton, Pennsylvania, sent me about fifty photographs. Among them was one that appeared to be of the same dog. Scribbled on the back of the photo was the word "Mutt." Eager for information on Mutt's fate, I phoned Mr. Clawson. He said:

> Well, my memory's not too good. But wasn't that in Germany? I don't remember any Recktenwald and I only vaguely remember the dog. The German soldiers, they were cooking their dogs for food. But us, we just kept him as a pet. He was a mutt, but I don't remember his name.

MAX VORON

I THEN RECEIVED A LETTER from Max Voron, seventy-seven, of Phildelphia, a GI whose name was on the gambling debtor's list in my grandfather's notebook. He wrote:

> Dear Jeffrey, I was both amazed and delighted to receive your letter. I was in the 978th, unfortunately, your grandfather's name is not one that I recognize … I do remember Spekholzerheide and having my laundry done by Hube and Tilla (surnames forgotten) in exchange for rations that I shared … Although I didn't know your grandfather, if you would be interested in continuing to correspond, I would be happy to do so.

Voron proved true to his word, and we exchanged several letters and spoke on the telephone. During a phone conversation, he explained how he ended up in the unit:

> Before I entered the service, I worked for Ford. We were assembling 1941 and 1942 Fords. I was in charge of 17 men. Then we switched over to tanks and jeeps. When I entered the service, I was put in an engineering unit because I had some technical competence.
>
> I was what you call a parts foreman. I was in charge of 18 men and 8 trucks. And we were there to service the front line with ordnance. We had spare parts and a full machine shop in our trucks: lathes, drill press, milling machine, grinders. We were always a couple of miles from the front, and the contact platoon would go out and retrieve equipment—generators, guns, cranes from the bridge sites, tanks, anything. They'd bring it back and we'd fix it. We had a truck full of spare parts. We also had a big stock of cold-rolled steel, so what we didn't have we'd make up in the machine shop.

An excerpt from one letter reads as follows:

> My best buddy was John "Mac" McElroy. The last I heard was that he had a high position in his church. (I don't know what denomination.) A top-quality human being. He and I were trapped in an ammunition dump amid exploding small arms. Another experience with "Mac" was at the Roer River, an attack by retreating Germans from across the river. We both sought shelter behind a 2½-ton truck. Mac joked about how nice a pastrami sandwich and a kosher pickle would be.
>
> On a personal note, I'm married 54 years to the same wonderful woman, have 2 children, son, daughter, 4 grandchildren, 3 boys and a girl—I retired 6 weeks ago after operating my own food market and then working for Bloomingdale's Dept. store for 17 yrs.

After a while, our correspondence became more serious. An excerpt from another letter reads:

> Jeff, I think I've covered all the "pleasant" parts of my stint in the service (I did go to the Univ. of Arkansas under the Army specialized training program). Other than this, Jeff, I'm afraid my memories of the service were not entirely pleasant. You see, I'm Jewish. Yes, I had some good buddies, but there were quite a few whose practice of anti-Semitism was relentless and painful. Some good buddies were, of course, "Mac" McElroy, Howard Cushing in the flower business in Newcastle, DE. Others hard to forget in a different way. In that vein the name Cooper[1] comes to mind.
>
> Another bitter memory of the Roer River was Pvt. Ronald Davees who insisted that I cry because president Roosevelt, the Jew Lover, had just died. Davees was an open anti-Semite. Incidentally, I encountered more anti-Semitism from my own "buddies" than the enemy and am still bitter about it …
>
> Davees—his job was to row communication cables across the Roer River. The Germans were sending over artillery, and there was some machine-gun fire … I remember hoping he would get hit and even toyed with the idea of doing it myself. I was going to shoot him in the back of the head. Of course, I didn't. Life was pretty cheap in that environment …
>
> You have to remember what it was like then, I don't want to forget the sign "No Jews, dogs or niggers allowed" as I entered Elgin, Texas.

From a phone conversation:

Times are different now. But you have no idea what it was like. I felt alone. There were only two Jews in the outfit. I had plenty of friends. But some guys just couldn't get it out of their minds, the fact that I was Jewish. Especially Cooper. There were always malicious comments, and things would sometimes get physical. One time a bunch of 'em went into town and came back looped. Cooper was stinking drunk. And he kept pushing me, and the other guys would catch me. Finally, he pushed me into a radiator. He hated me so much, would refer to me as "Jew Boy," but not to my face. Another time, on the train, I had an attack of appendicitis. I was in the latrine, with pains in my stomach, and he came in and punched me three or four times in the gut. Another time I got in a fight, a boxing match, with a guy that had eighteen inches on me in reach and outweighed me by a lot. But I was so worked up. That was a terrible decision. [laughs]

My buddy John McElroy helped me to cope, would calm me down when I got upset. He'd help me get over the next hump, helped me become a man.

I tried to forget it all and have been pretty successful in forgetting it pretty well. But there are just too many Jack Coopers in this world.

Jeff, I didn't really realize what a big part of my life the war was. It took some time to realize it. But after talking to you, I'm absolutely amazed, after not thinking about it, how things come back. It makes my life more interesting now. I think the war had a big impact on me. When we talked the other day, after we hung up, I couldn't talk for a while. You've opened up volumes of memories in me I never would have revisited. You're an excellent interrogator. [laughs] You get people to open up. And I appreciate your bringing out my feelings.

I asked Voron what he thought Cooper would say about things now.

I mean, I'm not a cynic. Maybe things have changed. The country has changed. I mean, [vice-presidential candidate Joseph] Lieberman was Jewish, and Gore received the majority of the votes. [laughs] I don't know what these guys would say today. But I doubt they've changed.

During the time I was in contact with Voron I tried to find Davees and Cooper. A search for Davees in the phone book yielded no listing. I tried the Social Security Death Index and found only a single match listed for the entire United States. His birth date and death date checked out with somebody who would have served in WWII, and his middle initial and home state agreed with the information I had. This was most likely the right guy. I later interviewed several veterans who remembered him, but only vaguely. One veteran sent me hundreds of photos, and among them were several of Davees in body-building poses at Camp McCoy. The GI who sent them remembered Davees as "a feisty little shit, a real knothead. He'd flare off at the drop of a hat. He was a tiny little guy, but all muscle."

I then tried searching for Jack Cooper and came up with hundreds of listings. I decided it would take too many letters and phone calls to plow through this list, and I tried to let it go.

But I just could not get these men's names out of my mind. It looked like Davees was dead. But what about Cooper? If he was still alive, what would he remember about the war? And what would he remember about Max Voron?

A few months later I dug through my photos and notes again. I found two photos of Jack Cooper. I tried hard to be objective, but I could not help but notice his snarly expression in both of them. Perhaps it was just my prejudice. Finally, in my notes from a conversation with another GI, I found a scribbled comment stating that Cooper was from the Midwest. I searched again for the name Jack Cooper in the phone directory. I found one, in Missouri. It was a long shot, but I sent a letter anyway.

A few weeks later I received a telephone call.

Hello, this is Jack Cooper from the 978th Engineer Maintenance Company calling from Missouri!

Mr. Cooper and I spoke for about two hours. I had formed a rather nasty picture of this man. But in fairness to him, I had to—and did—keep an open mind. Cooper recalled:

Well, Jeff, I have to tell you, I wasn't what you'd call a great soldier. I mean, I absolutely never shirked my duty. But I was out for a good time. We were drinking a lot. Probably a bit too much. [laughs] And we were always chasin' those German girls. And if you saw me, Jeff, you'd think I'd never have a chance. I'm short and certainly no handsome devil. But I did all right.

I remember my buddy Portman and I met up with some German girls. He was quite a ladies man and always good to go out with. Later, after the war, he contacted me. Things weren't going well for him. He was having problems with his wife. And he wanted to know if I still had the addresses of the girls in Germany. He was going to go back there to look 'em up. And he was dead serious. After that I never heard from him again. [laughs]

The people in Spek, they were wonderful people. I stayed with a family, and they had two little girls, Annie and Ellie, who were four and six years old. The husband was away in Amsterdam, in the Dutch underground.

I also had a brother who was in the infantry, in the Pacific. Looking back, it was just something I had to do. A lot of nice men. Couldn't have asked for a better bunch of guys. I was never bitter about it.

Toward the end of the conversation, I felt that I just had to broach the subject of anti-Semitism. I tried to be indirect.

Mr. Cooper, were there any blacks in the unit?

No, the Army was segregated at that time.

Were there any Jewish guys?

Yeah, there were two Jews. Probably more. But two that I knew of. Silverman and Voron. Both swell guys.

And did the Jewish guys get any hassle for being Jewish?

No, no. There was nothing like that.

I left it at that, but later in the conversation I read through a list of names of 978thers I had already contacted. I asked Cooper to tell me what he remembered about each man. I was curious about what he would say about his relationship with Voron, but I did not want to lead with Voron's name.

How 'bout Cable?

He was a real good-looking man. That's about all I can remember.

And Recktenwald?

He had a dog.

Yeah, the dog's name was Mutt. How 'bout Mangham?

He was from Texas. We called him Tex.

How about Silverman?

He was in the supply line. I was close to him. A Jewish fellow, from Chicago. I heard he passed away a few years back, was really sorry to hear that.

Finally, when I came to Voron, my voice was almost shaking with anticipation.

How 'bout Voron?

I knew him well. We were just friends. He was from Philly.

What else do you remember about him?

He was a Jewish fellow. A nice guy to know, but we didn't buddy around.

And Davees?

He was a physical fitness guy. Into barbells and such. That's about all I remember.

I had one more conversation with Cooper, during which I again mentioned anti-Semitism, but I quickly saw that nothing was going to come of it. In the end I could not help liking Cooper. Looking back, I should have known that Cooper was not going to come across as some sort of raving bigot. I have no doubts that Max Voron was telling the truth. I also know that anti-Semitism was prevalent in the Army during WWII. I was tempted to probe Cooper further on the matter. But I recognized that he was an elderly man who had most likely mellowed with age, who had perhaps changed his attitudes and remembered what he wanted to remember, and I decided it was best not to revisit the matter.

Some time later, I was visiting a friend in southern New Jersey. Voron had already invited me to visit him several times, so Eric and I drove up to his condominium in Philadelphia and had dinner with him and his wife,

Figure 11. Max and Dottie Voron, Atlantic City, 1944. (Photo courtesy of Max Voron)

Dottie. Fit and energetic, Voron was a friendly, down-to-earth, and lively character who came across much younger than his age. He insisted I call him Max and got slightly irritated when I unintentionally kept calling him "Mr. Voron." We had a wonderful evening. We talked only briefly about the war and Jack Cooper. Voron was interested in what Cooper had to say but did not dwell on it. As I left he gave me a photo of him and his wife taken in Atlantic City in 1944 before he was shipped overseas.

Figure 12. Max and Dottie Voron at their home in Philadelphia, 2000.

————————

Voron recalled only two Jewish GIs in the unit. In fact, there were more than that, and I spoke to several of them. Voron, however, may not have had contact with them because they were not in his platoon. In addition, I got the impression that several of the Jewish GIs either kept quiet about their faith or did not openly broadcast it, both during the war and today.

William Musiker, one of the other Jewish GIs, also commented on the anti-Semitism in a phone conversation.

> While we were still in the U.S., one guy tried to give me crap once, called me a Jew bastard. I told him, "It'd be dumb for me to do anything now while we're still in the States, but as soon as we get overseas, I'm gonna kill you." And I meant it. You know, I was smart and had really good test scores and a high score on the IQ test. They wanted to make me an officer. But I saw the way they treated the Jewish officers and I didn't want any of that. It was my way of saying *screw you* to the Army.

My correspondence with Voron, Cooper, and Musiker was among my most interesting. Voron and Musiker were fighting an openly anti-Semitic enemy while trying to cope with the more subtle anti-Semitism in their own society—fighting a war on two fronts.[2] Cooper's prejudices were nothing I had not encountered before, in various forms, most notably with Anglos' prejudices toward Hispanics in south Texas. The people who hold these views seldom come across as raving bigots. In fact, they're typically good, decent, likeable people who love their families and are usually oblivious to the lasting damage their words and actions can cause. I felt sad for what Voron had to endure during the war, but I was glad that he had the grit and fortitude to soldier on and make such a successful life afterwards.

1. Cooper, Davees, and Portman are pseudonyms.
2. For more information on the experience of Jewish GIs in WWII, see the book *GI Jews: How World War II Changed a Generation*, by Deborah Dash Moore (Cambridge, MA: Belknap Press, 2004).

GEORGE PATRIAS

GEORGE PATRIAS, EIGHTY-SIX, WAS THE first veteran I found who had known my grandfather. After receiving my letter, he tried to reach me by telephone at my parents' home in Texas. I wasn't there, but he spoke with my mother, who relayed the conversation to me. Just before we hung up, she said:

Jeff, Mr. Patrias said that my dad saved his life during the war, twice in fact.

Did he say what happened?

No, he just said that my dad saved his life. But when I asked him for details, he changed the subject. A little while later I asked him about it again, and he changed the subject again.

Well, Mom, perhaps it's just too painful for him to talk about. When I call him tomorrow, I'll see if I can approach the subject in such a way that he'll tell me about it.

At this point in my search I did not know what kind of action—if any— my grandfather had seen in the war. I assumed that he and George Patrias were in some sort of battle or skirmish and that it was in those circumstances that my grandfather, as Mr. Patrias said, saved his life. I spent the next day thinking about how to approach the subject in a way that would get Mr. Patrias to open up.

The next evening I telephoned Mr. Patrias. His demeanor was somewhat rough, and he did not volunteer a lot of information. I asked him if he could tell me a little about my grandfather and the war. Occasionally I had to prompt him to keep the conversation going. He said:

Now, you keep in mind, I got a bit of that Alzheimer's stuff, so I don't know how much I'll remember.

I was twenty-one or twenty-two when I got a letter from the draft board. I didn't volunteer. But in the end I figured I was lucky to get drafted. Things weren't going well. I didn't have a job. It was tough to get a job. And when I got in the Army, they promoted me right away to Corporal, and I worked my butt off.

Leo and I met at training camp at McCoy, in Wisconsin. We hit it off right away. Leo had a lot of guts. He wasn't afraid of nothin'. He'd do anything on a dare. We palled around at McCoy and on the boat, but when we got to Europe I didn't see much of Leo.

I was a wrecker driver. A wrecker's a big flatbed tow truck with a winch. We had three of 'em in the unit. I don't know why they put me on the wrecker. I guess 'cause nobody else wanted it. They couldn't handle it. So, I would go around and retrieve damaged equipment, usually by myself, but sometimes I brought somebody else along if I needed help hooking it up. But usually not.

We were always, oh, I don't know, a couple of thousand feet behind the front lines. We could hear gunshots and stuff. I was glad that I wasn't up there with a rifle, was lucky that I never had to kill anybody.

So, there'd be a damaged tank or something stuck in a ditch somewhere, and I'd get the call and head out there. I'd hook it up to the winch and drag it out. Then we'd take it back and they'd fix it. I was all over the place for days on end. One time there was a tank that was stuck nose-deep in sand. They didn't know how to get the thing out. Every time they hooked up the winch, it'd end up pulling the truck toward the tank. The top brass were there, and they didn't know what to do.

So, I told 'em to dig a hole and put the end of the wrecker in the hole, so it couldn't go anywhere. Then I took the rope and ran it back and forth several times. It's slower, but it gives you more strength. Then we hooked it up to the winch. I told the guy running the winch to hide behind something, 'cause if it snapped I didn't want it to kill the guy. And it worked. We managed to pull the tank out. I was surprised and the brass was also. They watched me doing this stupid thing, which I thought it was also, but then it worked and we pulled it out of there.

We did a lot of other things too. Towards the end of the war we had to deal with surrendering Germans. We'd load 'em up on the back of a wrecker. I'd stand guard on my 50-caliber mounted on the truck, and my partner would pack in as many as he could on the back of the wrecker. They never gave us any trouble.

Toward the end of the conversation, I hinted about the matter of my grandfather saving his life.

> Mr. Patrias, did you guys ever run into any trouble?

Well, we didn't have it as bad as the infantry, but we weren't on no picnic either. The Germans were always strafin' us. And there were snipers. One time in Germany we were driving in a jeep to go play football, and I heard what sounded like a couple of bees whizzin' by my head. At least, I thought they were bees. I looked at the other guys, and they heard it too. Turns out it was some German on top of a hill hidden in the trees takin' shots at us. I gave it all I had and we got the hell out of there. We didn't go lookin' for that guy. [laughs] We never knew what was going to happen.

But we never really had time to think about it. We were too busy. Now, on the boat to the Pacific, that was another story. We had nothin' to do but sit around and think. We were going to Japan. And I don't think we woulda won. They woulda killed us all. We were scared. I mean, you worry up to a point, but there was nothing I could do to get out. And then they dropped the bomb. We were sure glad that happened.

Finally, I decided to ask Patrias outright about my grandfather's life-saving heroics.

> Mr. Patrias, my mom said you told her that my grandfather saved your life twice. Is that right?

Yeah, that's right.

> Mr. Patrias, I know it might be difficult, but do you think you could tell me what happened? I would be very interested in hearing about it.

Well, I didn't want to tell the lady. But the first time was when we were in Marseilles, in France. This was after V-E Day. Leo and I had a couple a days' leave. And we didn't have any money for the bars. So Leo and I bought some homemade wine, and we were roaming the French countryside. Boy, we were lit up on that French wine.

And, well, we were lookin' for something to do.

So what did you do?

Well, we busted into a cathouse.

Can you tell me about it?

Well, we snuck in through a back room. We went in through a window. I went in first. And when I got in, there was some dame in the bed. Then all the sudden we see some guy come out from under the covers, and he pulls out a .45, points it at my head.

Well, then there was a bit of a scuffle. Leo finally managed to wrestle the guy down and get the gun away from him. Then we decided it might be better if we got the hell out of there. [laughs] We hitched a ride back to the base with a couple of MPs. They didn't give us any trouble though.

And how about the second time?

Second time? We only busted into the cathouse that one time. What do you think we were, some kind of troublemakers?

No sir. I mean, the second time my grandfather saved your life.

Well, that was in Manila. We had nothing to do. We were just sittin' around waitin' to be sent back home. We heard about this bar that served drinks out of a coconut shell. Have you ever had a drink out of a coconut shell?

No, sir.

Well, neither had we. So we went down to this bar, and we went up and ordered two drinks out of a coconut shell. [laughs]

And did you get them?

Hell no. Those goddamn gooks wouldn't serve us. All we wanted was a drink out of a coconut shell.

So what did you do?

We wrecked the place.

Then there was a bit of a scuffle. And Leo and I decided it might be best if we got the hell out of there.

Leo and I went back to our jeeps. I got in my jeep and Leo got in his, but I couldn't get my jeep started. Then this little gook comes running out, he had one of those six-inch knives like they used to carry. And I was trying like hell to get my jeep started, but it wouldn't start.

Then Leo took a pipe out of the jeep, you know, that type you have on the windshield? And Leo swung that pipe and cut the son of a bitch almost in half. Then I finally got my jeep started and we got the hell out of there. The MPs found out and we got in a bit of trouble. [laughs] I got knocked down in rank. I didn't see much of Leo after that.

Heck, we couldn't behave. We had nothin' to do.

Figure 13. George Patrias at training camp in the U.S.
(Photo courtesy of George Patrias)

Figure 14. George Patrias and his wrecker.
(Photo courtesy of George Patrias)

Several of the GIs I corresponded with remembered Patrias very well. They described him as one of the most valuable men in the unit. He was also considered the strongest, "strong as a mule," as one GI described him. Another described him as "a natural leader, the type of guy that you would feel confident going out with," "a good guy to have on your side," and "a hell-raiser, but not a mean-spirited one, a likeable hell-raiser."

My grandfather's discharge paper says that the highest rank he achieved was a Tec 3 but that he was discharged as a Tec 5, which is a lower rank. At some time during the war he got bumped down a rank. Considering that both my grandfather and George Patrias were described as "hell-raisers," I think I have a good idea of when, where, and with whom this happened.

I was also having to contend with the gradual formation of an image of my grandfather that was less than perfect, something I knew was inevitable if I was going to dig deep enough. In a war zone thousands of miles from home, living with the risk of death, young men are not always going to behave appropriately. But so far I could live with what I had discovered. After all, wasn't busting into a cathouse through a back window less incriminating than simply walking through the front door?

Figure 15. George Patrias, right, at a café in France. (Photo courtesy of George Patrias)

During my conversation with George Patrias, I asked him about Ski, my grandfather's Polish friend from the photo.

> Mr. Patrias, did you recognize the guy in the photo I sent you. His nickname was Ski.

No, I didn't know him.

> They called him Ski because he was Polish. Did you know any Polish guys in the unit?

Hell, I'm a Pollock. But that guy in the photo, never seen him before in my life.

Considering how well Patrias knew my grandfather, I was losing hope of ever finding Ski. Nevertheless, I continued to pay special attention to Polish-sounding names on the roster, particularly those ending in "ski," and send out letters. Every time I received a letter that had a Polish surname on the return address, I tore into it eagerly.

First had come Elroy Nowitzke's response: *I will say this I AM NOT the 'Ski' he referred to.* Next came a letter from the daughter of Edward Zewicke of Michigan: *My dad is not Ski.* Then my letter to Joseph Jablonsky was returned: *No longer at this address.* Chester Lesneski of Massachusetts was next; he sent lots of photos and shared some interesting stories, but he was not Ski and had never seen him before. Next, I found the address of Harry Nareski and sent a letter. Weeks and months went by without a reply; then I received my letter back with the notice *No longer at this address.* And now George Patrias, who had known my grandfather, didn't recognize the photo of Ski at all.

Whoever this Ski fellow was, nobody seemed to know him. Perhaps he had been in a different unit. Perhaps he and my grandfather had met in France after the war in Europe and became friends there. If that was the case, I would probably never find him. And with two letters returned *No longer at this address*, there was a pretty good chance that Ski was dead.

DAILY LIFE IN A MAINTENANCE COMPANY

FROM MY DISCUSSIONS WITH GIs like George Patrias, I learned about the work of noncombat soldiers in WWII. It gave me a perspective that is not often seen in books and movies about warfare.

For every man at the front, there were five to ten more who were supporting him: truck drivers, machine repairmen, radio operators, cooks, cleaners, clerks, mechanics. All went through basic training and learned basic infantry tactics, but afterward each received additional training in his specialty. In the case of the 978th, the additional training was in the repair and maintenance of a broad array of engineering equipment.

Thomas Orton, whom I found later in my search and who also knew my grandfather, was one of the most articulate and reflective men I corresponded with. He had an amazing memory for details and could recall the height, physical characteristics, eye color, hometown, background, and personal details of many men who had served in the unit. He also was able to provide many details about daily life in a maintenance company:

> Most of the men [in the 978th] had some sort of background in mechanics and heavy machinery. I had training before the war as a machinist. Early on in the war I was drafted while I was still doing my apprenticeship. So I went to the Army and made them a deal where the Army could have me, but they would let me finish out my schooling.

During the war I was in charge of a machine-shop truck. In the back were lathes, a milling machine, a drill press, bench grinders, and such. Your granddad was a mechanic, had a three-quarter-ton truck with toolboxes on the back. He was more mobile, going to sites, and did a lot of different things, general repairs and such. My truck was larger. We set up shop and the work was brought to us.

We were mostly a repair unit. The infantry and armored and some other units would bring us their damaged equipment and we'd fix it. It could be almost anything. A broken-down jeep, a crane that needed to be welded, a damaged piece of artillery. Some of the men acquired German equipment and needed to modify it to fit our own equipment.

I asked Orton to tell me about his most difficult task.

Well, I think the constant go, go, go, never being sure what was going to happen, or even where exactly we were because we were always on the go from one job to the next. Sometimes we'd be up for days on end. And having to drive at night to avoid German planes. It was exhausting.

When we were really busy doing our work in Germany, it was wake up, work dawn to dusk and even later, eat dinner, go to sleep in our trucks, and get up the next morning and keep going. And this went on for weeks on end.

Tommy [his partner] and I had a large machine-shop truck. When we bivouacked someplace we always tried to be in a wooded area. If we were going to stay a few days we always put up camouflage. So, we'd arrive at a location. Sometimes it'd be just Tommy and I in our truck, but usually it was a group of 8 to 10 vehicles. We wouldn't all park together, because if there's too much of a concentration, you'd have nowhere to run to if something happened. We'd park within walking distance of the other vehicles.

Our truck had four camouflage nets. They were about 50 feet square, one-quarter mesh woven out of string material rather than thread, and we'd peg them to the ground or to our trucks or wherever. You couldn't see us. We'd just disappear into the trees. We had 'em up when we did our work too. We'd be working on a truck or a tank, and we'd camouflage it too with the nets.

Orton also provided details about meals, water, and hygiene.

Figure 16. A light machine-shop truck, Camp McCoy, Wisconsin. The 978th's vehicles traveled with them from Camp McCoy to England, France, Belgium, Holland, Germany, the Philippines, Japan, and back to the U.S. (Photo courtesy of Thomas Orton)

Generally, the day when we arrived someplace it took the cooks a half a day or so to set up. So if we arrived in the evening we had C or K rations. Tommy and I accumulated rations and kept them in our truck so we'd never have to worry.

Rations are made in the U.S. and shipped over. A K-ration is a snack. About four K-rations would fit in a shoebox. It was cold food of some kind. Spam or something. C rations were in cans and meant to be eaten hot. There were six varieties: meat and beans, stew, hash, chicken—I didn't care for that—and something else, I can't remember.

Eventually Tommy and I acquired a hot plate. Before we acquired that we'd heat up our rations with a blow-torch. Or, when in convoy, when we were stopped, Tommy would jump out and stick a couple of 'em on the engine and next time we'd stop they'd be hot.

If we were off on our own, then we ate rations for a couple a days. Or, if we were attached to another company, they took care of us. We were lucky that we had good cooks. We had a good Mess Sergeant. He was a chef at a hotel in New York. One time they located some deer and shot 'em and took 'em to the cooks.

We didn't shower very often. It depended on the amount of water available. We had eight canteens between Tommy and I. Wherever we were, the last thing we did before we moved was to fill those canteens. Often we took a canteen of water and a gallon bucket. Our K rations came with two little bars of soap, about hotel size. So we'd take those and wash up in the bucket. The water was always cold.

One time an Inspector General came up and saw us and said: "You guys are a mess." He was upset. I mean, not at us or for morale, but that it's bad for hygiene. So the next day up came a convoy of trucks that were equipped with showers. And we washed, got clean uniforms. It was the first time since France that I had a real shower, three or four months earlier. And then we went back and continued work.

We never took our clothes off. I had a duffel bag full of clothes. We had three of everything. Socks we washed daily, other things less often. We did laundry at least once a week, in our little gallon buckets. And we had a clothesline hanging in the truck. Later, when Tommy was on one of his scavenging forays, he came up with an old farm-style washing machine. In Germany, if we saw something we needed, we took it. What was there, well, I wouldn't say it was free for the taking, but anything that we needed we had.

Tommy and I slept in the back of our machine-shop truck. We had blankets. The truck had a gasoline-burning furnace in the back work area, so we were able to keep somewhat warm during the winter. We were better equipped than the infantry. For them it was a different ballgame. We took our boots off when we slept, 'cause if you don't your feet swell up and you get problems; but we had all our clothes on, never really took them off because there was too much happening. We were fortunate. We never had any enemy action, except for the strafing. But we always had our rifles by our sides when we slept. Most of the time we were close to the front and the ground was shaking. It was nerve-wracking. Some guys couldn't sleep through it. I got used to it. You just get so tired you curl up in a corner and fall asleep almost immediately.

I asked Orton if any experiences near the front lines stood out in his memory.

I think one of our most important tasks was getting those outboard motors up and running. You see, during river crossings in Europe, small boats were used to ferry troops and supplies, both during an attack for the infantry and engineers and afterwards for more troops and supplies. These boats were fitted with outboard motors.

Unfortunately, during the Roer River crossing in Germany, a lot of the two hundred outboard motors on the boats failed. The motors had been shipped over from the U.S. and had been packed away for months. Those types of motors need a tune-up before use. But they didn't get one. So when it came time to cross the Roer a lot of those motors just conked out or didn't even start. And, of course, when that happens, soldiers die.

So before the next crossing, which was the Rhine, we were given about two hundred or so of these 25-horsepower motors to get in good working order. Our platoon, which had about five or six trucks, scouted out a little lake in Germany and we set up camp alongside the lake.

For the next ten days or so we spent all our time getting the engines working. Some of them needed to be tuned up. Some were damaged during the first crossing. Some of the wrecked ones we scrapped for parts and used on the other engines. We also had to make some of our own parts on the lathe or drill press or grinder.

It was pretty grueling 'cause we were going all day, dawn to dusk. Then we had to test them out. We had about a half dozen or so boats. So we'd put the engine on the boat and take it for a test run on the lake. And we'd only pass them if they'd start on the first pull.

There was one guy, he got a rope and took an old door or something like that, and he made a makeshift surfboard. We pulled him around the lake on his surfboard. [laughs] Anything to break the monotony. The war had its light moments too, you know. Even if you had to manufacture them.

So when it came time for the infantry to cross the Rhine, they had 175 engines in perfect working order. And of those 175 engines, not a single one failed. Not one. Our unit received a presidential citation for that.[1]

When the opportunity presented itself, the men of the 978th also took what they needed for their work, particularly in Germany. Several veterans

Figure 17. Training at Camp McCoy, Wisconsin. As part of its training, the 978th rebuilt this tractor shovel. According-ing to a local newspaper clipping, "the rebuilding job took two weeks of 24-hour a day schedules. It was done in the company's mobile shops—a task comparable to what is expected in combat zones ... Rebuilding the shovel necessitated replacing track roller shafts, bushings, adjusting bolts, stabilizing rod bushings, replacing a dipper tooth, rebuilding track and drive chain sprockets and rebushing of saddle block bushings."
(Clipping and photo courtesy of Thomas Orton)

told me the 978th was an effective unit because, one way or another, they could find what they needed to get the job done. William Musiker said:

> Jeff, you know why the 978th was so good at its job? Because we were resourceful and showed initiative. There were times during the war when we had absolutely no supervision. But we didn't need it. We were mature people and knew what we needed to do. We were responsible for the work we were sent to do, for finding a place to sleep, for feeding ourselves, everything. In Germany, this went on for days and weeks on end.
>
> One of our jobs was to set-up a bunch of inflatable boats for a river crossing. But we didn't have any way to inflate the boats. We had an air compressor, but no attachments. But we were good at improvising stuff, and one of the guys figured out how to make up these little attachments, grind them down to the right size, and hook 'em up to the compressor. And it worked.

We were always looking for ways to make life easier. At Mariagrube we had warm showers. There were some boilers there and we fixed 'em up. It was a coal mine. So what'd we burn to make hot water? Coal. And if there wasn't coal, we'd find something else. We used anything we could find to do our job. In Germany, if we couldn't use it, we wrecked it.

There was destruction everywhere. Bombs, concussions, looting, anything. Sometimes it was just plain vandalism. If it was in Holland, it was the Germans who had done it. If it was in Germany, it was us. In Germany, if it wasn't all knocked to hell, we'd knock it down. We'd wreck anything we couldn't use. We were tough bastards. We didn't give a damn. We didn't want to be there and a lot of guys resented it.

Heck, I hate to admit it, but I had a good time. When you think about it, you wonder how we ever won the war. But the Americans are smart. We got our training in the field. If we needed something, we'd make it. If we couldn't make it, we'd steal it! We were the best bunch of thieves in the Army. Heck, it all belonged to Uncle Sam anyway. We had several tractors. We needed some tractors to do our work. So how'd we get 'em? We stole 'em. Do you know from where? From the Army! We

Figure 18. "One of our jobs was to make this traveling Gin Mill for a General." (Caption and photo courtesy of William Musiker).

were a better unit because we were better thieves. [laughs] That's why
the Army liked us so much, because, one way or another, we could get
things done. We were resourceful and we showed initiative.

My background in mechanical engineering helped me appreciate the
type of work the men did and ask the right questions in interviews. My
expertise is in the industrial process of grinding, a machining operation similar
to turning and milling. I've worked with many manufacturing companies
and know that a good machinist is invaluable. In a current production
environment, when a machine breaks down there's enormous pressure on
the machinist to make the replacement part quickly and accurately, as an
out-of-operation machine can cost a company thousands of dollars an hour.
I can't imagine the stress of a situation where soldiers' lives may depend on
the quick and accurate production of this replacement part, done thousands
of miles from home in a mobile shop with limited resources under the strain
of war and the constant threat of the enemy.

1. The unit actually received a Meritorious Service Unit plaque, not the Presidential
   Citation as Orton remembered. Many other men of the 978th made the same error.

ALL IN A DAY'S WORK

THOMAS ORTON ALSO RECALLED AN event that might not be as citation worthy, but gave me insight into some of the peculiar situations the men of the 978th found themselves in:

> One of our jobs was right in the center of a town in Germany called Mönchengladbach. The Germans had retreated, but before they did they buried two blockbuster bombs right in the middle of the main intersection. These things are a couple of tons apiece. They call them blockbusters because they can take out an entire city block. The Germans had wired them together and had booby-trapped them. They were wired to what looked like a clothesline, with a couple of blankets hanging off the line.
>
> So we were called in. There were about four of us. George Patrias was there with his wrecker. We had to first excavate around the two bombs. It was a slow and meticulous process. And they could've gone off at any moment. You didn't make any false moves. It was almost as if you were afraid to take a breath, for fear that it would detonate the thing. It was as if, oh, you'd take a breath, then dig around them, and then take another breath, and then work some more.
>
> Once we had them about 90 percent exposed, we put chains around them. George operated the winch on the wrecker, and we pulled them out. The entire job took the better part of a day.
>
> Then the bomb disposal unit took them away.
>
> After we finished, I bumped into Dave Jensen,[1] one of the welders. He asked me where we'd been and I told him about the bombs. Then I asked him what he was doing. He looked at me and said, very casually, "We're going down to do some work on a bank."

I was completely blown away. Up to that point I hadn't had any experience with looting. I was a pretty serious individual. I was a newlywed and very serious about my job. I didn't stray. I didn't sit in judgment of those who did, but I just didn't have any interest in it.

That night, about seven or eight of us pulled our vehicles into the bombed-out remains of a bank in Mönchengladbach. The town was totally deserted, and we pulled our trucks right into the bank, into the lobby, where nobody could see them.

Dave was a welder, and he spent the next hour or so burning a hole in the vault door with a welding torch. I can still picture it. We had to burn through the steel door, then there was all this anti-inflammatory powder we had to get through before we got to the inner door, which we had to burn through. The whole job took several hours. Then we crawled through the hole in the door and spent, oh, about six or eight hours breaking into safe-deposit boxes. There was about seven or eight of us in the vault.

But I didn't find anything. [laughs] Just a couple of packs of Lucky Strike cigarettes that turned to dust when I picked them up. I heard one guy got a bunch of diamonds. Apparently he hid them in the barrel of his rifle. I don't know if it's true.

We did get piles and piles of German marks. But it was absolutely worthless. The next evening we built a fire in the forest. You dig a hole and build the fire in the hole so it wouldn't give off any light, so German snipers can't see it. And we sat around throwing German marks into the fire, used them to feed the fire. A month later we were being paid in German marks, the same currency that we were burning the month before. But at the time, we thought it was worthless. That was a big boo-boo. [laughs] God knows how much we burned, but it was mucho.

That incident at the bank was my only escapade with looting. For a while we were in the XIXth Corps of Engineers. It was a respectable outfit. Our patch had a tomahawk and a 19 on it. And some people used to say "the one-nine corps: one shootin', nine lootin'." [laughs] It was just a catch phrase, but it clicked.

Thomas Orton was typical of the veterans I interviewed. They were very proud of the work they did but had no hesitation about telling me of their rule-breaking antics and made no apologies for them. I seldom got the impression that the veterans were trying to "spin" their stories to show themselves or the unit in a favorable light. They had a matter-of-fact, tell-it-like-it-is approach to the interviews. Several times I asked veterans if I could put their antics in the book, and the typical answer was, "Well, that's what happened, so put it in there."

1. The name Dave Jensen is a pseudonym.

MERLIN CLARK

I CORRESPONDED WITH SEVERAL MEN who had been assigned to the 978th only at or near the end of the war. During the fighting in Europe and the Pacific, they had served in other units, often in the infantry.

Merlin Clark, eighty-seven, a retired mechanic from Houston, Texas, was in the 37th Combat Engineer Battalion. He sent me a short letter stating that he "was one of the first men to land at Omaha Beach" and signed the letter "an unknown friend." I telephoned him. He said that he had never spoken about the war to anybody and mentioned several times that I was welcome to stop by his house for a visit. Although he did not say so outright, I got the impression from both his letter and our telephone conversation that he wanted—almost needed—to finally tell his story.

During my next trip home to Texas, I drove to Houston to visit Clark. I chatted with him and his wife in their living room for a while, and then Mrs. Clark left us alone. On the wall hung a large, framed photo of Mr. Clark in his uniform. He began:

I have Parkinson's disease. I have some good days, some bad days. Some mornings I wake up and can't hold a cup of coffee; other days are ok. Today's a pretty good day, although I was a bit sluggish this morning.

In his long Southern drawl, Mr. Clark spoke matter-of-factly about his experiences in a "That's just the way it was" tone of voice.

We boarded an LST [Landing Ship Tank, a boat designed to land battle-ready tanks, troops, and supplies directly on the enemy's shore] from Portsmouth and went straight from the dock to the beach. It took two or three hours to cross the channel. It was still dark out when we landed, at St. Lo. Everybody was scared. But we were just functioning on automatic, like robots.

I drove a bulldozer. We were there to clear paths for the tanks and vehicles that would follow the infantry. There was one bulldozer in the back of the landing craft and one in the front. I was the driver of the one in the front. I also had a stack of pierce planking on the back of the dozer. It was like tracks, for the airplanes to land. I was supposed to drop that off on the beach, and the engineers would assemble it, and then I'd continue on.

And as we were coming up to the beach, I hid behind the pierce planking. The Germans were up on the ridge, and we were just targets for 'em. That's when the shells started to come in. One landed in the back of the boat, an 88. The guys in the back were wiped out, along with the other tractor.

We got to the beach and I drove off. As I was coming up the beach, I raised the blade on the front of the dozer all the way up and that protected me somewhat. I could hear the ping, ping of machine-gun fire on the blade.

I managed to get my tractor on the beach. I dropped off my pierce planking so the other guys could assemble it. But the others were an awful mess, all scattered about. And I started to clear trails. A chain attached to the front of the bulldozer would set off the booby traps and land mines.

While I was working I could see the infantry coming in. There were so many bodies in the water, like corks in the water. Ten there, five here, twenty there. And I just continued on, clearing trails. This went on until the area was secured, about five or six hours or so. Seventy-five percent of my unit was wiped out. Almost all casualties happened before they got to the beach. If they could get up the beach, then they had a chance.

Clark survived Normandy and moved with his unit through France, Belgium, Holland, and Germany.

We crossed the Roer, the Elbe, and some other river, can't remember the name. The bulldozer was the U.S.'s secret weapon. The Germans didn't have 'em. The bulldozer would go over anything.

We'd work for a while, dig a foxhole, take a nap, and then keep going. One time this little old French lady came out yelling at me for tearing up her orchard. Another time, during the Bulge, I had to hide out with a Belgian woman. Her husband was dead. She had three kids. This was during the Bulge, and the Germans had overrun us. I had nowhere to go, so I just hid out in the cellar until the Germans were driven back again. Then I just walked down to the American lines and rejoined my outfit.

Did you have to use your rifle?

Rifle? Well, yeah. I used it quite a bit. You'd carry that rifle with you everywhere, to bed with you, when you took a crap, everywhere. You'd see some movement, you know it's not ours. And you shoot. I don't want to say if I killed anybody, but you shoot them before they shoot you. Then I'd get back on my dozer and get back to work.

One time I stepped on a concussion mine. Blew off a chunk of my big toe. [laughs] I was in the hospital two or three days. I shoulda got the Purple Heart but never bothered to apply.

I asked him if he had any idea, before actually getting into the war, what it would be like.

Oh no. I had no idea. I volunteered. I had an uncle who was in WWI. He said to make sure I don't get in the Combat Engineers. And that's right where they put me. [laughs]

After what I experienced in Europe, I knew it was going to be even worse in Japan. Then I started to think about it on the boat over [to the Pacific, for the invasion of Japan]. I was so tempted to jump off the boat in Panama. [laughs] But I didn't.

After an hour or two, Mrs. Clark came in and joined us. She commented that in sitting with us for only a few minutes, she had heard more about her husband's experiences in the war than she had in the past fifty years. I asked Mrs. Clark what it had been like for them when her husband returned from the war.

When Merlin got home he just didn't want to talk about the war. Then we got on with our lives, work, our son, our grandchildren, and seemed busy with other things.

I asked Clark what it was like after the war.

Well, the first year was tough. I didn't talk about it. I had nightmares at least

Figure 19. Merlin Clark, 1945 or 1946, when he was with the 978th in Japan.
(Photo courtesy of Merlin Clark)

*once a week for three months. But we got other things going and got on with
our lives, didn't we, honey? There was this one time we were at a Fourth-of-
July celebration and they had fireworks. That sort of troubled me. We had to
get the police over, and they helped me settle down, didn't they, honey?*

*Then I got your letter and I thought, this fellow has some interest, so
I then decided, well, it'd been a long time, so I decided I was going to talk
about it. And I did.*

Clark mentioned his disappointment in young people today.

*Young people, they're just not patriotic. I see these protests in Italy, in Seattle.[1]
They just want to protest. Don't know what for. Don't even know what
they're protesting about. And they're just not interested in what we did. It's
like all we did was for nothin'.*

Clark dug through some drawers and came up with an old envelope containing souvenirs from the war—a photo of himself, plus some Japanese, Dutch, and German paper money and coins. He insisted I take the photo and the paper money. I respectfully declined; he insisted, and finally I accepted. Then he asked me to come into the garage, where he dug out a Japanese sword that he had taken off a dead Japanese soldier. He insisted that I also take the sword.

He walked me to the front porch, where we shook hands and said goodbye. He seemed to be beaming with enthusiasm. Clark then turned to his wife, his body language and tone seeming almost giddy with excitement, and said:

> *Honey, I did it. It's been over fifty years now, and I've been talking about the war for almost the whole evening. And you know what? I feel pretty good! Even my Parkinson's has calmed down.*

A few weeks later I telephoned Clark to thank him for the visit and the things he gave me. Mr. Clark was not much of a phone talker, but he thanked me for the visit and closed our conversation by saying, "Well, I appreciate all you've done. You're the only one I opened my heart up to. And I feel relieved. It's sort of, well, sort of brought an end to the whole thing for me."

1. Clark is referring to the protests at the World Trade Organization's conference in Seattle in 1999 and the G8 summit in Genoa, Italy, in 2001.

DIFFERENT PERSPECTIVES

I don't think of the war as a difficult time in my life. To me, it was a great adventure. Even with 39 months overseas, I was fortunate enough to somehow miss actual combat.

—Excerpt from a letter from 978ther Russ Thayer of Florida

A FEW MONTHS AFTER I visited Merlin Clark I started going through my list of names and calling men who had not replied to my original letter. Melvin Brandstatter[1] was one of them. Brandstatter said that he never received my letter, but he was willing to talk to me. His tone was somber, and he seemed cautious with his words. Like Merlin Clark, he had been in the 37th Combat Engineer Battalion and was placed in my grandfather's unit near the end of the war. He mentioned having landed at Normandy on D-Day but did not offer any details of the experience. He did tell me that he had had a pet monkey in Manila that he named "Monkey." I found it interesting that, like Francis Recktenwald, also a man of few words, one of the first and only things he brought up was a pet.

I asked Brandstatter if he remembered Merlin Clark or if he had any contact with any of his old buddies from the 37th.

No, I don't remember Clark, and I don't have any contact with anybody. I know that the 37th has been having reunions every year; I think the last one was in North Carolina. I've never been to one and don't think I ever will. I'd just as soon forget about the war.

But I would like to receive your letter and any other information and a copy of your Web page about your search. It sounds interesting.

I promised to send them to him. I mentioned my meeting with Merlin Clark and asked Brandstatter if he also would be willing to share his experiences with me. His voice instantly became tense and started to crack. In a very grave and shaky voice he said:

No, I don't want to talk about any of that. So if that's a condition you have for sending that information, then don't send it. I don't want it. I won't talk about that.

I assured him that I would send it regardless of what he was willing to share with me. The conversation faded. I sent him the information.

A few weeks later I called Brandstatter back to see if he received the things I had sent him. He was curt. He told me that he had received them and thanked me, but said that he was in a hurry and was awaiting another call. He did not ask me to call back.

After we hung up I made another phone call, to Elmer Kulback of Pennsylvania. Mr. Kulback was a talker. He was in the 38th Infantry Division of the 1st Army. He also had landed at Normandy, shortly after which he was transferred to the 978th. His tone, however, was quite different from Brandstatter's. His voice was filled with enthusiasm and bravado.

Jeff, I've had a great life. Really. I'll be eighty-five soon. I'm not an old sourpuss, if you know what I mean. I've had a wonderful life. I have five grandkids and a great wife. She died three years ago and that was really rough. But, oh well, you can't live forever. I meet all these young women now, and they all want to get married. But they're only after my money. [laughs]

As for the war, there's just so much to it, I could go on forever. I was twenty-nine months overseas. I never discussed the war with my wife or anybody else. I never kept in contact with anybody, never went to any reunions or joined the VFW or American Legion. I just wasn't interested. When I see all these guys who belong to the Legion who served in the Army for three months, got asthma, and were transferred out. Then they say, "We won the war." [laughs] I got no time for them. I'm not a flag waver.

We landed at Normandy, at Omaha, two days after D-Day, and I was the first man off of my LCI [landing craft infantry boat]. It's something you'll never see in your life. I can still picture it, sitting in that boat holding my gun. There wasn't any small-arms fire, but the 88s were whizzing by.

Heck, if they told me that they needed me, that I had to go out and do it again, I'd be there tomorrow. And I could do it too. I'm not joking. I still have my uniform, and it doesn't fit me half bad. I'm 6'4", a founding member of the original Tip-Toppers, a club for tall people.

You know what? I even spoke to General Eisenhower, in Dorchester. He came up to me and asked: "Soldier, how do you sleep at night?" I looked him in the eye and said, "Sir, with a touch of my toe and away I go." Heck, I also got to guard General De Gaulle. And I sat below King George at the Palladian Theatre.

I had two brothers in the war. One brother was in the airborne, completed 260 jumps. I lost the other brother on the Rhine. He went out on patrol duty and never came back, and they never found him. A year later they claimed to have found his body, but who knows. So, I said to my mom that I thought he should be buried in France. Edward J. Kulback.

Later I asked Kulback if he could tell me more about Omaha Beach. There was a pause, as if he was contemplating the experience. His tone became more somber, and he replied:

Well, that was horrible; let's forget that.

And then he continued:

Heck, a lot of guys were looting for souvenirs. German Lugers, or anything valuable. Not us. Me and my buddy, Jack Cable, we were drinkin' buddies. And we were both Republicans. We didn't like Roosevelt. We'd get to these German houses, and everybody else would go searching the houses for valuables. But not us. We didn't mess around with souvenirs. We'd go straight to the cellar. [laughs] We loaded up the trucks with liquor. Anything we could find.

Later, Mr. Kulback mentioned being in Mönchengladbach. I thought back to Thomas Orton's incident with the bank.

Mr. Kulback, do you remember anything about a bank?

His response was very serious and brusque:

Who told you about that?

I heard about it from a couple of guys.

Yeah, of course I remember. I was the guy holding the torch! [laughs] I burned a hole in the safe door. But the thing was empty. Germans must have moved everything out beforehand.

I heard it was Thomas Orton, Dave Jensen, and a couple of other guys. And that one guy got a bunch of diamonds.

No, it wasn't them. It was Mascero, Wright, and Webster. And we didn't get anything. [Pause] It must have been a different bank. [laughs]

You know, I had four battle stars, a Presidential Citation, and could've gotten a Purple Heart. But I never bothered to apply. I even got a ruptured duck, which is a good conduct medal. Hard to believe. [laughs]

Later on, the subject drifted back to his job in the war.

In the Army, you're only as good as the men behind you. Food, water, clothing, gas, etc. They always told us to take care of our equipment. People are easy to replace. But not equipment. That was true then and it's true now.

I was in the chemical unit. We were trained in the use of mustard gas. But the Germans never used it. I also had to use a flame-thrower. The Germans, they were in a pillbox shooting out at us. And the flame-thrower could shoot about fifty feet or so. So we'd aim for the windows, and we'd burn 'em out of there. You could hear 'em in there, you know? You know what I mean? You know what I mean?

After Kulback's comments on the pillbox, there was a brief pause (of which there were not many in our conversation). It seemed from my end as if he was either reflecting on it or deciding whether or not to discuss it any further. He changed the subject.

But I don't want to tell you about that. Let me tell you, son. You've got to believe in yourself. You can do anything you can make your mind up to do. And you gotta blow your own horn. Gotta have a little politics. It's just the way it is. And if somebody double-crosses you, don't get angry, get even.

Look at him and think, "I'll have your job."

We talked for quite a while. Eventually, I needed to politely extricate myself from the conversation. Then the battery on Mr. Kulback's phone started to die.

Jeff, I'm losing you. The battery on my phone is dying. But listen, don't let your boss tell you what you do. You tell your boss what you do.

Oh, there it goes again. Listen, if we get cut off, you'll have to call back tomorrow. OK? I'll charge the thing tonight. But if we get cut off, call back tomorrow. So, you tell your boss what your job is. Jeff, you know 80 percent of your job and. Are you there? It's dying. One more thing, You know 80 percent of your job, and the other 20 percent you can bluff. So Jeff, what I'm trying to tell you is… [line goes dead]

After our conversation ended, I thought about the different ways that Clark, Brandstatter, and Kulback viewed and discussed their experiences in the war. I also wondered if I could have managed the conversation with Brandstatter differently to get him to open up. But I think I spoke to all the men in pretty much the same way, and it would be naïve to think that I could have evoked a willing response from every GI I contacted. I was learning that the GIs' reactions to the war and how they coped with their experiences were based on many factors. Of course, the amount of hard combat and death that they saw played a large part in how the war affected them. But an even bigger factor didn't seem to be external at all; it was something inside. All the men I talked to were changed by their experience with war—they all brought something home in their memories and their makeup. But whether they came back a Brandstatter or a Kulback also had something to do with what they took with them into battle in the first place.

1. The name Melvin Brandstatter is a pseudonym.

FARRAN HELMICK AND DIFFERENT TRUTHS

IN A SIMILAR VEIN TO my experience with Kulback and Brandstatter, one of the more interesting insights I gained from conversations with the GIs was that different men from the same unit who had been exposed to essentially the same or very similar wartime experiences could have drastically different reactions to, and even vastly different recollections of, those experiences. The case of Max Voron and Jack Cooper is an obvious one. But even subjects less volatile than religion, even specific incidents, could be remembered in such different ways. After a while I focused less on finding out what had happened and more on simply listening to what the veterans told me and taking it at face value. I came to understand that I could never hope to realize "the truth" about the war, the 978th, or even a single event, and that continuing to probe some issues more deeply provided few answers—rather, it raised more questions.

Nobody contributed more to this awareness than Farran "Hank" Helmick, seventy-seven, of Arizona, whom I first spoke to by telephone. Helmick was filled with enthusiasm about his friends in the 978th, about life in general, and about his fifty-four grandchildren. Of his fellow soldiers in the 978th, Helmick said, "As far as men go, I could not have asked for a better bunch of guys." However, while some men of the 978th spoke proudly of the excellent training they had received and the important work they had done during the war, Helmick held a very negative view of what he saw as poor organization, training, and use of personnel in the Army.

I was bored to death most of the one year I was with the 978th. We had a lot of very competent, very knowledgeable people with experience in heavy equipment. But the younger fellows received absolutely no training whatsoever.

My conversation with Helmick prompted him to write his memoirs, which he sent to me. He began with his assessment of the training at Camp McCoy:

> Pardon my French but the 978th was a bastardized outfit. We were castoffs from all over the United States. We had people from every unit imaginable except the Infantry and the Airforce. This was typical of Army efficiency in never assigning qualified people to the right slots at the right time. Most of us were square pegs in round holes …
>
> I believe our platoon was most likely the worst qualified of the four platoons. However, that might not be so, because I was not present in the others … All I know is the First Platoon just did not get any worthwhile training. In our unit, there were hardly any qualified people. We were mostly green kids, few of whom even had any experience in puttering with their own jalopies …
>
> I was assigned as a diesel mechanic. I went to school for three days. I learned that diesels use diesel fuel, and that they are fuel-injected. I never saw a diesel engine in a workshop. I never worked on one in my life. However, there were two diesel grader machines parked in the rear of our shops and before we began our three-day school, we sneaked off and were trying to learn how to operate them. [I never received an official lesson.] It was great fun, and I would have been delighted to learn how to operate heavy equipment, but was never given the opportunity. We ran out of fuel. We were so ignorant we filled them up with gasoline. Needless to say, they did not work. Needless to say, we departed in a hurry. Needless to say, we never confessed to our dastardly deed. A few days later in school I was chagrined to learn that tractors used diesel fuel. I have no idea why we received no training, but we lay around all summer and did absolutely nothing. We did become experts on KP and guard duty, and nearly went bonkers with boredom. So to speak, "we sat the summer out" in the huge garage to which we were assigned …
>
> To ward off utter boredom, and on my own initiative, I took charge of the so-called tool room. Tools! What a joke??? A few old alternators,

starters, part of a transmission, and a handful of tools that would not have filled a toolbox the size I carry for emergencies in the back of my car today …

The officers were good in the sense that they were fair and left us strictly alone. They were not good in the sense that we never received any training. I had no duties whatsoever. One day I was so fed up I went over to the carpenter group and told the Sgt. "I'm going nuts with nothing to do. Can I join you?" He laughed and said, "We have a lot of nothing to do, also. Come ahead if you wish." Therefore, in effect, I reassigned myself. I figured if nothing else, I could swing a hammer, drive a nail, and saw a board. Of course, this never happened, but at least I tried.

Helmick traveled with the 978th to Europe, where he "wandered around with nothing to do" and occasionally passed his time by taking potshots at German airplanes flying overhead.

An aerial dogfight broke out off in the distance, and of course, we decided to help. Our logic was simple. The planes being chased were Germans so we fired on the lead planes. Believe me they were not in danger. We were too far away to be a threat. Suddenly we heard a spent round come zinging through the air … One of our fellows was hit in the shoulder by a .30 or .50 machine gun bullet … He was our first casualty that I knew of … So much for stupid kids with nothing to do in a war zone.

Our platoon did nothing while here [in Germany] that I know of … Our group had a fifty-caliber machine gun mounted on a two and a half-ton truck ring mount … On 24 Dec [1944] … we were all packed up and in convoy when two German planes at about two hundred feet went zooming by … Sgt. Lickey and I sprang to the gun and he swiveled it around and had a perfect shot at about two city blocks. One was a Messerschmidt ME 109, and the other a Folkwolf 190. Sgt. Lickey cut loose, and I was so mad I could have belted him. He had not snapped the automatic butterfly switch into the automatic position and he fired a single round. Perhaps we were lucky. If the Germans had seen us they would have swung around and strafed our convoy. Such were the fickle fingers of fate during a war.

It was during this time that some men from our company retrieval section were going up to the front lines and working under fire to

Figure 20. Lt. Farran "Hank" Helmick (left) and unknown, Berlin, 1946.
(Photo courtesy of Farran Helmick)

repair and bring out tanks etc. We heard that a couple of guys had been wounded, but the details were lacking. Our company was supposed to have been doing this type of work all along. How effective the other platoons were, I have absolutely no idea. I just know our platoon did nothing, at least anything that I was aware of.

When we were in Germany there was a rumor that we were going to be sent to the front lines. On 16 Dec. the Germans launched their Ardennes offensive and we were put on alert. Apparently the American defensive line was thin and rumor was that we were going to be called up as infantry and put on the front lines when they broke through. Heck, I was looking forward to it! Anything to break the monotony. That's the kind of young fool I was.

Helmick remembered the looting as well:

When we got the chance to liberate German weapons and such paraphernalia, we kept it and never thought anything about it. There was a wall-safe in one of the rooms of this house [in Walheim, Germany], and we all had dreams of riches. We taped a grenade to it.

I hate to admit it, but I was the ringleader and the brains behind this heist. We blew the safe and split our loot. I believe I got four pieces of very old silverware as my share. In turn, a couple of months later, I lost all my gear, including my ill-gotten gains when I passed through Paris … An entire railroad cart full of duffel bags, including mine, was stolen by the French black marketers. It serves to prove, "Crime does not pay." If anyone had accused us of looting we would not have known what they were talking about. We were all pretty naïve.

In another house, I found four beautiful stemmed glasses. The house was all shot to hell. How they survived, I will never know. All the rest of the chinaware was small piles of glass. I lifted the glasses in good second-story fashion and three of them got home [to Virginia] intact. Yes, the officers signed off on all packages without checking … I honestly did not realize that what I did was wrong. Later, when I got older and had time to reflect on my misdeeds, I realized the error of my ways … This episode ended my criminal career, and I am happy to say I never had to pay the piper. It was looting pure and simple. At the time, not a one of us would have agreed that it was.

The 978th was not assigned to the infantry, and Helmick eventually asked to be transferred out of the unit. This was just before the 978th became more extensively involved in the war.

Again, I was transferred to a unit in which I had no training. I was there such a short time; I do not even remember the unit designation … I was a loner while there. I slept in the attic of an Old French Chateau all by myself … I had a lot of time to think here and had no chance to goof off, which was good. I had been in the Army from May 3, 1943 until March 1945 and was obsolete in everything for which I had been trained. True, I had gained a lot of general knowledge, but on Jan. 29, 1945, I turned twenty years of age and as far as I was concerned, I was as useless as the tits on a boar hog. One day, posted on our bulletin board, was a notice that the Infantry was in need of gun Fodder. They needed Second Lieutenants. I decided that I would rather fight in the Infantry than go on like I had been doing. I volunteered, and was sent to Infantry OCD in Fontainebleau, France. In eight weeks, I was commissioned a Second Lieutenant, only three months from the time I left the 978th. I moved from the rank of a Model T Corporal to the rank of Second Lt. I was commissioned on May 14, 1945, six days after the war ended.

Helmick stayed in occupied Germany and married an American woman who was stationed in Berlin at the State Department. They returned to the U.S. in September 1947. In June 1951, while in the reserves, he was recalled to active duty during the Korean War.

I also spoke with Helmick on the phone:

> Heck, I thought it would be a war. I thought that everybody would be going. I didn't know it'd be just a police action. I went over in the infantry. I was a platoon leader and was immediately sent up to the front lines. When I got to the front I went to the Captain and said, "I have no experience in combat, can I go out with the first patrol?" He said no. But the next day I was called up. And I got my experience real quick. [laughs] I was involved in the Koje-do prisoner of war conflict that erupted when the Chinese prisoners inside Compound 76 captured General Dodd. I won two Bronze Stars for valor. We were ambushed and I pulled out two people. It was an exciting time.

Helmick's stories about his combat experiences in Korea were often graphic. Yet he talked about them with enthusiasm, even when recounting some of the more terrifying incidents and gruesome details. I commented to Helmick that the men I interviewed had such different reactions to what they saw, that some men got choked up about seemingly less traumatic incidents while others talked unemotionally and matter-of-factly about hard combat. He said:

> Of course they did. Everybody finds a way to deal with it and handles these things in his own way. But I'm just a different caliber person than a lot of them. I don't know why, but I never let things bother me.
>
> You know, in Korea, I sent men out on patrol, gave orders for them to do such and such. And they died. It doesn't make you feel good, to know that you're responsible. Things happen. One time I sent a man out to patrol something that was only about one hundred yards away. The normal procedure is to send two. But I didn't want to send two men. So I sent only one. The other guy stayed. What I didn't know was that the Sergeant had already seen some enemy and was getting ready to attack when the man went over there and walked right into them, and they killed him. That gives me very bad feelings. But the man who didn't go, he had it even worse than I did.

I mean, it just didn't affect me as much as some guys. But those who were emotional went through hell. But, then again, I remember one time my wife and I were watching a war movie, and the men were getting emotional when remembering what happened. And I said to my wife: "What's their problem? It doesn't bother me." And she said: "What are you talking about? In the first three months after you got back from Korea, you were up in the middle of the night giving orders and yelling out." [laughs] So who's to say it didn't affect me?

Helmick was one of the most articulate men I interviewed. In spite of his negative feelings about his time in the 978th, his tone was not one of bitterness or cynicism, but rather of bemused curiosity, with a respect for the uniqueness of his experiences. He did not speak in absolutes, but in a tone that seemed to say, "This is what I remember. Take it or leave it."

When Helmick sent me his memoirs, he also included a short, handwritten note. It is one of my favorite pieces of correspondence because I believe it articulates an understanding of the nuances of individual experiences and memory. It reads:

> Dear Jeffrey,
> I hope this is what you are looking for. I realize I am rather negative, but the facts speak for themselves. I am sure the unit did well the last three months of the war.
> My anecdotes are written from the eyes of a GI and are as truthful as I can recollect.
> Truth has many origins …
>
> Good luck, Jeffrey,
> Hank Helmick

Most of all I enjoyed Helmick's choice of words and phrases: "anecdotes," "from the eyes of a GI," "as truthful as I can recollect," and "truth has many origins." In a few sentences he summed up what I had learned about the war, about the World War II generation, and about history in general: individual stories are not definitive truths, but rather "anecdotes" written from the perspective of one person; another person may remember the same event in a vastly different way; fifty-year-old memories are as truthful as the person can remember, but time can alter these memories; and truth can be an abstract concept. History can never hope to be truth. At best it can strive to be a collection of anecdotes and recalled events assembled and processed in a responsible way that hopefully creates some picture and an understanding of what happened.

Several years after interviewing Helmick, I was trying to find another veteran of the 978th, Daniel Burford. I never found him. However, in the course of my search I came across WWII veteran Maxwell Burford, eighty-nine, of Pennsylvania. Burford was not in the 978th; he was in a bomb-disposal unit. He told me over the phone: "When we started we had a Captain and six noncoms. I was the only survivor of the squad that started. Then we got four replacements. They all died too. I was the only one who made it."

I told Burford about my book and asked him if he would be willing to share his experiences about the war. I enjoyed his reply:

If I can tell you what the war is like? Well, it's like the men from Hindustani, all blind, who went to see the elephant. Each one felt the elephant. The first one felt the leg and said, "It's like a tree." The second one felt the trunk and said, "It's like a snake." And the third one and so on, you know the story. And they all were right, see, all partly right. But they were all completely wrong. I could tell you about the war, but you couldn't get a picture of it. Everybody has a different story. The generals in the back with their maps had one story. The guys in the middle, another one. And it all comes back to the dogface up front. That's exactly why I say I can't tell you what the war was like. I can just tell you what I experienced. The private. The general. Whoever. It'd be just like the blind men looking at that elephant.

INTERVIEWING VETERANS

You know, when I look back on it, the war was the most interesting part of my life.

—William Musiker, from a phone conversation

INTERVIEWING MEN OF THE 978TH was not always easy. Some were hard of hearing, some had a wealth of experiences but were not good at communicating them, and others were suffering from the preliminary stages of Alzheimer's—or so they often warned me. But in general, the better the GI's memory, the more he complained that it was not what it used to be. There were awkward yet poignant moments too. One time I called one of the GIs who had not replied to my letter. An elderly woman answered the phone. I told her who I was and said, "I was hoping to speak to a Mr. Carleton Griffith."[1] Her voice suddenly grew sentimental and she replied, "Boy, I'd sure like to talk to him too. It's now been over twenty years, bless his heart."

Sometimes I had to contend with protective wives. William Musiker said he was thrilled to speak to me, but after a while I could hear his wife in the background.

Jeff, I'm eighty-eight. I recently had triple bypass surgery. You should have seen it. They crack you open like a chicken. My wife's always harassing me. Watches me like a baby. Won't let me do anything. But let me tell you about Spekholzerheide. We arrived and …

> [in the background]
> Bill, why are you getting all nervous?!

Never mind that, Jeff. Now, we arrived in Spek and …

> Bill, you're getting nervous. Tell that young man that
> you can't talk right now.

*Hold on, Jeff. [to wife] Listen, I'm not getting nervous. I'm just fine! I'm just
telling him what happened.*

> No, you're not. I can hear you, Bill. You're talking
> louder than usual and getting all excited.

OK. Maybe I'm getting excited. But it doesn't mean I'm getting nervous!
    *OK, Jeff. Now, we arrived in Spekholzerheide and I met this beautiful
Dutch girl. I was gonna marry her. I probably should have [laughs]. But
then …*

> Come and get dinner. You don't need to be talking
> about the war anymore. It's making you all nervous. Tell that
> young man to hang up. You know what your doctor said.

*Damn it. I'm not getting nervous. The doctor said not to overexert myself,
but he didn't say I couldn't talk on the phone.*

> Yeah, and you're getting all nervous. Bill, I don't want to
> have to call the ambulance again.

*[whisper] Listen, Jeff. Can you call back in about an hour and a half? My
wife goes to bingo then.*

A few weeks later I telephoned Musiker again. This time his wife
answered.

Hello.

> Hello, this is Jeff Badger calling. May I speak to…

Is this the Mr. Badger who's always calling about the war?

> I have called a few times, yes ma'am.

Mr. Badger, listen. My husband's kind of an old man. He had a triple bypass a few years ago, and the last thing he needs is to be getting all riled up about the war. Every time he speaks to you he talks louder than usual and gets all excited. And that's exactly what he doesn't need. Do you understand?

Yes, ma'am. And how is he doing?

Not well. He's not able to get up and get around. All his friends are dead. He has no one to visit and nothing to do. He's basically a prisoner trapped in his own house. Do you know what I mean? It's not an exciting existence. And that's not easy for him. So he loves to talk.

Well, I see what you mean. It sounds like he's seen some tough times. But perhaps that's a good thing, that he enjoys talking to me. If discussing the war is something that still interests him and gives him pleasure, then why not let him do it?

Figure 21. "A bar in somewhere in Germany."
(Photo and caption courtesy of Thomas Orton, seated center, with eyeglasses)

But with his health, he doesn't need to be discussing the war. And you know something? I'm not so happy with his war days. In fact, I am sick and tired of the goddamn war. It's been over since forty-five. But Bill, he's made the war a continuous part of his life. He loves to sit and talk about the war. He watches the war movies, and there's so much of it on the news. My husband has made this war a huge part of his life for fifty years, and I am sick of it. It's been over for more than fifty years. But Bill, he still goes on and on about the goddamn war.

Well, I really enjoy talking to your husband. And he has
so much to say.

Let me add something to that. Bill is very bright. Both educated and bright. You can be bright and not educated, but my husband is both. He's bright, and he was at that time in his life [during the war] also.

Yes ma'am. I noticed that right away. That's why I enjoy
talking to him so much.

The other men, I don't know what their thoughts are. But, let me ask you this. Have you spoken to anybody else, anybody other than my husband?

Yes, ma'am, about forty men.

And do their stories jibe? I mean, do they tell you the same thing?

Absolutely not. One of the most interesting aspects is
that men remember the same events in so many different
ways. And react to them so differently.

Exactly. That's the baloney of the whole thing. So when you write this book, is it going to be factual?

Well, I really appreciate your point. I'm not telling the
story of the war, or even of the 978th. I'm just going to say
what the men told me.

We talked for a while longer. Once she was able to vent her frustration and then hear me out, she warmed up to me. She even took up my cause, giving me advice about writing my book. Finally, she said:

Okay, Jeff. It was nice talking to you. I'll let you talk to my husband. And feel free to call anytime. But don't tell Bill you were talking to me. Oh, heck, I don't care. Go ahead and tell him.

1. The name Carleton Griffith is a pseudonym.

A TIDBIT ABOUT SKI

MY CONVERSATIONS WITH WIVES AND children of the veterans were often as interesting as my conversations with the veterans themselves. The men gave me one picture, their friends in the war gave another, but their wives and children gave me a view from another time and place, a separate set of circumstances. All were different, but all contributed to the picture of the men's personalities I was able to piece together.

My mom told me the following story many times when I was growing up:

All during my childhood there was a boy named Bucky who always bullied me. We lived in the little apartment complex on 74th Street. Most often, it was when he would not allow me to participate when playing cowboys and Indians or marbles. We'd usually end up fighting. Bucky would clobber me, and I'd come home bawling. Finally, when I was around seven or eight, my dad got fed up. He said that I'd either have to learn to defend myself or "get used to being beat up."

My dad learned how to box in the service. He took me down into the basement of our apartment building, put boxing gloves on me, and taught me how to fight. He taught me how to close my fist with my thumb outside, and we practiced keeping my fists up. And he insisted I "go for the nose."

A few days later, Bucky again kept me from playing with the gang. We got into a pushing match and the usual name-calling. He was pushing me, and I could feel myself starting to cry again. I looked up and saw my dad standing on the second floor of our apartment building. His arms were crossed and he gave me a stern look, as if to say, "You're not coming back into this house until you take care of that

Figure 22. My grandfather and my mom.

bully." At that point I think I was more scared of my father than I was of Bucky.

We got into a fight. I think I was losing. Then I looked up at my dad, and he kept pointing at his nose. I finally let Bucky have it in the nose and gave him a good punch in the chest. Down he went and tears came to him for a change.

I walked up the stairs to my dad like a champ. Bucky never laid a finger on me again.

My mom sometimes jokes that such an undiplomatic approach could get a kid—and especially the kid's parents—into trouble these days but that "times were different back then."

Little did I realize that my grandfather's confidence in the diplomatic potential of his fists would enter into my search for Ski. After much anticipation, I finally received a response from somebody who did not know Ski but at least recognized him in one of the photographs I had sent along with my letter. An e-mail from the daughter of Donald Mazzera read:

Jeff, my dad said, "I don't recognize your grandfather, but I do recognize Ski with him." My father said this Ski fellow was always trying to get my dad to do some competitive boxing. He never obliged.

It seemed that all was not lost. At least somebody recognized Ski and placed him in the 978th, and the reference to boxing was indeed a reasonable association with my grandfather. This news raised my hopes that I might be getting closer to at least discovering Ski's identity. But I was still left with the apprehension of wondering if he was still alive and, if so, whether I would ever be able to find him. Still, this tidbit gave me a glimmer of hope, and I sent off a new batch of letters.

SPEKHOLZERHEIDE

WHILE I WAITED FOR MORE news of Ski, I kept up my correspondence and interviews with other veterans. As I got to know them and hear their stories, particularly about events overseas, my thoughts drifted to Europe, particularly the Netherlands, Germany, and France, where many of the experiences most important to the men took place.

The place that probably left the strongest impression on the men of the 978th was Spekholzerheide, in the southern province of Limburg in

Figure 23. The Spekholzerheide Post Office, November 1944. (Photo courtesy of William Musiker)

the Netherlands. The 978th arrived on November 7, 1944, and spent three weeks there. The people of Spekholzerheide had suffered for several years under Nazi occupation, and the 978th arrived just a few weeks after the town was liberated. The Dutch people welcomed the unit with open arms.

Without exception, every GI I corresponded with spoke warmly of "Spek"—the friends they made, their romances with local women, and the strong impact that the deprived conditions made on each man's psyche. Of the hundreds of photos I received from 978thers taken during their tour of duty—England, France, Belgium, the Netherlands, Germany, the Philippines, and Japan—the vast majority of photos with civilians in them were taken in Spek.

Leo Pecker's company history talked a great deal about the unit's time in Spekholzerheide.

> The ordinary Dutch people were very enthusiastic over the Yanks, and expressed their gratitude in every way possible. In a short time, many soldiers had made friends and were enjoying home hospitality … In general, the men of the 978th seemed to like the Dutch people best, of all the countries they visited and all the kinds of hospitality they were exposed to … Months after the 978th left Holland, a flourishing correspondence with Dutch friends continued and after the 978th had advanced deep into Germany, a pass to Holland was more highly prized than a pass to a GI rest center.

William Musiker shared his recollections of Spek in e-mails and telephone conversations:

> In Spek, there were empty houses everywhere, most had their windows knocked out from vandals or the Germans or people just stealing things to survive, and we were camped in a corner building that still had glass in the windows. We did our work in the day, mostly getting our equipment together for our move into Germany. We had no supervision whatsoever. We did our work. And when we had some free time, we went fooling around.
>
> Me and my buddy, Lomax, we were wandering around one evening, and we saw some people. And you never know, so we always had our carbines ready. Well, it turned out to be a couple of girls, the Walters sisters, and they invited us over to their parents' house. I know a few words in French and German, so we were able to talk with 'em

reasonably well. It was the mom and dad and the three daughters. The dad owned a junkyard, but the Germans didn't leave him much. And the oldest daughter was married and was there with her husband, the middle one was seventeen or eighteen, and then there was a younger one, who was just a kid, maybe fourteen or so.

And for the next couple a days we'd stop by in the evening and visit with them. They'd fill us in on what had been happening the months and weeks before, during the occupation and the liberation. The Captain told us that we weren't allowed to go there empty-handed, and that we shouldn't take anything from them, so every time we visited we went there loaded: food, chocolate, and stuff. Oh, the chocolate. They loved the chocolate. It didn't taste all that great, but the kids in Spek loved it. They'd never had it before.

That was something I never got used to, the starving children. Every evening the unit would eat dinner out in the open, and the cooks put the slop in these big cans. After a while you couldn't eat it anymore, got sick of it, and would just eat the crackers, chocolate, and coffee. Well, some guys liked it. Lomax loved it. [laughs] When we'd finished eating, we'd throw away whatever scraps were left over. But there were always these little Dutch children, they were so polite. They would gather around the trash bins, some six years old or even younger.

Figure 24. William Musiker and the Walters sisters, November 1944.
(Photo courtesy of William Musiker)

And they'd look at you with these hungry eyes, I mean, literally, these hungry eyes. And we'd give it to 'em.

But the kids wouldn't eat it. They'd put it in their pails and take it home to share with their entire family. So we made 'em eat. We sat 'em on our laps and made them eat until they were full. Then we'd fill up their pails and send 'em home.

We'd been eating the stuff for so long we were sick of it. It was hash to us. But to them it was nectar.

And heck, we had a bunch of rough guys in the unit, coal miners from Kentucky. And they'd sit down and start to eat, and then they'd see the kids waiting for their scraps. And these rough coal miners would say, "Ah, shit," and I mean that in a good way, 'cause how can anybody eat when they see that? And they'd go give them everything they had. They just couldn't say no. Everybody did it.

It's something that one never gets used to. That was over fifty years ago, and it still bothers me when I see a hungry child.

I mean, have you ever been really hungry, I mean *really* hungry? People can't imagine it in the U.S. When people are really hungry,

Figure 25. Caption on back of photo: "On the way back to Valkenburg, Dutch-German Border. Girl charged the equivalent of $10, after all 'all Americans are rich.'"

they'll do anything. Some of the girls would do anything for food. The cooks, they always had broads. You know why? 'Cause they had food. So you can't really call the girls whores, because they were just plain, unadulterated hungry.

Farran Helmick also touched on this point. An excerpt from one of his letters reads:

[In Spekholzerheide] we were barracked near the mine buildings. This was our first experience with hunger. The civilians were on starvation rations. There was very little food and no cosmetics or soap. Two candy bars or two bars of soap and you could buy a girl. Most chose not to. Those who did claimed that the girls would only participate standing up. The girls believed that if they lay down it would make them a whore. War creates strange rationalization when one is only trying to survive.

Our chow hall was about the same as those in the States. We ate well here, and when we came out of the hall, starving Dutch children were clustered around each can, hoping we would scrape our leavings into their containers. It is something one never gets used to.

STILL SEARCHING FOR SKI

BY THIS TIME, I WAS starting to get something of a feel for the 978th and their place in the war, and my focus shifted away from my grandfather and finding his buddies to learning about the experiences of the individual veterans, most of whom did not know my grandfather. But my search for Ski was always simmering on the back burner, and I continued to send out letters.

I had already exhausted all the surnames on the roster of the 978th with a "ski" suffix. With several letters to *ski*-suffixed surnames returned as undeliverable, I became reconciled with the fact that Ski was most likely dead and that I might not even discover his identity. Nevertheless, I kept sending out letters to men I could find, always valuing their responses for what they added to the portrait I was assembling.

Then I received a letter from Howard Cushing of Delaware. He did not write much—and did not include anything about Ski—but he did add at the end that another 978ther, John Powasnik, lived in Bayonne, New Jersey, and gave me the address. Just a few days before this, another veteran mentioned Powasnik in a letter, saying, "John Powasnick was from New Jersey and worked in a bra factory. John would drink and play poker on Saturday night and want me to go to church with him on Sunday." As usual, I sent a letter to this drinking, poker-playing, church-goer who worked in a bra factory.

A few weeks passed without a reply from Powasnik. Considering only about 5 percent of my letters yielded a response, I hardly took notice. Then one evening I returned home from the pub and there was a message on my answering machine from my mom.

> Jeff, we got a phone call last night from one of your war buddies. He lives in New Jersey. He knew my dad real well. They were good buddies. We talked for a long time. Jeff, get a pen and paper so you can write down his phone number. He wants you to call him right away. His name is John Powasnik. But during the war his buddies referred to him as Ski!

I had finally found the infamous and elusive Ski—and what luck that I found him at all. My records indicated that I had searched the phone book for a Powasnik but didn't find anything. It was through Cushing's fifty-year-old contact with him that I managed to track him down. Now I had to call. Would he be as forthcoming and communicative as some of the other veterans? Was he going to have even juicer stories of cathouses and barroom brawls that I may not want to hear?

The next evening I skipped the pub, went straight home, and telephoned Mr. Powasnik. I was greeted with a loud, friendly hello that sounded like it came from an elderly but very energetic man. Mr. Powasnik was delighted to hear from me. Eighty-three years old, he was extremely friendly and positive. I had been referring to him as Ski for so long that calling him Mr. Powasnik felt strange. We spoke for about an hour. He was very interested in what I was doing with my life and wanted to hear about my family, my job, my love life, and what I was up to. He was willing to talk about the war, but did not offer a lot of details about his experiences, nor did he philosophize over them. He tended to focus more on the good times.

> We were always out for a good time, Leo and I—and George [Patrias], especially George. [laughs] Leo was a daredevil; he'd do anything if you put him up to it. And George was always game. George was a happy-go-lucky guy, a strong guy, strong as a mule. Nobody putzed around with ol' George. Heck, Leo and George could've taken on the whole German Army themselves. [laughs]
>
> One of the best times we had was in Marseilles. Leo and I had a couple of days' leave. But we were broke, we didn't really have any money for the bars. So Leo and I got our few francs together and bought some homemade wine. And we had a few francs left and saw a little horse and buggy. And Leo said, "You wanna take a little ride?" So

Figure 26. "Leo and I rented this little horse & buggy and cruised all over Marseilles."
(Photo and caption courtesy of John Powasnik)

we rented it. We cruised all over Marseilles in that thing. I tried to pick up a couple of those French lassies, but didn't have any luck. [laughs] And, well, we had a great evening cruising around in that little horse and buggy. I think I have a photo of it somewhere.

Mr. Powasnik sent me the photo a few weeks later.

Ski talked about the work he did before the war and how some of it carried over into what he did during the war.

I worked for Maidenform bras before I entered the service. And I worked for them when I returned, right up until when I retired. Jeff, I can tell you everything you want to know about bras. What sizes they come in, what materials are best, how much they cost, which ones give the best support. You got a girlfriend, send her to me. I'll fix her up.

Heck, we even had an official Miss Maidenform contest. When we were in Spek, we spent all our free evenings at the beer hall. It used to be the Nazi party headquarters before the war. And we'd go over there and drink. Well, I didn't drink much. And I've never smoked. What I did was, I wrote back to Maidenform in the U.S., and they sent about twenty or so pictures of girls in their Maidenform bras. And we pinned them up and had a vote. Shirley Epstein was the girl who won. A Jewish girl—I met her later, after the war. And she was Miss 978th.

Heck, I even had a sign painted on my jeep of a woman in a Maidenform bra. Had my name written on it, just below the windshield. It said "The Maidenform Kid." Sort of like bomber art, only this was on my jeep, jeep art. [laughs]

I also organized boxing matches at the beer hall. At first we put numbers in a bowl, A, B, C, D, and drew them and the guys boxed each other. Then I recruited a local Dutch guy, I think he was an ex-prize fighter. And I asked for volunteers from the 978th, and Leo was the only guy who stood up. So Leo and him had a little exhibition match. It was a couple of rounds, and Leo did all right, gave this guy a run for his money. I mean, this Dutch guy was no slouch, he was a big guy. But then Leo got tired, and the Dutch guy ended up winning on points. It was a good time.

You know, Leo and I, we never got a chance to get an education. The Depression and all. Gotta get to work and support the family. That's how it was. Leo worked in the heavy machinery business, and I worked in the bra business. We didn't get rich. And it was hard work. But that's fine. I'm not bitter. I had a great time working for Maidenform. But I told my kids, you don't wanna be working in a factory your whole life. You gotta get an education. My son, he's a top guy in his company, worked as an engineer in Malaysia, on those big tall buildings. And my daughter got a real good education. And the family, that's important. I got two kids and four grandkids, and they all live in the area. And they're my pride and joy. They're what keep me going.

Ski and I spoke on the telephone several times, and later I visited him at his home in Bayonne. Our conversations always began with him asking about my family: Were they doing OK? Were they healthy? Were there any new nieces and nephews? How were my parents? He also had a sincere interest in me: What was I doing? How was my job? Was I going to marry the girl I was dating? He was willing to answer my questions about the war, and doing so did not seem to bother him, although he did talk more about his escapades than about the serious aspects of the war. In each conversation, he would talk about the war for a while, then seemed to get bored with it and changed the subject back to my family or his family. He especially liked to talk about his grandkids.

I could see that my grandfather and Ski shared a similar set of values. Both were Catholic, both came from working-class backgrounds, both valued family, and both valued education, even though neither of them had much themselves. My mom often said that my grandfather was frustrated at not having had the opportunity for more education, but he instilled his respect for education in his daughters. All three of them received college degrees at a time when women were not encouraged to pursue education the way men were.

It was enormously gratifying to find Ski. The war had been over fifty-three years and my grandfather had been dead for twenty-eight, but the faded black-and-white of Ski and my grandfather no longer seemed like it belonged to an unreachable bygone era in history. Here was the same guy in the photo I remembered as a child, now on the other end of the telephone line.

But instead of bringing a close to my search, finding Ski just brought more questions and a yearning for more information. Ski said one of my

Figure 27. John "Ski" Powasnik and his grandchildren, 1997. (Photo courtesy of John Powasnik)

grandfather's best friends was Thomas Orton, also from Chicago. I had to track him down. And my mistaken belief before I found him that Ski was dead, and then finding him alive and well at eighty-three years old, created a sense of urgency that I had to find other men before it was too late.

Ski's stories about the 978th's time in Europe shifted my thoughts overseas. I wanted to learn more about the men's experiences in Spekholzerheide, the Roer River crossing at Jülich, and the Mariagrube coal mine in the town of Mariadorf. And in the back of my mind I wondered what those places were like today.

---

1. Although George Patrias and Ski were friends, when I first asked Patrias about the photo of Ski and my grandfather, he didn't recognize Ski. Yet later Patrias talked about his buddy John Powasnik and referred to him as Ski. I don't know if this inconsistency was because of failing eyesight, spotty memories, or something else.

GETTING INTO THE WAR IN GERMANY

MARIAGRUBE

IN LATE NOVEMBER 1944, THE 978th left Spekholzerheide and moved into Germany. The unit set up operations in the abandoned buildings of the Mariagrube coal mine, near the town of Mariadorf, fifteen miles from Spek. The unit was based at Mariagrube twice, from November 29 to December 24, 1944, and again from February 5 to March 1, 1945. Looming in the distance were two large mountains of slag, waste product that had accumulated over the years from the coal refining process. Many GIs described the area as a "very spooky place."

A short time before the 978th arrived, the slag pile and surrounding area had been the site of a battle between the Germans and Americans. Most of the mine buildings had been destroyed, landmines were "everywhere," and American and German corpses were scattered about.

I was curious about the fighting between the Americans and Germans at the Mariagrube minefield before the 978th arrived. I searched the Internet and found two articles. The first, from the unit history of Company B of the 117th Division of the 30th Infantry written by Warren Giles, reads:

> In November, 1944, the 117th Infantry made substantial additions to its already voluminous record of victories and successes in the destruction of the German Army.
>
> In the great offensive that carried the Allies to the banks of the Roer River, the 117th, in the initial assault, carried out what was termed by higher headquarters as three perfect infantry attacks with artillery, tank, direct fire and other supporting weapons faultlessly coordinated. Although engaged offensively for but a short part of the period, the

Figures 28, 29, and 30. Heil Hitler? A break from work at the Mariagrube coal mine. The 978th set up shop in the bombed-out ruins of the abandoned Mariagrube mine near Aachen and spent several weeks working there. The buildings afforded shelter, hiding places, and hot showers. (Photos courtesy of William Musiker)

Regiment captured more than 800 prisoners, large supplies of enemy ammunition, weapons, and other equipment.

On November 16, the Regiment jumped off in a perfectly conducted attack and gained the town of Mariadorf, Germany. The Second and Third Battalions held positions in Alsdorf and supported the attack

Figure 31. Ready for action, in the ruins of the Mariagrube coal mine.
(Photo courtesy of William Musiker)

by fire. Within fifteen minutes form the inauguration of the assault, this section of the hostile main line of resistance had been taken.

This was the attack that newspapers the world over, as well as Corps and Army Headquarters, termed the Perfect Infantry Attack. It was necessary to cross an open field of 1000 yards to attack Mariadorf, but this was done so rapidly that the troops were already fighting in the town when the German defensive artillery fire started falling in the field....

Dense enemy mining was encountered by the attacking force. The foe made extensive use of the wooden "box-type" mine which was extremely difficult to detect. Numerous casualties were suffered while crossing the mine fields and considerable mortar and artillery fire encountered later. However, strong concentrations of friendly artillery and mortar fire had neutralized the bulk of the enemy resistance prior

Figure 32. At the Mariagrube coal mine. During this time in Germany, town officials were required to wear top hats during official functions. Consequently, it was common to find these hats in vacant German homes, and many GIs obtained them as souvenirs to be "Burgermeister of the Day." (Photo courtesy of William Musiker; information on top hats courtesy of Frank W. Towers, president of the 30th Infantry Division Veterans of WWII, Inc.)

to the attack. 104 German prisoners were taken during the day's activities.

The attack was resumed at 0700, November 17, with the First Battalion jumping off from Alsdorf and cleaning out the remainder of the town of Mariadorf.

While this account was filled with enthusiasm and bravado over a great victory, the second, from the 30th Infantry's February 1945 Scrapbook, provided a more sobering account:

The unit of infantry from the 30th division was advancing toward the town of Mariadorf at dusk Friday evening when it encountered a box-minefield. The unit was hurrying to take Mariadorf before darkness was complete. Suddenly mines began to explode; the unit went on and more mines exploded as the unlucky soldiers stepped on them. Soon the mines were exploding too often to continue the advance and the unit attempted to withdraw. But the men were too far into the minefield. As they fell back more mines caused more casualties. Dusk had faded to darkness, the unit was trapped and unable to move in any direction.

The Germans discovered their predicament and pasted the area with mortar and artillery shells. All night the unit stayed in the midst of the minefields, men digging themselves in as best they could. All night other men tried to get to them to bring out the wounded. Engineers tried to break the path with light bulldozers, mines blew the tracks off and crippled the bulldozers. In the pitch dark, mechanics put tracks on again only to have the mines blow the tracks off again and again.

Toward the morning engineers brought up a giant bulldozer which was able to plow a path through the mines. In the meantime during the night five infantrymen, by putting their hands on one another's shoulders and walking in one another's footsteps, managed to feel a pathway through the mines to the unit. However, two of the "lock-steppers" were wounded by mine explosions while on the dark trek.

Not until the bulldozer was able to shovel a clear path through the field were most of the wounded taken out. They lay among the mines in the open on a cold rainy night, with only the first aid their companions were able to give them under mortar and shell fire.

But the morning after the day fight, remnants of the unit advanced to their objective, Mariadorf.

Once again, it was interesting to note the vast differences between accounts of the same events. I was also able to find a photo of the open field near the slag pile.

Figure 33. Photo of the Mariagrube slag pile taken from the northwest, where the 117th Infantry crossed into the minefield. (Photo courtesy of the National Archives, used with permission.)

Farran Helmick, who helped me appreciate these differences, remembered when the 978th arrived on the remains of the battle:

> We arrived at the coal mine about a few days to a week after a battle had taken place between the American infantry and the Germans. Don't ask me how I know this now, I have no idea, but it was Company F, the 117th Infantry Regiment of the 30th Infantry. The Americans had attacked across an open field at night. You can't attack across an open plain like that in the daytime because a machine gun can take out an entire company. So, they attacked at night and they ran into a minefield.
>
> And when we arrived there were about fifteen or twenty bodies of American GIs in the minefield. Most of them were killed by mines, or they were wounded and just laid there and died of their wounds or the cold. And some were killed by machine-gun fire. I didn't see any evidence of mortar fire.
>
> The minefield was laid out so there were about two feet by two feet between mines, and they were done in a grid, with another mine in the center. The entire area looked sort of like a crime scene with tape around the minefield and signs posted everywhere so you wouldn't go in. And you could see the bodies in there.
>
> The Captain called for volunteers to go in and retrieve the bodies. I volunteered but wasn't chosen. I was a damn fool kid, would volunteer for anything. [laughs] These little mines are called Schü mines. They have a quarter block of explosives, about the size of a quarter pound or a quarter of a stick of butter, and it's in this little square wooden box. And they're buried an inch or two beneath the surface.
>
> The idea is that when you step on them, they don't kill you right away. They're meant to incapacitate you, to blow your foot off. Because, for every man who's crippled, it takes ten men to take care of him. That's the strategy. So, it's better to cripple ya than to kill ya.
>
> We'd been trained in basic on how to probe for mines with bayonets. What you do is, you inch forward on your hands and knees digging in the ground. And when you hit something, you dig all around it and take out the little wooden box. And there's a little cap that sets it off, and you take out the little plunger to diffuse it. Once you find it, defusing it's the easy part.

They took about half dozen to a dozen guys and set out across the minefield. The way you do it is you start out from the edge of the minefield and move your way in toward a body, making a path about the width of a man. And once you get there you take the shortest path to the next one. So it sort of looks like a spider web. By the time they were finished they had a big pile of mines about three feet high.

I was stationed in Germany for quite a while after the war. There were millions and millions of mines. They used German prisoners to find 'em and dig them up. It took years and years.

What saved a lot of guys was that the ground was frozen, and I think that prevented a lot of the mines from going off. There were a lot of other bodies in the area that we were picking up. I came across one American GI lying on his back who had a letter sticking out of his breast pocket. Foolish me, I read it. He looked to be in his mid-to-late twenties. He was married and the letter was from his wife with a picture of her and two or three kids. He was from Kentucky, my neighboring state. That hit home quite hard. I got pretty choked up. After I read a few lines I suddenly felt like a thief. That letter belonged to him, and I was intruding on his privacy. I put the letter back and believe me, I was one sobered young man. The war was real.

Another scene that will stay with me the rest of my life. One GI had been running across the field. He was a machine-gun assistant. He was carrying a metal case of ammo in each hand. He had been shot and killed in his tracks. He had fallen slightly forward so that he was in a position on one knee and both hands holding his two cases of ammo. His body hung and froze in that position. He was like a sprinter getting ready to leave the starting line at the sound of the gun. It was weird.

There were also a lot of dead Germans in the area. I remembered finding two of them dead in a foxhole. There was one old man, about fifty-five or sixty, and a young kid, about fourteen or sixteen years old, in the same foxhole. During the fighting they were shot and killed there. For the entire month we were there we didn't do anything with them. The American bodies were picked up as soon as we could. The German bodies, they were frozen there in their little foxhole, they would have laid there until after the war.

They brought the guys from the minefield over and we brought over the others we had retrieved. Then they called the GRS, the

Graves Registration, who came in a big two-and-a-half-ton truck. The bodies were frozen and they threw them onto the truck like they were cordwood. It's a job that, if you let compassion set in for each one of these bodies, it'd drive you crazy. These guys, they were smoking and wise-cracking. They became inured to it. But us, it was new to us, and we were all affected by it.

Mariagrube marked the beginning of a new phase of the war for most of the men of the 978th. Upon entering Germany, the sight of dead bodies and, in many cases, their retrieval, had a significant impact on the men's psyches. Some men got choked up talking about it. But it was a subject they brought up frequently and discussed in vivid detail.

A RIFLE AND A TUNNEL

ONE OF MY MOST PLEASANT correspondents was Austin "Jack" Cable, eighty-one, of Florida. He began his first letter to me with, "Well son, you really found a 'live one' this time. Yes, I was a proud member of the 978th, from its beginning to end. Not a very pleasant trip but I guess we all made it."

Cable's letters were typed on an old-fashioned typewriter on thin typewriter paper. After a page or so he apparently got fed up with the typewriter and continued on the back, writing with a pen. In his letter Cable wrote that, at the time of the war, he was married and had an infant son. His classification was 4F, meaning he was far down on the list of potential draftees. Since he was working in the construction business, he said that he probably could have gotten a deferment. But, he wrote, "in talking it over with my wife and both families, thought it better to be an American." He joined the service and, with his experience with construction equipment, was assigned to the 978th.

In several of the letters Cable mentioned a rifle that he acquired in Germany. When the 978th was on the boat to the Pacific, he had most of the men in the unit sign the wooden stock. It went with him to Manila, and he eventually brought it back home to the U.S. He had planned on passing it down to his son. However, he wrote, "We were extremely unfortunate to have lost our son last August 16, 1997. There are no words in the world to convey this. That's why I was kind of looking for another owner."

A few weeks later he wrote again.

> After much thought and fussing I have decided that the best home for *the ole German rifle* was with friends and family in Texas.

Naturally there were many reasons for this decision, which I will explain later. So I hope you will agree. After all its world travels, it was signed out through United Parcel and should reach its final resting place about next Thursday.

Cable's rifle arrived at my parents' house. A few days later came a letter describing how he had obtained it:

> [W]e moved to a large abandoned coal mine in Mariagrube. Around the south perimeter of the mine we found an opening leading underground. What this lead to was a tunnel, sloped to take a person down to about a depth of 25 feet below normal ground ... What we found was an average mine shaft, just enough room to stand up, with double wooden bunks and a very small gauge tracks running immediately alongside. This seemed to be a place to accommodate

Figure 34. Austin "Jack" Cable of Florida. (Photo courtesy of William Musiker, who remembered Cable as "a happy-go-lucky kid")

about a platoon of special guards, lookouts, or whatever. There were signs of living, cooking, etc. all over.

As mentioned before, the only fun a GI had was looting. There were three of us … When I arrived at the above-mentioned spot, I turned my head and at eye and bunk level, 10 inches away was a dead German, a hole in his chest and the rifle along his wall side, and I don't believe that red stuff was cherry pop. At that stage of the war the Germans were using everything they could find. As far as we could check that is a German rifle or it could be most anything. But after that experience I would not debate the issue.

Jeff thanks again. But I hope you realize that outside of my wonderful granddaughter you are the only one I write to. Excuse all the errors.

A. Jack Cable

I sent a thank-you letter. During the year after I received the rifle, I moved from Ireland to England to three different towns in Sweden, working short contracts. In addition, I was writing my Ph.D. thesis in the evenings and learning Swedish. It was also during this time that I found several other veterans and was spending time corresponding with them. Life was busy.

When things finally settled down, I decided to ask Cable for more details about the rifle. I sent him a letter. A week later I received a reply from his wife. He had died.

This was my first "war buddy" to pass away and it was troubling for me. I knew they wouldn't be around forever, and I would later lose many others I was close to, but this was the first and it hit home that this generation was fading away. I sent a letter of condolences to the family and then kicked myself for having not asked my questions sooner. I also kick-started my search and interviews into high gear, realizing every day mattered.

But I still wanted to know more about this tunnel where the rifle was found. I checked my notes and found some comments from Farran Helmick, who had spoken about the same tunnel in a letter and a phone conversation:

In one of our first scrounging forays, we found a tunnel leading down into and under one of the smaller slag piles. It was dug out like a coal mine and had wooden frames to help support the weight from above. Although it was dug in slag, the material was so compacted that the tunnel was reasonably safe. After fifty feet down, the Germans had hollowed out a huge room about ten by twenty. . . . They had built-in bunks, and they had interlaced communications wire to make beds for themselves. There were several bodies there. They had all died from gangrene-infected wounds. They were all big men and of course were swollen from gangrene, which made them appear even larger.

There were two or three bodies there, maybe more. They were all puffed up, bloated. There were all types of guns and ammunition belts and stuff. And we took what we thought was interesting. I picked up a carbine that was the nicest machined piece that I ever saw over there. It was a Steyer, made in Czechoslovakia. I also got a Mauser and some others. I packed them up and sent them home to my family. We didn't mess with the bodies. I'd seen some guys go through pockets and stuff, but we weren't that gross. [laughs]

It was a cool and pleasant place. What happened was, the 117th Infantry attacked during the night, and these guys were shot or wounded. So, they were taken down there, and the place was used as a makeshift hospital. Finally, the area was overrun by the Americans, all the able-bodied Germans left, and nobody knew these guys were there. The Americans went right through, probably didn't even notice the tunnel and weren't going to venture down there if they did. And the people were left down there and died of their wounds or just bled to death. And then a few days later we found 'em.

They probably lay there for the rest of the war, until the summer, five or six months. Then, I suppose either somebody went in there and got them, or they just took some explosives and sealed the place up at the entrance, made a permanent grave out of it. I don't know. That's what I would have done. But I'm too practical. [laughs]

Ski also remembered the tunnel.

We found the tunnel, and some guys were afraid to go down there, 'cause you never knew. It could have been booby-trapped or something. But we went down, and it was a nice little living quarters. Really well kept.

And we found several bodies of dead German soldiers. They had pictures of their families with them, their parents, their kids back home. And you knew that they felt the same way we did. They have these nice little families left behind. And here they were. One German was still in his bunk bed. There was one guy there with his shoes off. One guy was holding a little container of sauerkraut. And it still had some sauerkraut in it. They'd been there a couple of days. How they died, I don't know.

It gave me the shudders. War was about killing.

Hey, Jeff, don't get me wrong. That doesn't mean that you can't go out and fight and kill if you had to, you don't let it bother you. You can't take pity on that. You're in a foreign, hostile country. You're not gonna go back and worry about it. But, just that, at that particular moment, well, it brought back memories of home.

I could not find my grandfather's signature on the rifle—many signatures were blurred—but I did find several others that I recognized, including George Patrias—Detroit; John Powasnik—Bayonne, NJ; Thomas D Orton—Chicago; Richard G Snell—Toledo, Ohio; Francis Recktenwald—Seattle, Wash.

Some experts told me that the rifle is a 1914 Carcano. It is not valuable. An original 1914 Carcano can be purchased on the Internet for less than a hundred dollars. Yet this 1914 Carcano means more to me than any pricy WWII souvenir. It was a gift from a man who appreciated my interest in him and his experience at a difficult time in his life. And it has a story.

By 1944–45, it was already an antiquated weapon, thirty years old, perhaps used in World War I. Then, as far as I can reconstruct, it was the last possession of a German man who, as he lay in his bunk at the bottom of the slag pile bleeding to death from a bullet hole in his chest, surrounded by photos of his family, held onto it in the possibility that he might need it to defend himself.

The rifle then lay in the dead German's hands for a few more days before Cable took it and carried it with him for six additional months in Germany. It took the long trip to the Pacific and then back across the ocean to the U.S., where it lay in Cable's house for another fifty years. The weapon now sits in the guest bedroom of my parents' house in Texas. When I establish a permanent residence, I will display it with all of the other souvenirs and photos from my correspondence with the men of the 978th.

Eventually all the people from the war will be gone from us. Austin Cable is already gone, as is the dead German man who last used the Carcano rifle. I wondered about Farran Helmick's speculation that the entrance to the mine was sealed after the war. If so, then that German soldier still lies at the bottom of the slag pile in his bunk, his arms clutching for the now-absent rifle, surrounded by pictures of his family, next to the man with his shoes off and the man with the sauerkraut still in the can. His body is sealed off from us. But his story, albeit assembled piecemeal and incomplete, survives.

MARVIN MANGHAM

MY MOM SAID THAT MY grandfather did not talk much about the war. But the few times he did, there was one incident in particular that upset him:

> There was one incident my dad mentioned a few times, but he always got choked up when he did. He mentioned "the bodies in the water," how the water was red from the blood of the dead soldiers. I can still picture him telling me about it; his face would tense up and then he'd start to get choked up and wouldn't continue. I can't remember where this was at, if it was Normandy or somewhere else.

This was one of two questions that continued to nag me as I pressed on with my research. The other was one of the photos that my grandfather brought home from the war, a picture of him and an unknown GI standing beside an outside table. There was no caption.

Like my hope for ever finding Ski, it seemed certain that both the identity of the person in the photo and the details about the bodies in the water that upset my grandfather would forever remain a mystery to me.

However, after I received a letter from Marvin Mangham, seventy-four, of Waco, Texas, I felt like I had a chance to capture an elusive piece of history before it was too late:

> Dear Jeffrey,
> It was quite a surprise to receive your letter and I remember your grandfather, Leo, very well. At one time, we shared the same pup-tent.
> I remember the Roer River and the coal mine. Your grandfather and I were sent to repair a crane that was hit and damaged while

Figure 35. Leo Kavanaugh and unknown GI.

laying a pontoon bridge across the Roer River. The bridge was bombed and destroyed twice. I remember that while working one day something in the sky caught our attention. It was the first jet plane any of us had ever seen or heard. I was on guard duty at about 2:00 a.m. one morning when they began the offensive on the Roer River crossing with 2500 artillery pieces. What a show that was—Leo and I were strafed with machine-gun fire from planes twice. Once while in a truck and the other while in a building. Some time later, when we crossed the Roer River again there was not a building left standing that was more than 4 feet tall.

There were four platoons in our company of 398 men, Leo and I were in the contact platoon. Your grandfather was a very good mechanic and heavy equipment operator. I remember a few of the men from our company: W. D. Cross was from Palestine, Texas, he and I were close friends. Horace W Pitts was our first Sergeant and at one time so was Cross. Horace W Pitts was from North Carolina. John Powasnick was from New Jersey and worked in a bra factory. John would drink and play poker on Saturday night and want me to go to church with him on Sunday. I recall that we had a man killed while moving one night. He fell off the truck and was run over by a truck. Julio Ramirez from California

Figure 36. Leo Kavanaugh. A photo my grandfather brought home from the war.

Figure 37. A photo Mangham sent me of himself.
(Photo courtesy of Marvin Mangham)

was hit in the arm by a bomb fragment while standing in the chow line one day. He was out for 3 months before returning to us (his platoon).

Oh, by the way, that's me in the photo with Leo with us sitting on the table. Where it was taken I'm not for sure. I have enclosed a couple of pictures, you'll notice that one of them is at the exact same place as the photo of Leo that you sent me. I am returning your photos to you but have made myself a copy of them. Thanks for sending them.

Note: Our company holds the record for the most number of days at sea (69) and for the most number of miles covered by an Engineering Maintenance Company.

I wish I could be of more help but 54 years is a long time ago and I was only about 19 years old at the time.

When you have time I would like to know when and how Leo passed away. Unfortunately, I never saw Leo again after we left the Philippines for Japan. I thought maybe he got out earlier than I did...

Also enclosed in the envelope was a second letter. It was from Mangham's daughter.

Dear Mr. Badger,

My name is Laurie Brown. I am Marvin Mangham's youngest daughter and typed the letter from him you just read. Your letter was very interesting and I hope my father's few lines help you feel a little closer to your grandfather.

Recently, in May of this year, we lost my mom. She passed away on Memorial Day and dad, naturally, has had a difficult time. So, when your letter arrived it was wonderful to see him get so enthused when discussing it. He's been talking about the "old" days and trying to remember all the guys from his unit.

I just wanted to take a minute and let you know how much your letter had meant to dad (and me) so, if you are ever in Waco, give us a call. I'm sure he would love to tell you all about it in person ... Take care and many thanks.

Besides the photos, one of the few things my grandfather brought home from the war was a poster with the title "Roer River Crossing at Julich." From what I could gather, the Army must have given out these posters some weeks after the operation to the men in the units involved. When I first found it, I didn't know the context, so it didn't mean much to me. Now, with a little more information, I pulled it out again. In the center is a map of the town of Jülich with the Roer River running through it. Arrows point to the location of the six crossing sites. Next to each crossing site is an "action drawing." Engineers assemble the different types of bridges at each site—a treadway bridge, a Bailey bridge, a foot bridge, a heavy pontoon bridge, and an infantry support bridge. At the bottom is a list of the ten engineering units involved in the crossing. One of these is the 978th.

The simple drawings were very illustrative and conveyed the bridge building better than any text could have. They showed GIs at the edge of a wide river, with trucks and other pieces of heavy machinery nearby, assembling the pontoon boats, wire cables, and treadways to construct the bridge. With these drawings I was able to visualize to some extent the events of the Roer River. I hoped Mr. Mangham would be able to tell me more.

———————

A few months later, during my next trip to Texas, I visited Mangham at his home in Waco. I was greeted by a slim, fit-looking man whose neatly parted hair I recognized immediately from the photo with my grandfather. Mangham's daughter was also there. He offered me a Dr Pepper, and the three of us sat down at his kitchen table.

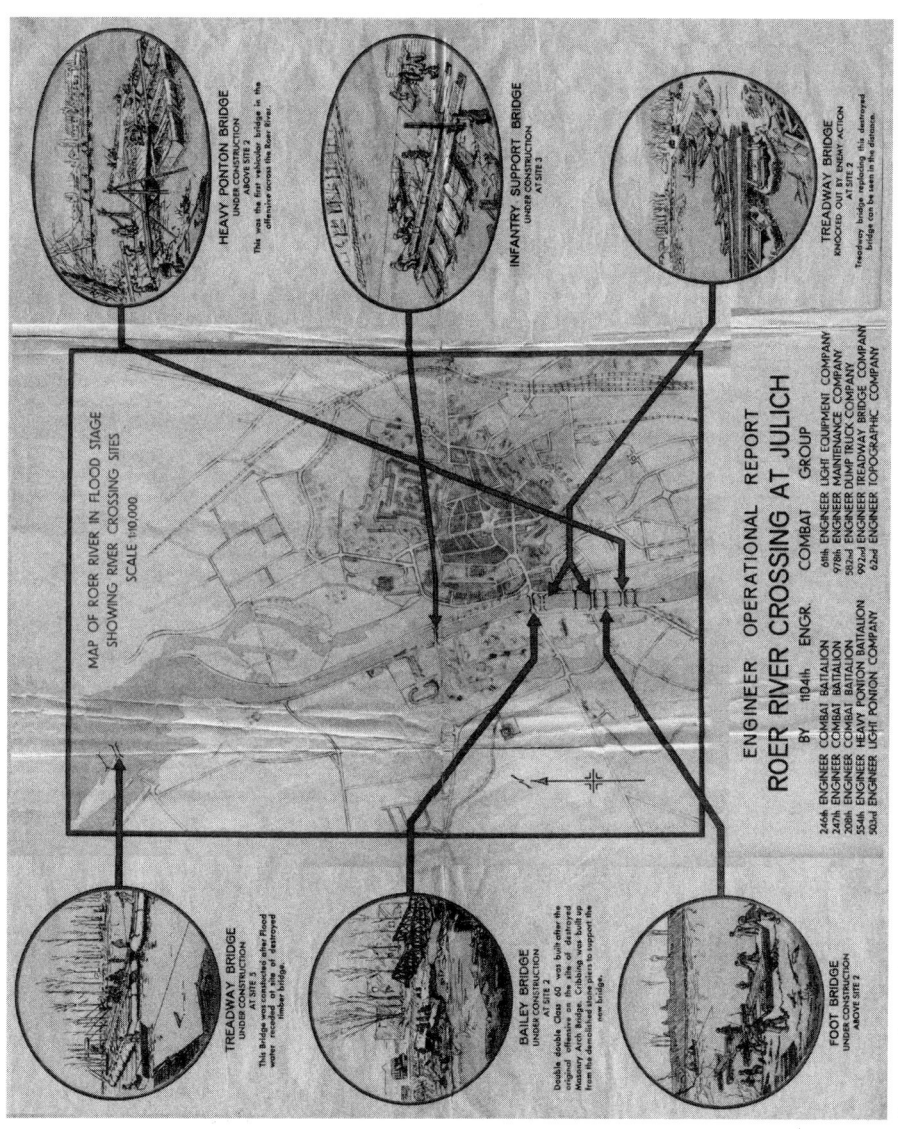

Figure 38. Poster of Roer River crossing at Jülich.

Mangham struck me as a sincere, hard-working, straight-talking, soft-spoken man, the type who let his accomplishments speak for themselves. After he returned home from the war he got a job at an iron works company as a welder, a skill he picked up in the service, working for fifty cents an hour. He stayed with the same company for his entire forty-five-year career. "Not many people can say that anymore, can they?" he said. He had raised three children, one of whom was also in the service. Now retired, he spends his time with his children and in the rec-room attached to his house, where he has a pool table and a dart board. He said, "Coors and King Edward cigars are what keep me goin'."

I asked him about my grandfather and about Ski.

Yeah, I remember Leo real well. He was an all-around good fellow. A tough, no-nonsense guy. He didn't take no guff off of anybody. We palled around, but he was a few years older than I was. I was only about nineteen at the time.

The guys from Texas, Arkansas, Oklahoma. We were more together, stuck together more. Powasnik and I were always arguing. He was always smartin' off about Texas.

Mangham spent a few minutes looking through the two hundred or so photographs that I had collected from other 978thers. He went through them one by one in a slow, deliberate way, seeming to take in many of the details. For the first time in almost sixty years he was looking at images that he had held only in his memories. He was a teenager the last time had seen the people and places in these photos. The expression on his face did not seem to be one of strong interest or any sentimentality—neither pleased nor troubled—but rather studied and curious. He did not say a lot about the photos. After looking through them he gave them back to me. I set them on the table. Throughout the rest of our conversation he did not look at them again.

Later, Mangham talked about what were for him some of the more difficult experiences of the war.

There were some guys who couldn't handle it. There was one guy when we were staying in a hotel in Belgium. He shot himself. There was another guy, at a railroad crossing. He jumped off a bridge to commit suicide. He damn near killed himself. Some said it was an accident, that he was drunk. Some didn't.

Another time we went into a tunnel where some Germans were when they got killed. There were photos of the guys' girlfriends and families, even their kids. They were lying dead in their cots. One guy was barefoot. That gave us some sympathetic feelings.

Continuing, Mangham told me about the Roer River crossing he had described in his letter.

Your granddad and I were sent to the Roer River on a job. The Americans were building bridges across the river to get troops and supplies over, and the Germans were trying to stop us. There was a crane there, had been knocked out by German artillery, and we were sent to repair it.

Mangham's words came more slowly, with pauses between the sentences.

The Americans had pushed the Germans back, but they were still within artillery range. We'd build a bridge, and as soon as we made contact, we'd send over as many troops and supplies as we could, and then the Germans would send artillery over and blow it up. And we'd do it again. That one bridge we were working on, they [the Germans] had blown it up twice already.

The crane we were sent to repair … [long pause] … the way it worked was, our job was to repair it on the spot … If we couldn't do that, then we dragged it back and fixed it back behind the lines.

His speech slowed even more, the expression on his face became more serious, and he seemed to retreat further within himself. During a long pause, I interjected:

> Mr. Mangham, please don't feel obligated to talk about anything you don't want to.

He continued, but I could see he was becoming choked up.

No, that's all right. Leo and I … your granddad and I, we were working on the crane…the guy operating it, he was still in his seat … he was dead … And we were trying to repair it … and the artillery was coming in … and … and … I'm sorry … I'm sorry …

I interjected:

> Mr. Mangham, I can't imagine how tough that
> must have been for you guys. I just appreciate your
> letting me come and visit with you. Why don't we
> talk about something else?

While he regained his composure, his daughter and I spoke about how we can forget that even after fifty years, memories of such a difficult time still can be upsetting and painful. He said, "Well, we had a walk in the park compared to what some guys had to do."

Mr. Mangham and I talked a little more about my grandfather and some other things. We then went into the rec-room and played a few games of pool. Eventually it began to get late. I said I would have to be leaving soon.

Are you sure? You're more than welcome to stay and listen to Rush Limbaugh with me.

> I'd like to, Mr. Mangham. But I still have a few hours'
> drive to my parents' house.

Well, all right. But Rush is on in twenty minutes.

> So you like Rush?

Oh, yeah. Old Rush knows what's going on. If there's ever something going on in the news, I just tune in to Rush. He tells it like it is and sets ya straight on the whole thing. I never miss ol' Rush.

A few days later, Mangham's daughter and I exchanged a few e-mails. She wrote:

> Jeff, I know dad enjoyed visiting with you, but he has mentioned
> that he feels like he didn't really have that much to say. He said it was a
> long time ago and that he's tried to forget some of it. I just can't imagine
> it and I hope this country never has to do anything like it again.

––––––––

After I received the first letter from Mangham, I figured out that it was the events at the Roer River crossing that upset my grandfather when

Figure 39. Marvin Mangham, playing pool in his rec-room in Waco, Texas, December 2007.

he spoke to my mom about "the bodies and blood in the water." So I knew that there was the possibility that Mangham would get choked up over it. But considering that almost sixty years had passed and that Mangham had invited me to his home, I naively assumed that this would not be the case. I quickly learned otherwise. In fact, Mangham was the first of many GIs to became choked up as they talked with me. At first it made me uncomfortable. I figured if I had not made contact with them, they would not have had to relive these painful memories. And I prefaced each subsequent conversation by saying that I did not want the GIs to talk about anything they did not want to. But the strange thing was that so many of them insisted on continuing, even when they did get choked up. Moreover, I never got the impression that they continued just for me. More often it seemed that it was cathartic for them. And later they told me so. One GI said he considered our conversations "a challenge" and decided early on that he was going to "take it on" and try to "push through it." Later he told me it "helped heal the wounds." Merlin Clark told me in a phone conversation a few weeks after our meeting that he felt relieved and that our discussion had "brought an end to the whole thing" for him.

But in Mangham's case, I got the impression that there was nothing cathartic about our visit, that, for him, nothing really good came out of it, just a dredging up of painful memories. A few years after our visit, I was passing through Waco again and e-mailed his daughter. She called her dad, and the next day I received an e-mail from her. She was upbeat and said she was looking forward to my book but that her dad had said "he would rather not go over any more war stories. He feels it's been too many years and his memory isn't good and he can't remember all that much of it. Or maybe (to me) he just doesn't like talking about it any more."

Another few years passed. In December 2007 I was in contact with Mangham's daughter regarding the release forms for the book. She invited me for a visit. I stopped by again and spent a few hours at Mangham's house with Mr. Mangham, now eighty-four and in good health, and his two daughters. We talked briefly about the war, but spent most of our time drinking Coors and playing pool.

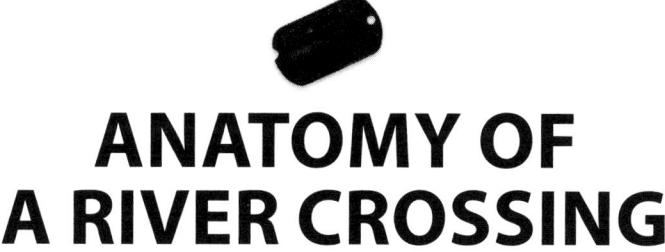

ANATOMY OF A RIVER CROSSING

IN THE YEARS AFTER MY first visit with Marvin Mangham, I was able to find more information on the Roer River crossing at Jülich. One useful source was the March 12, 1945, issue of *LIFE* magazine, which had an article and pictorial essay by photographer George Silk of the 29th Division's crossing of the Roer at Jülich. The *LIFE* article gave a short introduction to the action:

> The Ninth Army's crossing of the Roer was a short, violent struggle against the Germans and the river. Forty-five minutes after the night barrage had begun, assault boats and amphibious tractors started across in a great wave. In some of the boats were combat engineers, ferrying cables to moor their pontoon bridges in mid-stream. It was an excruciating few hours for the engineers. The flood had lessened but the current was still swift and strong. Runaway boats and pontoons careened downstream, crashing into bridges as they were being built. As the work went on the Germans kept up a blind but deadly machine-gun and mortar barrage through the smokescreen. But in spite of the difficulties there were two footbridges across the Roer in the morning. Later the engineers put in bigger bridges for trucks and tanks.

———

Many of the GIs from the 978th remembered this night barrage that was unleashed on the city of Jülich at 2:45 a.m. on February 23. Mangham was on guard duty a few miles away. "What a show that was," he said. Farran Helmick wrote:

The sky was lit up so well that you could read a newspaper outside. The planes roared overhead, and I thought the artillery would never stop. The very ground shook where we stood and we were all awe struck. When the artillery stopped the silence was deafening, and we all knew our troops were crossing the Rohr [*sic*], and we all mentally said a prayer for them.

The troops crossed the river and began to clear out enemy resistance. Meanwhile, work began on building bridges—first footbridges for troops and then pontoon, treadway, and Bailey bridges for vehicles. Work continued for several days, and so did enemy gunfire and artillery. The units directly involved in the crossing were the 84th and 29th divisions. Numerous other engineering units acted in support, including the 978th.

The 978th's company journal, a copy of which Theron Snell had obtained from the National Archives, said that on two occasions—at 9:00 a.m. on

Figure 40. Photo from *LIFE* magazine article. Dead American soldier who was hit by German mortar-shell fragments lies fifty feet from east bank of footbridge across Roer River. (© Time & Life Pictures/Getty Images)

February 24 and at 10:30 a.m. on February 25—a wrecker and an emergency repair crew with six men were sent from the contact platoon to the Roer River to repair damaged equipment. I presume that Marvin Mangham and my grandfather were among those men.

Thomas Orton gave me a more intimate picture of this action:

> Before they began, the Americans would send an artillery barrage over to the other side. But they tried not to blow out the area where they were going to touch down at the bridgehead. After the barrage, the Germans would come out. Some were surrendering, some were putting up a fight.
>
> The way it works was, after the artillery barrage was over and the infantry had cleaned out at least some of the Germans in the near proximity, the first guy then takes the hand rope over in an assault boat and attaches it at the other end of the river. He's lucky if he survives. Once they get that wire over, then they start assembling the footbridge. They take the two boats and the treadway off of the trucks and assemble them on the ground. Then a crane would lift the entire assembly into the water and they'd affix it to the guide wire that's stretched across the river. Then they'd continue, taking sections off the truck and assembling them on the river's edge. The crane would lift each one into the water and the assault boats would float it over to where they affix it to the guide wire. If the current was swift, that made it all the more difficult. The guide wire is there to keep the entire thing from floating downriver.
>
> The town of Jülich was mostly cleared out, but the Germans still had the Citadel [a large medieval fortress]. It was about a mile or so from the river. And they had lookouts there. They were well fortified there and they were there long after we had crossed the river and moved further into Germany. From there they [the Germans] could see what we were doing [at the crossing sites]. And, of course, there were German spotters hidden everywhere. The Germans were on the other side, but they could also have even been on our side hiding out in American uniforms. Those things went on too.
>
> And the instant they make contact with the other side, they're sending troops across to cut off any resistance on the other side. It'd be either the infantry or the combat engineers, to stop any Germans on the other side with rifle grenades or mortars.

At the beginning there were bodies everywhere. Guys who got hit in the water and washed downstream, guys that were hit upstream and were washed down to where we were, guys who were on the shores and were hit. Sometimes there wasn't time to pick them up.

So, I suppose your grandfather was there to repair a crane. It probably got hit by artillery or something, and they needed to get it fixed then and there, or take it back, get it fixed behind the lines, and then get it back up again.

During this time, it's a chaotic mess, absolute pandemonium. There's constant gunfire, either on you or in the area. The combat engineers are clearing away any resistance on the other side. And then there's small-arms fire coming in at the guys who are assembling the bridges, 'cause you can never get all the snipers. And with the mortars, there were these long gaps. The Germans wanted to know where we were, and they'd wait until we had almost reached the other side with the bridge, and they'd send over an artillery barrage and blow it up, and the engineers would start again. And 99% of the time it's raining, because when it's cloudy, cannon fire brings on rain. It seemed as if they'd planned these things when the weather was at its worst. It's hard for the enemy. Of course, it's hard for you too, but even harder for the enemy. And, you'll see all the houses are missing their roofs. That's because the concussion of the mortar when it lands, even if it lands a fair ways away, the concussion blows the tiles off the roof. So, there's constant gunfire, even in the distance or right in your vicinity. So you do a lot of flinching. But after a while, you can't flinch all the time, so it's sort of just one continuous flinch, you just don't flinch as hard.

Once they had the area semi-cleared, they started on the dual-treadway bridges to get the vehicles across. And they were done the same way. So, a day or two later, we [the 978th] crossed on a vehicle bridge. Now the Germans were a little farther away, but things still happened. The bridges collapsed, or the Germans sent over artillery. So, the entire unit crossed at the same time, but we didn't all go over in convoy. We went one vehicle at a time, about 50 yards spacing, so if you lost anybody, you'd lose only one.

Later, I was in contact with a man on the Internet about the Roer crossing. He obtained Signal Corps footage of the Roer crossings from the

Figures 41 and 42. Americans shell Jülich and Linnich to soften up resistance and to lay a smoke screen to hide bridge -building from German artillery spotters.
(Photo stills from Signal Corps footage)

Figures 43 and 44. Engineers from the 309th Engineer Battalion, Company C, and members of the 334th Infantry carry assault boats to the river near Linnich and load boats at edge of Roer.
(Photo stills from Signal Corps footage)

Figures 45 and 46. Engineers string cable across Roer. Pontoons will be affixed to cable.
(Photo stills from Signal Corps footage)

Figure 47. Troops from assault boats make it across to east side of Roer River where cable is attached, exit the boat (in background), and prepare to root out Germans on eastern side of river. (Photo still from Signal Corps footage)

Figure 48. More troops get into boats on river's edge upstream of bridge location and furiously row across in heavily loaded boat, probably at Linnich.
(Photo still from Signal Corps footage)

Figure 49. Engineers lose control. Boat caught in cable, about to capsize. (Photo still from Signal Corps footage)

Figure 50. Boat capsizes (not shown in film). Engineers try to salvage capsized boat on river's edge.
(Photo still from Signal Corps footage)

Figure 51. Cold and exhausted men return ashore from capsized boat. (Photo still from Signal Corps footage)

Figure 52. Bridge now assembled halfway across Roer.
(Photo still from Signal Corps footage)

Figures 53 and 54. Engineers carry assembled pontoon from shore, attach it to guide cable on near side of river, and push entire assembly further across river. (Photo stills from Signal Corps footage)

Figures 55 and 56. On western side of river at bridge site, soldiers and medics take cover from sporadic incoming artillery and machine-gun fire in foxholes and behind discarded bridge material. Bridge can be seen in distance. (Photo stills from Signal Corps footage)

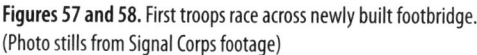 

Figures 57 and 58. First troops race across newly built footbridge. (Photo stills from Signal Corps footage)

Figure 59. After crossing footbridge, member of a mortar squad from the 29th Division waits to advance just east of the Roer River at Jülich. (Photo still from Signal Corps footage)

Figure 60. Division soldier waits to advance on Jülich after crossing the Roer. (Photo still from Signal Corps footage)

Figure 61. Troops advance carefully through the ruins of the city. In Jülich, the Germans were putting up a defense of the city. (Photo still from Signal Corps footage)

Figure 62. 29th Division soldiers cross footbridge. (Photo still from Signal Corps footage)

Figure 63. Crane in background unloads bridge supplies, most likely at 29th Division crossing site. (Photo still from Signal Corps footage)

Figure 64. More troops, having recently crossed footbridge, advance through ruins of city, probably Linnich. (Photo still from Signal Corps footage)

Figure 65. Later, men cross heavy-pontoon bridges. (Photo still from Signal Corps footage)

Figure 66. Vehicles cross the Roer. Photo taken from footbridge, most likely Site 3 at Jülich. (Photo still from Signal Corps footage)

National Archives and sent it to me.[1] The film, which had been transferred to DVD from 16-mm silent, black-and-white footage of the crossings at Jülich and Linnich, was about ten minutes long.

From this footage, I was able to piece together a rough picture of what constitutes a river crossing and what my grandfather and Marvin Mangham might have seen. The work of the 978th in the Roer River crossing was as important a contribution to the war effort as that of the men doing the front-line fighting—and it was also hazardous. Ninety percent of soldiers overseas worked primarily in support roles, but watching men assemble a bridge across a flooded river while the enemy shot at them from the other side gave me an appreciation for the contributions of these "noncombat" soldiers.

The following photos are taken from the Signal Corps film footage. They provide a rich visual record of the crossing of the Roer. The footage covered several crossing sites, no clear chronology was given, and none of the crossing locations or units involved were identified on the film. Theron Snell and I reviewed and discussed the footage, and the captions of the photos reflect our best estimates of units, locations, and events. But even if the time, place, and units involved are indefinite, the photos do illustrate what the men endured as they crossed the Roer River, battling not only the current but also the enemy.

1. *29th Division Crosses the Roer*. 23 February, 1945. LIB 3278. 111 ADC 1868. Source: AFCF (M-1310-1313) ARCH MP & APC MP, 821' silent.

EXPANDING RESPONSIBILITIES IN THE COLLAPSING REICH

THE 978TH CROSSED THE ROER in convoy on the recently built pontoon bridges on March 1, 1945. As they traveled deeper into Germany, the collapse of the German military was well under way. In the wake of the defeated and retreating German army was chaos, and the men of the 978th found themselves having to perform not only the responsibilities for which they were trained but also numerous other tasks, some military, some municipal, and some social.

Pecker's history of the 978th describes the process of taking surrendering German prisoners:

> In this type of fast moving warfare, where armored columns forged ahead on main roads at top speed, and other slower units followed to clean up, it was inevitable that small pockets of German soldiers be isolated. Except for a few fanatical groups, most of them experienced a rapid decrease of food, ammunition, morale, and fighting spirit. Tens of thousands surrendered. It was a common experience to be driving a vehicle along a well traveled highway and to see Germans come out of the woods beside the road with hands up, yelling "Kamerad." Some of them showed themselves briefly, then fell to the ground, and eagerly came out after you fired a few rounds in their general direction. This

was a procedure apparently adopted so their military honor would be vindicated and they felt that they had surrendered after a struggle. It was an ordinary sight to see our ration truck, or messenger vehicle return to the company area with bedraggled German soldiers sitting sadly on the hoods. After a while it became a nuisance to bring them in, because there were so many of them. Once a company officer saw a complete platoon of German soldiers being marched in cadence on a highway by their Lieutenant. They had their chests stuck out and were doing their best to show that they were still German soldiers, although their facial expressions were none too cheerful. American medium tanks were coming up the road in the opposite direction, making the ground tremble and raising clouds of dust. The scene was symbolic of the disintegration of the proud German Army…

Whenever [German] prisoners showed up in the company area, they were placed in a room to wait until a vehicle could take them to the rear. Three newly freed Polish soldiers volunteered to guard them. They got all dressed up in their Polish uniforms with their ridiculously long overcoats and conducted a genuine military guard. They enjoyed their job very much.

As the 978th moved through one village and town after another, the men regularly encountered German civilians. Pecker's history talked about this:

Any German who tried to ingratiate himself with the Americans would have the same old story trying to excuse the German people of war guilt. The same old excuses became so standardized that "Me no Nazi" became a humorous expression. The conventional story went something like this: the Gestapo, Nazi Party, and militarists had seized power, terrorized the honest, hard working, peace loving German people and forced them to support the war. Some even assured us they were underground workers against Hitler, had sacrificed themselves in the cause of liberty, and served time in concentration camps. But those who talked the loudest usually had their sons in the SS troops, and their daughters in the Germans WACS. The best way to silence them was to show them pictures of scenes in liberated concentration camps, the gas chambers, crematoriums, torture chambers and mass graves. That was rather difficult to explain away.

During this time, the 978th encountered several prisoner-of-war camps. Pecker's history included this account:

Figure 67. Sign placed at German border. (Photo courtesy of Leo Packer)

Figure 68. "The German pep signs were everywhere." (Photo and caption courtesy of William Musiker)

A young British medical officer came to the company and told of several hospitals in Brunswick [Germany] full of Allied prisoners of war, many of them seriously ill. He begged transportation to move them to the rear where they could be taken care of. He himself had been captured after jumping with the British paratroopers in the unsuccessful attack at Nijmegen... The next morning ... the 978th Engineer Maintenance Company sent five trucks to the hospital to evacuate as many patients as could safely be moved. Many of them, in their eagerness to go, pretended to be well although they were too weak to climb into the trucks. One British soldier who had been prisoner since Dunkirk was violent and had to be tied into a stretcher. The men of the 978th who were on this detail felt a deep satisfaction when they delivered their passengers to the efficient care of an army hospital.

On the way back to Brunswick our men saw long convoys of American trucks carrying German prisoners to the rear to a place of safety where they would eat American chow, get proper medical care, and receive all the privileges of the Geneva Convention.

Pecker also recorded some of the social interactions between his command and the Germans:

> Late one quiet afternoon, a young German farmer came pedaling furiously on a bicycle from the direction of the next town. He stopped, obviously very excited, and related that his little son had just been hurt in an accident, and in the name of humanity, would we get the civilian doctor in our town and take him to his farm to treat the child. The doctor was summoned and a jeep was dispatched to take him to the farm in the next town. The boy, about 8 years old, had been playing with some grenades left behind by soldiers, and an incendiary grenade had gone off in his face. Actually nothing could be done. The child died in a hospital a few hours later. In the midst of his grief, the father tried to show his gratitude by offering fresh eggs and meat as a gift. It was tactfully refused. Later on, in thinking about the incident, it was interesting to wonder whether or not German soldiers occupying an enemy country would have taken so much trouble to try to save a child's life. Are we Americans more soft-hearted than other people?

––––––––––

Some men of the company tried a very interesting experiment while at Goslar. At that time, *Yank Magazine* ran a series of pictures of concentration camps discovered by the onrushing allied armies. These pictures usually showed piles of corpses, mass graves, torture chambers, crematoriums, and other extermination equipment which the Germans brought to such a peak of efficiency. We posted the most shocking of these pictures on the main road running by the company area. Under the pictures was a sarcastic caption in German, praising the new achievements of German culture in the field of murder. Hundreds of Germans passing on the highway stopped to look at the pictures, and we were able to watch their facial expressions and reactions, without being seen by them. To those men who expected some reactions of guilt or remorse, it was a disappointment. Most Germans seemed not to believe the pictures, others became angry and resentful, a few seemed genuinely amused. After three days our guard caught a German boy ripping the pictures down. That little Nazi found out that Americans can be tough when they are angry.

"MY NICEST EXPERIENCE DURING THE WAR"

DURING THEIR TRIP THROUGH GERMANY, the men in the 978th came across liberated slave-labor camps, many of them only hours after the guards had fled upon learning of the imminent arrival of the Allies. Thomas Orton described one of the camps as "a gruesome sight." Although it was not the job of the 978th to care for the survivors at these camps, the GIs felt obligated to help. The people in these camps came from all over Europe. Since many men of the 978th were first- or second-generation immigrants, they were able to converse with these survivors in their native tongues.

John "Ski" Powasnik remembered one of the camps:

> We were in Germany, and the unit was moving very fast. We'd usually drive at night, find a place to bivouac, and then spend anywhere from a day or two to a couple of weeks there doing our work. Then we'd get orders to move on.
>
> One time we were bivouacked in a new-car dealership in Germany, I think it was Blomberg.[1] It was pretty close to a recently liberated slave-labor camp. And there was a bunch of Polish people from the camp that used to visit us. The Germans drafted 'em in Poland for slave labor and I guess they were liberated just a few days before. There weren't any elderly people. So, they were all about, oh, I'd say 18 to 25 years old. Young people that could still do some work, could still do some labor for the Germans.

They were stayin' in a little house up on a hill. They were on their own up there, about 15 to 30 of 'em, all bunked in this little house. Mostly men, a couple of women. They were safe there, and they couldn't go back to Poland yet, and didn't have any way to get back, so they were just waiting until they could go home.

While we were there they used to come down and visit us. My parents came from Poland, and I speak Polish, so I talked to 'em. And we became friendly with 'em.

One evening they invited a bunch of us up to their house. So we went up there. I spoke Polish to 'em and translated for the other guys. I can't remember if Leo was there, but he must have been as we were always together. I'd already taught him a couple of Polish phrases and stuff, and he must've used 'em on 'em to see if they understood. He always got a big kick out of those types of things. The Polish people gave us something to eat. They didn't have much themselves, but they shared with us what they had. But they did have something to drink. Boy, that was powerful stuff. [laughs] I don't know where they got it. We spent the evening with them and had a hell of a time, just eating and drinking and talking to them.

The next day, the C.O. [Commanding Officer] found out and said that we couldn't go back. You know, no mingling with locals and all that. 'Cause you never knew what was really going on, if somebody might be German or something. So it was just that one night.

I think that was my nicest experience during the war.

I saw 'em again the next day. And, in the car dealership we were in, there were a bunch of cars in the showroom, beautiful ones, brand new. So we took a couple of 'em out of the showroom, filled 'em up with gas from our supply truck, and gave 'em to the Polish people. I don't know if some of 'em could even drive. [laughs] But I suppose they needed 'em to get back to Poland or wherever they needed to go. Boy, were they happy.

And the Polish people took off in those cars and we never saw 'em again

Another GI, Charles "Ki" Wojcik of Wisconsin, also recalled meeting Polish survivors of a slave-labor camp, although I couldn't ascertain whether these were from the same group Ski talked about:

Figure 69. "Met two Polish women at camp... I would give them candy (it was hard to come by)."
(Photo and caption from Charles "Ki" Wojcik)

We were in Germany. This was after V-E Day and we were making our way down to France to be shipped to the Pacific. We'd drive at night to avoid die-hard Germans and such. So during the day we had a bit of free time. Me and a buddy of mine[2] were going fishing at a little lake in Germany, and we saw these women on top of a hill. So we walked up there. Turns out they were from a nearby slave-labor camp and were Polish, so I could talk to 'em in Polish 'cause my parents came from Poland. We talked to 'em for a while. I gave 'em some candy—it was pretty hard to come by for them. Before we left to go fishin', I took their picture.

1. Thomas Orton also remembered the car dealership, yet thought it was located in the town of "Brunswick." He believed the dealership was selling either Opels or Mercedes. The company history says the 978th was in Blomberg from April 5 to April 9, 1945, and in Braunschweig April 13 to April 19, 1945. *Brunswick* is probably the Anglicized term the 978th used for *Braunschweig*.
2. Wojcik's buddy was W. D. Cross from Texas. Both Wojcik and Cross were friends of my grandfather. After the war, Cross came to Wisconsin with Wojcik. He died in the 1970s in a car accident. Of all my grandfather's buddies my mother remembered or I had a photo of—John "Ski" Powasnik, Thomas Orton, George Patrias, Marvin Mangham, and W. D. Cross—Cross was the only one I was not able to interview.

FAVORITE QUOTES & ANECDOTES

MY INTERVIEWS BROUGHT OUT MANY memorable anecdotes of the GIs' experiences during the war—such as Ski's fond memories of the Polish family. And some of them were funny. Hearing the veterans talk about the lighter moments during the war was in most respects just as interesting as the more dramatic moments. These stories gave me more of a feel for the time and what the men experienced. They also humanized both the men and the situation.

English Girls

Farran Helmick recalled time the 978th spent in England before leaving for France, the Netherlands, and Germany:

> We were billeted in Bournemouth England at the Royal Exeter Hotel … Bournemouth was a vacation resort for the idle rich. We were given leave … A few of us met some local girls and took them out one night … The girls were fun, but were all leery of soldiers and their "lines." They had some peculiar expressions. At least to us they were. To "knock someone up" was to go to their house and knock on the door. The one that put us all into hysterics was, "keep your pecker up" meaning, keep up your morale … No one ever said the word "bloody" in front of a lady. It was tantamount to saying the "F---" word in front of a girl in the U.S.A. Yes folks the "F---" word was not in common usage when I went to High School. It was never used in front of girls. Women were treated like ladies, and we fellows treasured them. However, we soldiers learned all too soon to use

the word prolifically among ourselves. Of course, there were a few decent exceptions.

An Embarrassing Moment

Medical examinations were a standard part of life in the military, and general examinations were often group affairs. One GI recalled the following incident during one of these get-togethers:

> A big thing in the Army was to be inspected for VD, you know, venereal disease. We had this little guy in the outfit, he was married, about 28 or so. And we were all lined up for our inspection, totally naked, and it was his turn to walk forward. And the guy had a hard on. His face was absolutely blood red. I felt sorry for him. But it was funny as hell. He was a real nice guy, too. We had a lot of nice people in the outfit.

The French and "the GIs"

Several of the men talked about "the GIs," the Army acronym for "gastrointestinal disorder," or diarrhea. According to several veterans, it caused a lot of problems, particularly when the 978th was in France. From Farran Helmick's memoirs:

> About this time [in France], the "GIs" reared their ugly head. Everyone had diarrhea. The inconsiderate kind that keeps everyone running. Our toilet was in the middle of an adjacent hedgerow field, and the backend was open. The small French children used to congregate about a hundred feet back from the toilet. When we sat down the water flew, the kids would laugh, and point and no doubt were making crude jokes. They used to "root us on" when we poor GIs came dashing across the field "hoping against hope" that we would get there in time.
>
> I finally came down with it myself … I went to the First Sgt. and asked him if there was something he could do to help me. I was sick enough to die. He sent me back to my tent and came back with a brick of cheese … I ate the cheese and, in no time at all, that did the trick.

I asked Thomas Orton about it:

> Oh yeah, I was just as lucky as everybody else. In France, in Les Pieux in the hedgerows, just about everybody had diarrhea. It was the

water that caused it. They had well water and we weren't used to it. It'd just nail you. I had them in France, but once we got out of France, into Holland and Germany, I was OK, didn't have any trouble. But some guys did. I know some guys had them throughout the entire war.

I remember one time [in France] I was having one of my daily—not daily, momentary!—trips. There was a French family that lived off of our garbage. They made three trips a day to our feeding area to get our scraps. At any rate, it was raining and the farmer, his wife and three little girls saw me and came traipsing across the open pasture. The family stopped about 15 feet from me. The man knew a little English and was very congenial. And we chatted away while I was doing my business.

In France, it's common practice. In cities it's not uncommon either, to see somebody in a latrine and the person outside just chatting away with them.

Figure 70. A photo from William P. Pappan, location unknown.

The troops were friendly with the French. The French people in the countryside, they'd give you the shirt of their back. The French people in the city, well, they'd take your shirt.

A Gas Attack in Holland

Carlyle Parsons remembered an incident in Spekholzerheide that turned out to be an amusing incident:

We were located only five miles from Aachen, Germany. We were warned that the Germans would do anything to keep the Allies from entering Germany. Their last resort was to possibly use gas … One morning about 5:30 the gas alarm sounded. The sentry saw the "gas" coming down the street he was patrolling. I woke up trying to find my gas mask when I realized that it was under the front seat of my truck, which was parked out in the driveway. I took a big gulp of air and headed for the truck. I could see the mist as I got outside. I finally got the mask out from under the seat and was trying to unravel the straps when I could no longer hold my breath. I took a little air and a little more and finally said "the hell with it" and started breathing normally. What happened was that the sentry had seen this "gas" coming, but it turned out that it was just the morning mist doing its thing.

"A Little War All Their Own"

When the 978th was camped near the slag pile at the Mariagrube coal mine, tensions were high. They had just entered Germany and the slag pile was the "spookiest place" the 978th encountered. Several men said they dreaded guard duty at night at the slag pile. Helmick remembered one incident there:

The slag piles were always breaking away in little patches and sliding down and making a noise. This condition never bothered me, because I knew what it was, and I never joined in the foolishness. Twice, a guard thought he heard something because of the sliding slag and opened fire. When they did it created more slides and of course, more noise and to them it sounded like they had a squad of enemy pinned down on the slag pile. They had a little war all their own and shot the hell out of that slag pile before someone wised up and made them quit. Most of us were laughing at them. I do not remember who was doing all the shooting except for the Sergeant who was firmly convinced that he had a German patrol pinned down. It was fun. It broke the monotony.

Odd Jobs of the 978th

During a phone conversation, William Musiker commented on the type of work the 978th did in Germany:

Toward the end of the war, the Germans were stringing cables across the road. They'd take thin metal wire, string it across the road and tie it to the trees. The Americans in their jeeps, they couldn't see them. And the Germans would put them at about the level of your neck if you were in a jeep. The idea was that the guy driving the jeep couldn't see it, and he'd drive right into it and it'd decapitate him.

So the 978th's job was to fix up a little bar that extended in front of the jeep, and then went up in front of the jeep with a little knife to cut the wire. The idea was that if there was a wire there, it would cut it.

So, was this common, Mr. Musiker? Did guys actually die because of this?

Well, when you get your head chopped off, you die.

We made quite a few of those. We'd set up shop and other units would bring their jeeps in to get fixed up. By the end of the war, every jeep was affixed with one of these little bars to cut the wire.

Another GI offered the following on events in Germany early in 1945:

Our unit was one of the first to come across one of the buzz-bomb factories when we came into Germany. The buzz-bombs, they ran on alcohol, and a bunch of the guys found the stuff and drank it—and they went crazy. This one damn fool took a .45 and was chasing the Captain around. We caught him and had to hold him down. But the Captain, he was a full-blooded American Indian and one tough cookie. Nobody messed with the Captain, so we were expecting the worst. But he just laughed and let the guy go and told him not to drink that stuff anymore.

William Musiker offered the following recollections on the process of procuring supplies in Germany:

I remember a General came up to our unit and told us: "A good soldier takes care of himself," meaning that you find what you need anyway possible. And we took it to heart.

One day in Germany the Mess Sergeant went off one day with his M1 carbine and shot up a bunch of geese. He came back an hour later with a wheelbarrow full of them. But that evening, what's the S.O.B. do? He makes stew out of it. [laughs] We could have killed the guy. We were expecting a feast of roast duck or something—and he makes mush.

There were two types of guys in the unit. Some were innovative, could do anything. Some guys were shitheads, that's the only way to describe 'em. [laughs] Every outfit has losers.

Another time a truck driver was going around Germany doing his regular work, retrieving disabled tanks and vehicles and stuff, you know, and he sees a cow in a barnyard. So he took his rifle, goes over to the cow and shoots it. Then he threw it on the back of his wrecker, drove it back to the cooks, and continued on with his work that day. A couple of men in the unit were butchers back home and knew what to do with the cow. And that night we had a feast.

George Patrias and His Monkey

One of the photos William Musiker sent to me was of a GI and a monkey. Later, Thomas Orton sent me another photo of himself with what appeared to be the same monkey. I thought back to George Patrias, who a few years earlier had mentioned that he had had a pet monkey in Manila. I phoned him again. Unfortunately, by this time his memory had faded, and he could not remember much about the war. So I called Ski and asked him about the monkey. He said:

Yeah, that was in Manila. Those damn little monkeys were everywhere. We just wanted them to stay the hell away from us. They were cute, but they were little bastards. [laughs] They were always stealing our food. They'd sneak into our tents and steal our food and just mess things up. They were hoppin' all over the place and screeching like mad—eeee, eeee, eeee—and we didn't know what the hell they were going to do.

The other guys wanted no part of them. But not George. He was able to catch one of 'em and keep him as a pet, in the tent. He'd play

Figures 71 and 72. Matthew Kelts (top) and Thomas Orton with George
Patrias's monkey in Manila.
(Photos courtesy of William Musiker and Thomas Orton, respectively)

with him. He was the only guy in the unit who was able to keep one.

Later, during a visit with Thomas Orton, I showed him the photos and asked him if it was Patrias's monkey.

Yeah, that's George's monkey with me in the photo. He got it in Manila, and it became his pet monkey.

Did anybody else have a monkey?

Oh, no. Only George. [laughs]

And why did George have a monkey?

Why did George do anything? Why did George go out and get beat to hell with a bamboo stick by a bunch of Filipinos? I don't know.

You heard that story? He was with my grandfather.

Figure 73. George Patrias, at eighty-five, in his house in Detroit, 2004, with wood carvings. Patrias's hobby in retirement is carving exact wooden replicas of mechanical tools. He collects modern and nineteenth-century tools, such as wrenches, screwdrivers, and vices; researches the dates they were made; and then carves a replica. He said: "Everyone carves fish or ducks or some darn things. Nobody else in the country that I know of is making these." He prefers hardwoods with pleasant grain patterns, such as birds-eye maple, black walnut, oak, and mahogany.

I saw 'em when they got back to camp. He and Leo came back with giant welts all over them. At first they didn't look that bad, and then they swelled up several inches high, all around. Apparently he and Leo went to some kind of bar, got into a fight, and the locals got the best of 'em.

That's not the story he told me.

Of course not. George never lost a fight. [laughs]

A Haircut in Japan

By the time the 978th reached Japan, the war was over and the unit was being dissolved. Carlyle Parsons recalled the time that he and a buddy got a civilian haircut under unusual circumstances:

> One other thing that happened in Japan was on a trip to Tokyo. A buddy and I were walking along a side street which had been bombed, and there was rubble all over the place. At the end of the street was a barber shop, and a barber was outside waving his arms at us wanting us to get a haircut. Neither one of us trusted the Jap but did know that we could use a haircut. My buddy said that he would go first, but I was to keep close track of the barber. He got into the chair and the barber got out the scissors and comb and started to cut my buddy's hair. About that time I put a shell in my carbine and aimed it at the barber's head. He was a little upset, but he was very careful with the scissors. After he was through with my pal, it was my turn. He flipped a shell into his carbine, pointed it at the barber and I got my haircut. I think that we gave him a pack of cigarettes for payment.

IN THE FOOTSTEPS OF THE 978TH

SKI'S FRIENDS IN SPEKHOLZERHEIDE

AFTER HEARING SO MANY STORIES of the veterans' experiences in Europe, my thoughts inevitably drifted there, particularly to the Mariagrube coal mine in Mariadorf and Spekholzerheide, both of which had made a strong impression on the men. During my search I was living in Ireland, England, and then Sweden and had been to the Netherlands and Germany for both work and vacation, but never to these small towns.

What really piqued my interest were several photos that Ski sent me. The first was of three young women, one holding a baby, who befriended Ski in Spekholzerhiede. The other was a photo of a young girl in Spek. Written on the back was the name *Maria Merx*, an address, which was scratched out, and a note to Ski's family: "This little girl in Holland sends her love to my family back home. Love, John." Ski told me about them:

> In Spek we became friendly with a local family. We'd take our laundry to them, and the mother did our laundry, and we'd give 'em candy.

> There were a couple of older sisters and one little girl, she was about ten years old or so. She was a nice girl and we used to joke around.

> I remember when we had to leave Spek, the little girl gave me a photo of herself. She wrote her name and address on the back. And I mailed it back to my family. The censors scratched out the address, as that was forbidden to send that type of info. But her name was still on it. I think her name was Merx.

Figure 74. Girls in Spekholzerheide who did Ski's laundry. (Photo courtesy of John Powasnik)

Figure 75. Maria Merx of Spekholzerheide, the Netherlands. (**Photo courtesy** of John Powasnik)

I searched the Internet for Spekholzerheide. This was in 1998, when the Internet was not as developed as today. I came up with only a few hits. The only interesting page discussed the genealogy of a family in California that had immigrated from Spekholzerheide in the 1950s. I e-mailed them, asking about Spekholzerheide and sending Ski's photo of Maria Merx and William Musiker's photo of the Walters sisters. The next day I received an e-mail from the daughter of the family, Tessie Rensen-Brouns. She wrote:

> My father didn't recognize anyone on the picture, but does remember the name Maria Merx. He says she lived in their street in Spekholzerheide. The name of the street was "Ons Limburgstraat"...
>
> All those towns, Chevremont, Spekholzerheide etc. are now Kerkrade. I'm not sure they still have the old signs up.

For the next few days, Spekholzerheide was running through my head—the recollections from Ski and William Musiker, wartime photos of a post office, a young girl named Maria Merx, and an elderly man in California who immigrated to America almost fifty years ago and remembered a Maria Merx living on Ons Limburgstraat. I had to find out more about the present-day Spekholzerheide, and knowing that it was now part of Kerkrade proved to be pivotal information.

Hoi Jeffrey.   8 november 1998

I Have graet news for you ?? I found Maria Merx,and here sisters, She is now 63
years old ,on the Photo she was 12 years on school the Photo is thaken in the war
time.
She ask if you and I will visit here when your coming to "Spek" .She live's three
streets away from my and there sisters too.
I hope you have some on it .

I have 4 Photo's get from here whit two G.I's and there big sisters in the war (Sept
44 / Nov 44) in there backgardt (Ons Limburgstraat) where the big Photo is thaken
there you sent to my, whit the 3 girls and the baby on the arm.
I hope the copie's are good

She gave my two name's from two G.I.'s 1) is Richard and 2) name is Janic now
backname's .onknouwn is what for Companie or Division.But I will find out. In the
History you send my there are several names there col Richard but now Janic
(Perhaps a Nicname) she don't remember other names maybe white te time will
come up some remembers.

Your are very welcome to stay wen you have some time.

Met vriendelijke groet,

Figure 76. Fax from Leon.

"I WILL BE DRESSED
IN ALL BLACK"

I SEARCHED THE INTERNET AGAIN, this time for Kerkrade instead of Spekholzerheide. I got a lot more hits. I found my way to the homepage of Industrion, a recently opened museum of industry and mining in the region. I sent an e-mail to the museum, telling them about my search, including the information I had.

When I arrived at the office the next day, there was a fax waiting for me from a man named Leon[1]:

> Dear Jeffrey.
>
> I'm Leon And work in Industrion I read your E-mail that you send us. You are searching for info of the Dutch town Speckholzerheide and the people Hub and Till and Merx their daughter … I self living in Spekholzerheide … My hobby is everything of story's or Photo's of the War in my area…
>
> Groetjes Terug. !
>
> Leon[2]

I sent Leon a letter that briefly described the 978th's experiences in Spek. I also included copies of the photos of the Walters sisters and the post office. A few days later I received another fax from Leon:

> Dear Jeffrey,
> Thank you very much for the letter you send my.
> Nice Photo's and History.

Photo 1) First to begin, I have found one of the girls on the Photo that William Musiker sent's you, One of the Wolters sisters it's te girl in the white blous sie is 14 years old on the Phto.

The other sister is dead, But the girl in the white blous live's today in one of the two houses on the background on the Photo.

The two houses still standing two streets away from my adress.

Photo 2) The Postoffics "Spekholzerheide" is on the Industriestaat near by the old mine wear your Grandfather was stationed,

The woman in the background on the Photo is dead.

The Postoffics is closet after the war. It still stands today 5 streets away from my adress.

When you come to visit "Spek" Your are very welcome to my home if you wil you can stay a copel of day's,

Than wy cane drink some beer in the pub's of "Spek" and cane visit the place's on the Photo's.

Jeffrey thanks agiain for the Photo's and the History of your Grandfather and Budy's.

Met vriendelijke groet,

Leon

In the meantime I had made copies of Ski's photos of Maria Merx and the girls who did his laundry. I sent them to Leon, along with the section about Spekholzerheide in Pecker's history of the 978th. A few days later I received another fax—one of my favorite pieces of correspondence from my project (see page 158).

———

I phoned Ski to tell him of my discovery and asked if he remembered a person named Richard or Janic. He remembered a Richard, but not a Janic, and said, "There wasn't anybody in the unit with that name."

In the meantime, Leon had sent me the photo that Maria Merx had given him. It was of Maria's sister Anna with two GIs. And, just as Leon said, it was taken in the same backyard as the photo Ski had given me of the girls who did his laundry.

———

Figure 77. Photo from Maria Merx of two GIs with Maria's sister Anna. (Photo courtesy of Maria [Merx] Mommertz)

During the Christmas holiday of 1998, I was visiting friends in Alphen aan den Rijn, the Netherlands. Leon had invited me to Spekholzerheide, and, being close by, I decided to take him up on his offer. I arranged to spend five days with him in Spek after visiting my friends in Alphen. He said I could stay at his house. I checked the train timetable and sent Leon my arrival time. He replied in a fax, saying that he would pick me up at the train station.

The evening before I was to travel to Spek, I began to wonder about Leon and if it was wise to spend five days in the home of a complete stranger whom I had met on the Internet. I decided to give Leon a call.

Hallo.

Hello. This is Jeff Badger. Can I speak to Leon?

Somebody said something in Dutch, and there was a long pause. Then another person picked up the phone and spoke in a dry, raspy voice.

Hallo. I am Leon. Is this Jeffrey?

> Yes it is. Hello, Leon!

Hoi Jeffrey! How are you?

> I'm OK, Leon. How are things in Spek?

Oh, all is OK. Thank you for asking to me. Kom you to Spek?

> Yes I am, Leon. My train arrives tomorrow afternoon at
> 3:31, in Kerkrade.

Yes, Jeffrey. We very happy that you to Spek komt. I pick you up.

> OK, Leon. Good. Leon, before I come, I'm just curious.
> How old are you?

I'm one and thirtig year old.

> Thirty one. OK. And who do you live with?

I live with my moeder and vader.

> OK, your mother and father. And Leon, what is your
> job?

I work at the museum.

> OK, Leon. Sounds good. I will see you at the train
> station. How will we find each other?

No problem, Jeff. We will see each other.

> Leon, what do you look like? How will I know it is you?

You will know it is me.

> And how will I know?

You will know.

> Leon, what will you be wearing?

I will be dressed in all black.

You will be wearing black?

Yes, I will be dressed in all black.

All black. OK, Leon. All black … I will see you then.

OK, Jeffrey. You are welkom to Spek. We are looking forward to you kom here.

My conversation with Leon put me at ease: thirty-one years old, lives at home with his parents, works at a museum, conservative dress. I felt reassured. Leon must be a good guy, probably a bit nerdy, but a good guy.

The next morning I boarded the train.

1. I have omitted Leon's surname for reasons that will become apparent later.
2. I enjoyed Leon's English. I thought it had an almost poetic ring to it and have left it entirely unchanged.

A KINDRED SPIRIT?

THE THREE-HOUR TRAIN TRIP TO Kerkrade was boring. The train was uncomfortable and empty. As we traveled through the southernmost province of Limburg, I saw that this was not the Holland of windmills and tulips. The landscape was flat and gray, and the trees were bare in the cold yet snowless Dutch winter. The train rolled into Kerkrade early in the afternoon. A bleak, gray Dutch sky was fading into darkness with the early setting of the winter sun. I grabbed my backpack and got off the train. There were a few people milling about on the platform, but nobody came up to greet me. After a minute or two they had cleared away. I looked up and saw a man standing at the front of the platform. He was dressed in black: black Levis, black belt, black t-shirt, black leather coat, black combat boots. He was about six feet tall, lean but not skinny, unshaven, with black hair and brown eyes. He was smoking a cigarette. He did not have any visible piercings, tattoos, or leather studs that would mark him as a middle-class youngster trying to look hard. He genuinely looked hard. Hard and weathered, but not mean or aggressive. He noticed me in the distance and put up his hand. I walked toward him. He yelled out:

Hallo, are you Jeffrey?!! I am Leon of Spekholzerheide. Welkom, Jeffrey. Welkom to Limburg.

Leon was with his brother, Jons, a tall, taciturn fellow. We threw my things in the back of Jons's VW bus and headed for Spekholzerheide. On the way Leon filled me in on the schedule for my visit. We were going to visit Maria Merx, one of the Walters sisters, the beer hall, the Spekholzerheide post office, and the slag pile at the Mariagrube coal mine, which Leon had located.

Spekholzerheide consists of row upon row of small, two-story brown houses lined up right next to each other. The roads are small—most wide enough for only one car—and many are paved with brownish-red brick. Shooting off the main roads are smaller, dead-end streets, each with more houses. A number of people were on the streets, but the town still seemed quiet. There are not many billboards or advertisements, and interspersed among the houses are small, low-key pubs and an occasional restaurant. I got the impression that these pubs had been there many decades and that Spekholzerheide had not changed much since the days my grandfather and Ski spent there during the war.

Leon's brother dropped us off at their parents' house, and he drove on. Leon's mother and father, a housewife and a retired coal miner, welcomed me into their home. Leon translated. Leon showed me the guestroom and I threw my backpack on the bed. Leon's mother had prepared a dinner of potatoes and stewed meat, and we ate and talked. Leon's father told me about working in the Sofia-Wilhelm coal mine in Spek. During the preceding few years, the demand for coal had decreased, all the coal mines had closed down, and the area had since faced hard times. After dinner, Leon's father headed off to the beer hall. I was told that we would be joining him later. His mother left to visit friends.

Leon called me into his room. Hanging on the walls of his room were framed posters relating to the war: movie posters, an announcement of a WWII museum exhibition, Nazi propaganda, 1930s-era Nazi recruitment posters. Stacked on his bookshelf and overflowing onto the desk, the bed, and the floor were books, magazines, maps, photos, and other paraphernalia about the war in Dutch, German, and English. On one shelf were dozens of videotapes of movies and documentaries about the war. In one corner of the room lay a model of a battlefield, with tiny collectible figurines of German and American soldiers and tanks. Scattered about were sundry souvenirs: an empty artillery shell, a metal military case, empty shell casings, a rusty German helmet.

Leon pulled out several folders and showed me the contents: hundreds and hundreds of original photos from the war, most of which had been taken in Limburg. Over the years Leon had collected these photos from the local people, by writing to American GIs who had been in the Limburg area, and from the Internet and eBay. There were photos of German soldiers during the occupation, American GIs with Dutch families after liberation, American tanks roaming the streets, destroyed buildings, children playing in the rubble, and just about anything imaginable relating to the war. One group of photos was particularly disturbing: Dutch women in the town square shortly after liberation forcibly having their heads shaved as punishment for allegedly collaborating with the Germans during the occupation. Several 978thers had mentioned witnessing this ritual, saying that they found it particularly troubling.

Leon gave me several welcoming gifts: a patch for the 30th Infantry Division, the unit that liberated Limburg; a patch for the XIXth Corps, my grandfather's unit; and a framed drawing of the Sofia-Wilhelm coal mine. Leon said:

> Jeffrey, we are very happy to have you here kom to us. We are very thankful for what your opa and his buddies did for us in the war.

Before we left I took a quick shower. Leon played at full volume the love-song theme from the movie *Titanic*: Celine Dion's "My Heart Will Go On." The house shook.

Then we walked to the beer hall. On the way Leon gave me a mini-tour of Spekholzerheide and its history—or at least its history as it related to WWII. Here was the place where the first American was killed, the road down which the first Americans came, the house where the Americans set up their communications center, and other points of interest. Leon also knew much of what must be the unofficial WWII history of Spek: the locations of the German brothel and the American brothel, which houses were those of Dutch collaborators and which were those of the Dutch underground. Every house in Spek seemed to have a story relating to the war, and Leon seemed to know them all.

We arrived at the beer hall, now called the Wilhelmina. I had heard many stories about it from the men of the 978th. It served as the Nazi Party headquarters during the occupation. After liberation, it became a favorite drinking ground for the men of the 978th. It was the location of Ski's Miss Maidenform contest and the exhibition boxing match where my grandfather boxed the local Dutch ex-champion. The locals, mostly older men, all seemed to know Leon. He later told me that he spent much time here as a child; his father would come to the beer hall after work at the coal mine.

Leon's father was already at the beer hall with several friends. Leon introduced me to everybody and told them about my grandfather having been stationed in Spekholzerheide. They nodded respectfully. Leon asked me to get out the photos of my grandfather, Ski, and the other men and pass them around in hopes that somebody might recognize something. Nobody did. Still, the people at the bar were interested. In fact, wherever I went during the following days, people showed a quiet, sincere interest in why I was there and what I was doing, and they tried to help in any way they could. The people of Spekholzerheide seemed to still carry the war with them, and I felt that they respected the magnitude and significance of that time. Many of the bars had memorabilia from the war—nothing flashy, a few photos, an old helmet or a rusty American machine gun mounted on the wall.

Leon and I spent the evening in the beer hall. In Limburg, beers are not served by the pint, but in very small glasses. The bartender keeps a tab and brings new ones continually. Leon started us off with three apiece and a shot of whiskey. The small glasses proved dangerous, as after a while I had no idea how much I had consumed. Leon had to translate most things that were said, as the locals either did not speak English or were reluctant to, a big difference from what I had experienced in northern Holland, where the young people are all fluent in English. Consequently, I sometimes felt outside the conversation, and there was little else to do but drink more tiny beers.

In fact, several aspects of this part of the Netherlands were different from what I had experienced in northern Holland. This part of the country seemed a little less modern and a little tougher, and the people did not seem to be in as much of a hurry. Leon commented that they were different: that the "Hollanders" think of people in Limburg as being more German, and their accent is very different from that in the north.

Leon's spoken English was much better than his written English. He had never studied English in school, only German. However, a lifetime of watching American war movies, reading war books in English, and talking to American GIs when they visited Holland had given him a pretty good command of the spoken language. When he spoke, it was with intensity—as if everything he was telling me was incredibly important and urgent, as if he must tell me right then and there. After he finished speaking he would look at me with an intense, penetrating, expectant glare, as if waiting for a reaction. It was not threatening or aggressive, just intense. He was extremely polite. If he did not understand something I said, he always answered with, "Please?" Although outwardly hard-looking, he seemed to have a very humane and intuitive side to him. He told me about the collection of photographs and letters he had shown me in his room:

> Jeffrey, I used to collect souvenirs. Nazi propaganda, bayonets, American weapons, German weapons, a Nazi flag, you understand. I had so many things. But after a while, I become bored. They are only things. They cannot really tell you about *the war*, the personal side about the war, the feelings of the people, you know. I sold everything I had. Now, I just want to collect personal accounts from people, to listen to their stories and their feelings. And to collect photographs. Nothing more. The souvenirs don't interest me now, Jeff. Just the photos and the stories. Because there, there is *the war*.

During the evening, Leon filled me in on his life. He became very interested in the war as a child and spent almost all of his free time reading books and watching movies about it. Later, he got involved personally, going around Spek and Limburg asking people for photographs, writing letters to American GIs and German soldiers who had been in Limburg and asking them for photos and information, and sending requests for documents to the U.S. and German archives. He had even helped two local Dutch people find their American GI fathers:

> Jeffrey, two times I helped Dutch girls find their fathers. They come to me and say, "Leon, my mother says that my father is an American GI. But I don't have a lot of information. Only his family name, and maybe the wrong spelling. Can you help me?" So, we find out which units were in Spekholzerheide nine months before she was born, we contact the government and write off for archives and finally get the name of the man. Then we write to the reunion association, get the address and phone number of the GI, and finally send him a letter. At first he gets scared and says, "No, that is not my child." But finally he says okay. And he is happy. He did not know he has a daughter and now he knows. And she knows who her father is.

Leon's curiosity about the past and skill at digging it up helps him in his job. He works for Industrion, a museum devoted to preserving the industrial history of Limburg, particularly the mining industry. His job is to find old machinery and industrial equipment, refurbish it, and get the mechanics operational so that the piece can be displayed in the museum.

The evening wore on. When it drew close to closing time, my conversation with Leon drifted back to the war. Leon stared at me with his trademark intensity and said:

> Jeffrey, I am happy that you are here. You and I, we share the same interest. You love *the war*. I love *the war*. You know, Jeff, all my life, I spend so much time learning about the war. I find thousands of photos about the war. I watch the movies about the war; I watch the documentaries and listen to the personal accounts about the war; I read the books about the war; I talk to the Dutch people who *were there*; I go to Germany and talk to the people who were there during the war.

Leon paused and looked down. His voice became slower, more reflective and less intense. He had a look of wistfulness about him. His tone sounded like that of an older man speaking about his one true love, a love that had escaped him, with a longing for what could have been.

> Jeffrey, I love *the war*, I love everything about *the war*. I watch the movies. I read all the books. I go to military reenactments. I collect souvenirs. I listen to the personal testimonies. I talk to people who were *there*. But no matter how hard I try, I can never know what it feels like *to be there*. I can never know what it feels like *to fight*.

Leon looked down and sighed. He then gave me his usual expectant glare, and I felt compelled to respond.

> Well, I suppose I know what you mean, Leon. I mean, I learned a lot from my war buddies. But we can never know what it feels like if we've never experienced it firsthand. But, you know, I'm not sure I'd really want to know.

Leon looked disappointed with my reply.

> *Yes, yes, of course. We can never know what it feels like. We can never know.*

But all my life I've wanted to know. And I needed to do something.

So what did you do?

I don't want you to think I a bad guy.

Leon, I don't think you're a bad guy. You helped me find all these people. You invited me to stay with you in Spek.

Yes, but I don't want you to think I a bad guy.

Leon, I don't think you're a bad guy.

OK. You know Yugoslav, where the Serbs and Croats and Bosnians are all fighting? I went there to fight in that war. But, Jeffrey, I don't want you to think I'm a bad guy. Some people fought for political reasons. Some Germans, they are neo-Nazis, they fight because they are against the Muslims, and because the Croats helped Hitler during the war. But not me. I don't care about politics. I like Muslims. I think Muslims are OK. It doesn't matter to me. I went for the experience.

Leon and I talked about his experiences in the Balkans, but he asked that I not pass along any details. I asked him what eventually happened. A look of disappointment crossed his face.

The war ended and I had to come home. But I would go again, for the experience.

The beer hall finally closed and we set off for Leon's house. The walk back seemed much longer. It was dark. It was cold. With my new friend—a sort of kindred spirit?—I staggered back to the house through the dark, deserted streets and alleys of Spekholzerheide.

SPEK

LEON AND I SPENT THE next few days visiting Spek and the local people. We visited the younger Walters sister, who now lives with her husband in her childhood home, the same house in the background of Musiker's photo (see figure 24, page 87). She had been about fourteen when the photo was taken, but she did not remember Musiker.

Spek had a relaxed atmosphere. Leon and I dropped in unannounced on his acquaintances. They offered us coffee and Leon chatted with them about people and places we were seeking. Usually, they sent us to an older friend or relative, who would help us find the person or landmark. Using this method, we tracked down Pierre Schlangen, the nephew of the Huub and Tilla who did Max Voron's laundry. Huub and Tilla were dead, but their nephew enthusiastically recounted the Americans' arrival in Spek and gave us several photos. He remembered going to the beer hall with his father to watch the boxing matches during the war. We found the wife of J. Krewinkel, the boxer who fought my grandfather in the exhibition boxing match. Unfortunately, he was in a retirement home and was unable to see us. We found the sites of all of Musiker's photos in Spek and Valkenburg, a nearby town.

We visited Maria Merx at her home. She was there with her husband, Sjef Mommertz, and her older sister Anna, who was in the photo that Ski gave me. We had coffee and chatted about the war.

Maria remembered Ski very well, but referred to him as Janic, the Dutch version of John—so there was one mystery solved: Ski himself was Janic. Although she had not seen Ski in over fifty years, she recognized him immediately in the photo. Sjef could speak a fair bit of English, and Maria and Anna could speak some, so the conversation was an animated mishmash of their English and Leon's translation. Maria, Sjef, and Anna all told their stories. Maria said:

> Janic was more of a father to me than a friend. He took a liking to me. He'd always say, "such a sweet child." We couldn't talk, had no common language. After the war, a few months after he returned, Janic sent letters. But I couldn't read them. I never wrote back. And Janic sent money to me, twice! Money for me to come to America. And it wasn't a joke. He was serious. But my parents said no. [laughs]

Anna also remembered that time:

> I was 21 in 1944. I was always making clothes. And every day Maria would sit by me while I worked. One day our little brother bring Janic to my mother. And my mother says we can do laundry for them, for Janic. But we had no soap. So the Americans brought soap to us and we did their laundry. They came several times. We would chat a little bit, and they would drop off their laundry and leave. But Janic wouldn't let the other GIs near us, near us girls, my older sisters and me. I guess he was protective. [laughs] Later, I would make clothes for the Americans. After they left, they needed warm clothes for the Battle of the Bulge. And I made them clothes and gloves.
>
> My husband, he was my boyfriend at the time. Just before the Americans came, the Germans took him because he was listening to the BBC radio, and that wasn't allowed, forbidden. They took him to the old school in Spekholzerheide. The Germans had made it into a kind of prison. When they took him we thought it would be months and months before we saw him again, that the Germans would send him to some kind of labor camp. But he was there for only ten minutes, and they, the Americans, started to liberate Spekholzerheide. The Americans came to the school and found him there in the prison. One of the GIs had some kind of drink, and they all started drinking together in the prison. The two GIs and my boyfriend got very drunk, and finally my husband said he wanted to go home, back to his family. So the two GIs brought him home. And they brought him home in a tank! [laughs] And they were all crazy drunk when my boyfriend climb out of the tank in front of our house. I was really surprised, thought for sure he'd be sent to Germany to a labor camp.

Sjef talked effusively about the arrival of the Americans:

I was about twelve or fourteen when the Americans come. After they come, I work with them every day, all the time. I even sleep in the same place as the Americans. My parents, they couldn't stop me. [laughs] They were my friends and needed my help, needed my help to meet girls. Then I know where two girls, about 17 or 18, where they live. So I take the Americans to them. And we go to the door and ask for the girls. And their oma comes to the door and starts yelling at us. [laughs] "You little…" I can't say the word, but you know. "You boys, what the hell are you doing here?" And she chases us off. [laughs]

We're very happy you come. It was unbelievable before that. Ooofff. The Germans always coming around, "bang, bang," with the iron on their boots. But the Americans, they had rubber boots, didn't go "bang, bang" when they walked.

The Americans taught me so many things. They even taught me how to shoot a gun. [laughs] And one day my brother finally comes to take me home, because I was there all the time, always with the Yankees. And I say, "No way! No way I'm going home." And I start shooting into the air and say, "There's no way I'm going home." [laughs]

It was wonderful. I can tell you that. I will never forget it, as long as I live. Never.

Figure 78. Sjef and Maria (Merx) Mommertz and Maria's sister Anna.

———

In the afternoon Leon's brother drove us to the Mariagrube coal mine at Mariadorf. Before my trip to Spek, I told Leon about the mine, and he had tracked down its location. Theron Snell had sent me a map made by the Defense Mapping Agency during the war. I sent this on to Farran Helmick, who labeled the location of the tunnel and other things and returned it to me. So, armed with our map and the stories of men trapped in minefields, dead Germans in foxholes, and bodies in a tunnel, Leon and

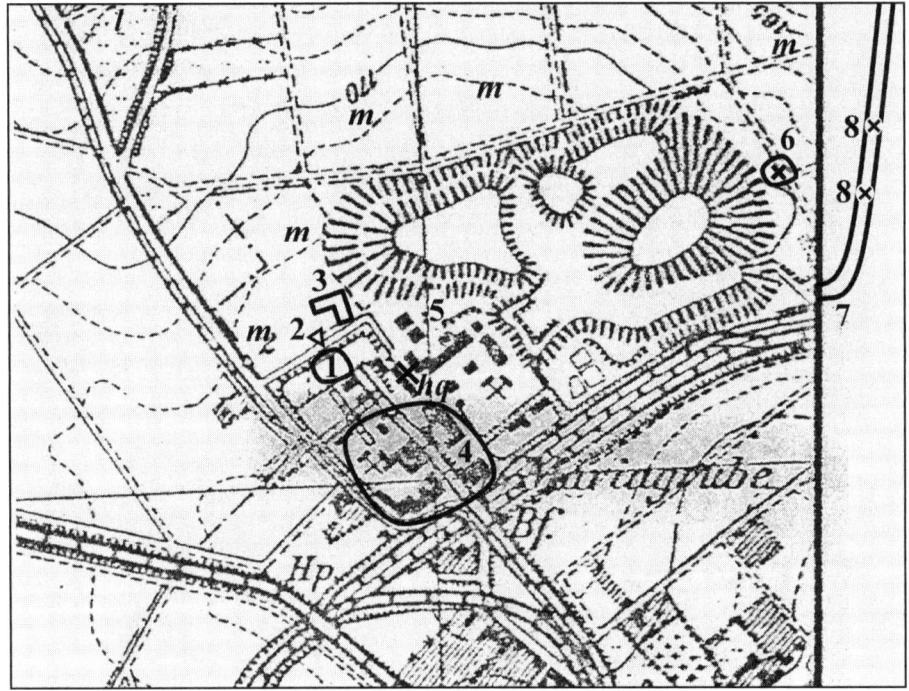

Figure 79. Map of Mariagrube, with annotations from Farran Helmick.

m:	**mines**
hq:	**headquarters** building, next to carpenter shop
1.	"**There** was a small slag heap in this general area."
2.	"**The** tunnel entrance was on this end."
3.	"**This** small area was cleared of mines. There were wire barriers marking the boundaries with signs on them: 'Mines.'"
4.	"**Area** where the rest of the company was located."
5.	"**Site** of the firefight with the slag pile." (pages 146–47)
6.	"**General** area of the assistant machine gunner." (page 105)
7.	**Railroad,** sketched in by hand, on cinder tracks.
8.	**Location** of dead Germans in their foxholes. (page 105)

I set off for the slag pile with grand visions of finding the foxholes where the elderly and young Germans lay and, perhaps with a little digging, the entrance to the tunnel.

As we approached Mariadorf we could see the large slag pile, which dominated the landscape. It was now overgrown with a mass of trees and vegetation. We parked the car near the train station, marked "Bf." for *banhauf* on the map. This was now a private residence, and we followed the now-overgrown railway tracks to the area where the mine buildings used to be (area 4). This was where the 978th established their base of operations. Unfortunately, the mine buildings had all been torn down, and we could find only a retaining wall. We identified the minefield where the "Perfect Infantry Attack" took place and where Helmick later picked up the American bodies. The northwestern part of the minefield was now built up, with many new buildings. The western part of the minefield was still clear. It was a vast, open field, currently being used as farmland, and was devoid of any cover. It was hard to imagine anyone trying to cross it in the face of enemy machine guns and mortars. We talked to some kids who were fishing in a small pond halfway up the slag pile and to the man who lived in the old train-station building. The man did not know much and did not seem to be interested in what we were looking for. We asked some of the locals if they knew anything about Mariagrube during the war, but they did not. We then walked down the railway line, which is now a road, to the small slag pile (area 2). This was where the entrance to the tunnel lay. This small slag pile was not on the original map, but Helmick had drawn it in, and we found it immediately, within a few feet from where Helmick had drawn it. This too was overgrown with weeds and trees, and, although we could pinpoint quite well where the tunnel entrance lay, it had obviously been filled in and we could see no signs of a former opening.

We then drove back to Spek. On our way back, I felt disappointed in our trip, or that it was at least somewhat anticlimactic. There had not been much to see. The Mariagrube coal mine seemed to be a lonely place. Or, at least, I found it that way, as I thought of the men of the 117th who died in what is now just a farmer's field, the dead Germans frozen in their foxholes and the others lying under the slag pile, and of all the things the 978th experienced there. And now there was no sign of any of it. Of course,

Figure 80. Leon in front of the Mariagrube slag pile, in the area where the mine buildings were located.

thousands of major battles and minor skirmishes took place in Germany during the war. Afterward, people cleaned up the mess and got on with their lives. The events at Mariagrube were hardly a footnote in history. But after hearing the stories of events there that impacted people so profoundly, I guess I had been expecting something more, something that would live up to the memories of the men who had been changed there.

WWII ARCHEOLOGY

IT WAS MY FINAL EVENING in Spekholzerheide, New Year's Eve. I had been away from home for several weeks, visiting various friends in Sweden and the Netherlands and making a work-related visit to a company in Sweden. I enjoy traveling and socializing, but I'm not a naturally extroverted person. Although physically well rested, meeting so many new people, usually being the center of attention, and having to be "up" all the time had drained me, and I was eager to get home. Nevertheless, it was New Year's Eve, and I felt I should be a good guest and go out. Leon and I set off for a local nightclub in Kerkrade.

It was a typical nightclub and lacked the charm of the pubs in Spekholzerheide. The only distinctive feature I noticed was a glass display case in the middle of the dance floor that contained several mannequins dressed in American GI uniforms. At midnight, we rang in the New Year. Half an hour later I decided to finish my drink and take a taxi back to Leon's house. Leon had given me an extra key. I said goodnight to Leon, who had a final question, which he asked with his usual intensity:

> Okay, Jeffrey. I stay here. But before you go, you must first tell me. Tomorrow is your last day here. What do you want to do? I think we have done everything. We visited Maria Merx. We visited the Walters sisters. We went to the beer hall. We visited Mariagrube. I don't know what to do.

> Well, Leon, do you have any suggestions?

> Yes, Jeffrey, we can go to dig.

Leon gave me his usual intense, expectant gaze, and there was nothing else to say but:

> OK. That sounds good. Let's do that... But, Leon, what do you mean, to dig?

My friend Jeroen and I, we go to Germany, usually in places for the Battle of the Bulge. And we ask the old people, "Where were they fighting during the war?" And then we go there and take a metal-detect machine. And when we find something, we dig.

> What do you find?

We find everything. We find guns; we find bullets; we find helmets; Zippo lighters, rifle oil cans, U.S. money, German dog tags, ammo clips, cans of food. One time I find an American GI wallet. I gave it to the American military base here. They contacted the family and gave it back to them. We find anything to do with the war: gasoline cans, medical supplies, bottles of morphine, razors, people, clothes, first-aid supplies.

> People?

Yes, Jeff. One time I found a German boot. It had a foot in it. But no body. I went home and give it to my sister. Two times I found American GI bodies. One time the GI was in a foxhole. I don't know what happened, if a shell came and buried him or he was shot or what. But he got buried in his foxhole. And it was raining when he died, because he is in like this [Leon curls up in fetal position], with a rain cover over him. His body is still there, mostly just bones and a little clothing, his boots, and the things with him. So, we dig around him, very respectfully. And then we call the American Army base close by. They know me. And they come and say, "Thank you, Leon." They take the body and give it a proper burial in Holland. Or they send the body back to the family in the U.S. And the family is happy. They finally know what happens.

> Sure, they finally have closure to the whole thing. Leon, that's beautiful. That sounds fascinating. That's a great plan for my last day. Let's do that.

Okay. I'll call my friend.

I have always been fascinated with archaeology. I suppose my search for my grandfather's war buddies was a sort of archaeological venture and my trip to Spekholzerheide a sort of archaeological dig. I figured that I might as well see it through and go on an actual dig with Leon.

As I finished my drink and was getting ready to leave, I got to thinking about Leon's hobby. I had read newspaper articles about French farmers inadvertently plowing up explosives in WWI trenches and battlefields. I asked Leon if they ever ran into anything that might be dangerous.

Yes, of course, Jeffrey. We find bullets; we find explosives; we find no-explode artillery shells; we find handgranaats. Sometimes we find ammunition for tanks and artillery. Sometimes we find landmines.

And what do you do when you find a landmine?

Well, we are very careful, Jeffrey. Very careful. We don't step on it. [laughs] We dig the dirt from around the mine. Then we take out the firing pin. Then we take out the explosives. And we take the mine away.

How do you know how the mine works? How do you know how to dismantle the firing pin?

We have books that show us.

Have you ever had any accidents?

Yes, it happens sometimes. One friend of mine, he was digging in Belgium in WWI battlefields and he finds something, we don't know what, we think a landmine. And it explodes. All they found of him was a foot. Another friend of mine, I went digging with him several times. He was in garage playing with some handgranaats he found, I think cleaning them. He tried to disarm them and they went off. The explosion caused a fire in his garage. And fire department comes, but neighbor runs over and tells them he collects ammunition, and they don't go in. He was killed by shrapnel from the granaat. But it has never happened to me, not yet. [laughs] So we go to dig tomorrow?

As much as I was fascinated by the idea of digging for WWII relics with Leon, I decided against it. I figured that if my grandfather survived the war, so should I. I told Leon that we should perhaps do something else. After some thought, he suggested that we visit the American military cemetery that was close by. It sounded safer than digging.

A VISIT TO THE CEMETERY

LEON WAS AN EARLY RISER and, despite having been out late the night before, was knocking on my door early the next morning. My train was leaving that afternoon, so we had to set off early. I had some quick breakfast at his house; Leon had a cup of coffee and a cigarette. We walked to the house of his digging buddy, Jeroen. The three of us then drove to Margratan Cemetery. During the trip, Leon explained to me that every American GI who died in the region of Limburg or close by in Germany has a grave marker at the cemetery.

That made me think of Thomas Kulick.

The 978th had approximately two hundred men at full strength. The war took the unit from Wisconsin to Boston, then on to and through New York, Wales, England, France, Belgium, the Netherlands, Germany, back to France, the Panama Canal, the Philippines, and finally Japan. Several veterans claimed that it was the most well-traveled maintenance company in WWII, and Pecker's unit history calculated a journey of 24,000 miles from training camp in Wisconsin to the unit's dissolution in Yokohama, Japan. Added to that would be the journey from each man's home state to training camp and his journey from Japan to California and back to his home state. During their travels, their convoy was attacked by German U-boats, and the men were strafed by airplanes, shot at by snipers, and forced to endure artillery barrages when working at the river crossings. They also had to endure the day-to-day risks of working in the hazardous conditions of a war zone. In spite of all this, only a few men were wounded, and only one man had been killed. Many of the men were amazed that the casualties were not higher.

PFC Thomas E. Kulick of Pennsylvania was the sole member of the 978th who was killed. Pecker's history mentions Kulick's death only briefly. Thomas Kulick fell off a truck and was run over, and a memorial service had been held for him in Gedern, Germany. I asked Ski if he remembered Kulick.

> Oh yeah, I knew Tommy. He was a young guy, a real nice kid. He used to pal around with us. I remember the night he died; it was a truck accident. He fell off the back of the truck and was run over. The next morning a couple of us had to take Tommy's body to Graves Registration.
>
> We took Tommy down. Gosh, there were a lot of bodies. There were hundreds. And they were all being stacked up on the back of a truck. There were four guys working there. And these four guys would take their dog tags and then load 'em up onto a truck. One guy on each arm, one guy on each leg. And they were throwing 'em up there onto the pile, throwing 'em up there like they were, oh, like they were garbage. It would have made you sick to see it, Jeff.
>
> And we got kind of upset. I mean, these were American GIs. But it must have been an awful job. And they had the detail, and there were so many of them coming in. They probably realized it wasn't the right thing to do, but they had to get 'em through.

Everybody in the unit I had talked to thus far was aware of Kulick's death, but nobody had offered any additional details.

Leon, Jeroen, and I arrived at the cemetery early in the morning. It was New Year's Day, and there was not a person in sight. I stopped by the office and checked the list of men buried at Margratan. I found the following, noting that Kulick had died four days after V-E Day.

> Thomas E Kulick   serial number 33608791
> Private First Class   U.S. Army
> 978th Engineer Maintenance Company   died May 12, 1945
> entered service from Pennsylvania
> location: Plot F, Row 8, Grave 22

Leon and Jeroen headed off to find the grave of one of their recent archaeological discoveries. I walked to Kulick's grave. The morning was dry,

Figure 81. Tommy Kulick, bottom right, with baseball.
(Photo courtesy of William Pappan)

crisp, and bitterly cold. The sun was shining just above the horizon but provided no warmth. The trees were bare and the landscape flat. The thin, white layer of morning frost was just thawing, and the green grass beneath provided the only color. In the distance some people were skating on a frozen canal. Aside from Leon and Jeroen in the distance, I was alone in the cemetery.

I thought I ought to say some meaningful words, perhaps to thank Kulick for his sacrifice. But for some reason, it did not feel right. At this stage in my search, I felt that there was much more to the war and to Thomas Kulick, and to utter some canned lines would sound trite. I stood silently for a few moments, took a few photos, and then joined up with Leon and Jeroen.

On the way to the train station I thought about my visit to Kulick's grave and how I felt that, like the visit to Mariagrube, it was somehow anticlimactic. I did not know Kulick. But his death certainly changed the lives of his family, friends, and perhaps a girlfriend or wife. In the fifty years since his death, I was perhaps the only person to visit his grave. Certainly others had walked by and read his name. But I may have been the only person with a connection, albeit distant, who had ever visited his grave. Certainly he left loved ones back home who wondered about his grave overseas. Had they ever made the journey to his grave marker? Probably not. Perhaps that's why I felt strange saying something at Kulick's grave. Those words belonged to somebody else. Others deserved to be there more than I did.

Figure 82. Grave marker of
PFC Thomas E Kulick, Margratan, the Netherlands.

A few months later I would meet one of those people, Thomas Orton, Kulick's best friend during the war. And I'd later make contact with a family in the Netherlands who also had a connection to Kulick. People and places all over the world were connected to the war via a giant web, and through good fortune I was gradually meeting many of them. And as was often the case during my search, everything just seemed to fall into place at just the right time.

THOMAS ORTON

MY SEARCH FOR THOMAS ORTON was a bit different from the quest to find my other war buddies. My mother remembered "a guy from Chicago who opened a Venetian-blind business after the war and came over to the house a few times with 'the guy from Detroit' to drink and play cards." Both George Patrias and Ski told me this was Thomas Orton. I had sent a letter to a Thomas Orton from Chicago, the only T. Orton in the entire U.S. phonebook, but never received a reply. So, I reluctantly put Orton on the "most likely deceased" list and moved on.

It was not until two years later, after I had heard Ski and George Patrias talk more about him and I was confident that I had the right T. Orton, that I decided to call his number. As it turned out, he was the right person and had gotten my letter—he wasn't deceased—but at the time he received it he had been hospitalized with cancer. Now that his health was better, he was more than willing to talk to me. We ended up spending many hours on the phone discussing his experiences in the war.

Shortly after we made contact, I was going to be in Chicago on business, and we arranged to meet at his home. Unfortunately, a few days before my visit, he was rushed to the hospital for emergency surgery on another cancerous tumor that had appeared. In spite of this, he insisted that I visit him in the hospital. During my visit he appeared frail and weak; he could hardly speak and he nodded in and out of consciousness. I was certain that he was close to the end. But in the coming months he made a full recovery and regained his health and voice. Of all the GIs I got to know, I formed the closest relationship with Orton. We talked on the phone numerous times, and he ended up being the most forthcoming and communicative of all my sources.

In subsequent years, I was fortunate to make several business trips to Chicago, and I always made a point of spending an afternoon with Orton and his wife, Lorraine, at their home. They did not have children—an illness during the war left Lorraine unable to have children. But I could see that they were still very much in love and extremely devoted to each other. At the time of my last visit they had just celebrated their sixty-second wedding anniversary.

Toward the end of our first telephone conversation, I asked Orton if he remembered Kulick. There was a long silence, and I thought we might have been cut off. I asked if he was still there, and he quietly said:

Jeff, I'm not sure I can talk about Tommy Kulick.

I did not push the subject and went on to other things. Later, Orton interrupted, his voice choking up:

Jeff, the reason I'm not sure if I can talk to you about Tommy Kulick is that … I … I was the one driving the truck that ran over him. But, I will write you a letter about Tommy, is that OK?

I never received the letter, but during our next telephone conversation Orton interrupted me in mid-sentence and changed the subject, saying in a slow, strained voice:

Let me try to tell you about Tommy. I've been preparing myself for it all week. I was going to tell you in a letter but then thought I'd just try to tell you outright. I've tried to block it out the past fifty years, and have done a pretty good job, but I'd like to try to tell you.

Tommy and I met at Camp McCoy and became friendly very quickly. We were both newlyweds. After basic training our wives came up to live with us in the couples housing, and my wife, Lorraine, became good friends with Tommy's wife, Theresa. They were from Pennsylvania. During our last furlough before we were shipped overseas, Thomas and Theresa came to Chicago with us.

During the war, Tommy and I were assigned to a single repair truck We were together just about every minute of the day. It was a six by six,

Figure 83. Thomas Orton and Tommy Kulick, Mönchengladbach, Germany. (Photo courtesy of Thomas Orton)

and in the back was a machine shop. We had three work benches. On two of them were all our equipment: lathes, a drill press, a grinder, a generator, and such. We slept in the back in our sleeping bags. Tommy slept on the floor and I slept on the third workbench. Our platoon would set up shop at a location for, oh, anywhere from a couple of days to a few weeks. We'd do our work and then travel on to our next assignment.

We always traveled at night, as the risk of traveling by day and being sighted by German planes was too great. Sometimes we'd be up for days on end—working during the day, driving at night. It was exhausting. Sometimes the convoy would stop, and guys would fall asleep at the wheel. Then somebody would have to go down the line and wake everybody up, and we'd continue on.

During that time we were still under what we called combat conditions, even after V-E Day [Kulick died four days after V-E Day].

There were die-hard Germans and bands of kids, Hitler Youth and such, mostly teens to their mid-twenties, who still thought they were battling the war. And the Bulge had just ended, so things were uncertain and could have flared up again. So nobody was really sure what was going to happen.

We couldn't drive with our headlights on 'cause the Germans would see us—either the planes or snipers on the ground.

Each truck had a set of tiny lights on the back. And you can see nothing of your surroundings except the tiny lights of the vehicle in front of you, 'cause we'd travel on these dark little country roads. So you just follow the lights, and when you see the lights ahead of you turn, you turn. It's exhausting. But you have to concentrate on those lights. And when the truck in front turns in the dark, you can't anticipate it, it happens all of the sudden so you just react.

Well, Tommy and I were talking. And I was concentrating on the truck in front of me. Then we took a sharp left turn, and the truck hit a shell hole or something. I bounced out of my seat and hit my head on the roof. I heard Tommy yell out, and he fell out of the side of the truck. I slammed on the brakes and veered left to avoid running over Tommy. But we were going pretty fast and it didn't matter. The rear wheels ran over Tommy. He was unconscious when several other GIs arrived. They put him on a stretcher, but he died a few minutes later.

The next day some of the guys took Tommy's body to Graves Registration. But they wouldn't allow me to go. I tried, but I was such a basket case.

Orton was very choked up throughout our conversation but insisted on continuing. Aside from the grief of losing a friend, he said that he still sometimes felt responsible for what had happened. In subsequent conversations, he added more details about Tommy's death:

That ruined me for quite a while. I blamed myself for a long time. But I've run it over in my mind so many times and I'm not sure I could have done anything differently. If he had been killed by a sniper or by an artillery barrage, then I think I could have handled it better. But this?

After the war, Tommy's wife, Theresa, came to visit me in Chicago. I tried to tell her how it happened. But I'm not sure she really understood. I think she visited looking for a reason. But there was no reason. I mean, he should still be here.

Figure 84. Thomas and Theresa Kulick and Thomas and Lorraine Orton, before the 978th left for Europe. (Photo courtesy of Thomas Orton)

Orton also talked about the lingering effects of the war:

Sometimes I'm around people who tell you one war story after another. And you begin to wonder—how many of those he READ. I mean, there are things you talk about, things I've told you about, and things that are best left over there. You don't talk about the bodies, the blood, the bodies with no faces. We saw that all the time.

It wasn't that it might be me. But that they were ours. I never thought about what might happen to me. I've always been a pretty positive person. Even today. I mean, except for with Tommy. I really beat myself up over that for a long time.

It didn't matter if it was Americans or Germans or whatever, one of the things that got to me more than anything else was when we were in convoy, I think it was at the Bulge. And a big Graves Registration truck was coming the other way. They were big six-by-sixes, no canvas top. There were four of those trucks. Each one has the bed of the truck and wooden slats going up the sides, with hoops. And the dead troops were up there, piled on top of each other all the way to the top, just like they were firewood. That affected me worse than anything else. [chokes up]

Sometimes now, today, that scene and other scenes from the war are going through my head. I have vivid memories of it. Over the years I've tried to freeze it out of my memory. But you never freeze it out completely because you still dream at night. Every year, two or three times a year, I dream the war all night. My wife says, "You didn't sleep." And I say, "No, I dreamt war all night." You can't get away from it.

Like all bad things, the older you get the less it bothers you. But you never forget it. It's not a subject I enjoy, but I wanted to tell you about it. And I'll just have to go through it all again, the blackout situation. I'll just have to black it out again.

Orton sent me his photo album from the war. It has one page of images with Orton and Kulick, together with their wives, at home before they were sent overseas, and several pages of the two of them together in Europe.

During my last visit with him in Chicago, he said to me:

Meeting you has improved my attitude. It was a challenge and I enjoyed it. Over all these years I've never really talked about it. I could hardly even say Kulick's name. But time, and going through it with you, has helped heal the wounds.

Figure 85. Thomas Orton and me at his home in Chicago, 2003.

Not Forgotten

During the time I was having conversations with Orton, I tried to track down relatives of Kulick. I found quite a few Kulicks in his home-state of Pennsylvania and made some calls. But none of them panned out. My next connection with Kulick, however, wouldn't be in the U.S., but back in the Netherlands, with a family who live not far from Spekholzerheide.

In November, 2004, numerous ceremonies and memorials were held throughout the Netherlands in celebration of the sixtieth anniversary of the country's liberation, including a visit by George Bush to Margratan. At this time, a program was developed where local families could adopt the grave of an American soldier buried there.

Louis Palmen and his family, who live about a mile from Spekholzerheide, in Heerlen, decided to adopt a grave. They were assigned the grave of PFC Thomas E. Kulick. During the ceremonies at Margratan, the Palmen family laid flowers at Kulick's grave.

That evening Louis searched the Internet for "Thomas Kulick." He found my site and e-mailed me with the story of his family's adoption of the grave, "a great honor," he said. Palmen asked for more information. I sent all of my photos of Kulick, along with the sections about him that were to appear in this book. The family was delighted to know Kulick's story and have a photo of him.

Louis is a member of his local Lions Club. He told them the story of adopting Kulick's grave and our correspondence. Afterward, all the members of his club adopted graves of American soldiers. Every Christmas Louis lays flowers on Kulick's grave.

"I PREFER LIVE AMMUNITION"

OVER THE YEARS I DEVELOPED contacts with numerous people around Spekholzerheide: a Dutch teenage girl trying to track down her grandmother's first love—an American GI during the war; a young man trying to find his American GI father; and local people curious about the war who stumbled upon my Web page.

I ended up visiting Spekholzerheide four times. Each visit was usually a few days long, tacked onto the end of a business trip to the area. During one of these visits, Leon gave me more details on his hobby of digging for relics in World War II battlefields:

> I've been searching many hundreds of times, mostly in Germany, but also in Belgium, France, and Holland. I have found four German bodies and two American bodies. And a foot. We were in Belgium, in Wijtschate, digging in WWI battlefields, and I found a German boot with a foot in it. I took it home and gave it to my sister.

At first I had trouble believing many of Leon's stories and tried to subtly corroborate them by asking him for more details or bringing them up with people who knew him. During one visit, Leon, his sister, and I were having a beer at Café Puccini in Kerkrade. While Leon was in the restroom I asked her if she knew anything about Leon's hobby of digging. She replied:

> Yes, one time I was at home sitting on the bed, and Leon comes in and says, "Here's something for you," and throws a boot in my lap.

Oooph. [Gives an expression of disgust.] The bones of the foot were in it, and the boot had five bullet holes in it.

I asked Leon about his other finds.

I also found an American in Belgium, in the Ardennes. A tree had fallen down, and he was lying under the tree. So we had to dig under the tree. It took maybe five or six hours, as we are very careful because of live ammunition. We hear the metal detector go beep, beep, beep. And we start to dig. The first thing we see is the helmet, with the skull and the hair inside. And my heart starts to beat. So exciting. Then we dig up the body. It is mostly just bones, maybe a little bit of material from the jacket. And the boots. The boots are usually preserved.

We found the purse of him, with one picture inside of a girl, and a driving license and a ring, a bracelet with a name on it, maybe of the girl, I don't know. A toothbrush, a razor. I think he was killed by a bullet, and years later the tree falls down. But maybe not. Maybe artillery causes the tree to fall on him.

We then call the police and the American military comes and take him away. He had a dog tag so they know who he is. They give him a proper burial and contact the family and tell them they found the body of their family member.

One of the Germans we found, his name was Adolf.[1] He was 43. We were digging near pillboxes in the forest near the town Krefeld in Germany. He was in an engineering unit and died from a bullet to the head. We could see the entry into his skull. We found a purse with two photos, one of his marriage day and one of his wife and child. The other papers were too old, they fall apart when we try to open them. He was lying straight on his back. I don't know if he died that way or if they buried him and never came back to get him. He had two medals on him, one ammunition bag, a belt, a backpack, a pistol.

The first time I found a body, a German before this guy, I called the Kriegsgräberbund, an organization in Germany that takes care of things from the war, and they never told me what they did with it or if they found the family. So this time I take the dog tag, ring, and photos. And I tell them that there wasn't anything there. And they take the bones away. Then I send the dog tag and photos and things to Berlin and told the whole story. They found a niece of him and sent the photos and stuff to her.

Leon had made other finds. A sixteen-year-old German named Hans-Joachim. The Kriegsgräberbund tracked down his brother. And then a German "medical guy who was missing a leg." And then a German named Hans who was in a Panzer division: "We found the foot first, then the rest of the body. He was lying in a ditch in the position like a baby. [Leon curls up in the fetal position.] He was married, had a gold ring and a crucifix." And finally another American, in Belgium, without a dog tag, next to two hand grenades.

I asked Leon if his digging was legal.

No, not really. But lots of people do it. One time we were digging in Germany and the police came. So we went running away. And the German police guy, what's he do? He starts shouting for us to stop and starts shooting his gun in the air. [laughs]

I asked Leon if he was ever worried about things blowing up.

Yes, it could happen. I have been digging hundreds of times and it hasn't happened yet. But it could. But you know, Jeff, there are two things in life that are very dangerous: women and live ammunition. Live ammunition you can take care with. You know how it works, you can guess what might happen with it. You can be careful. I prefer live ammunition.

Figures 86 and 87. Leon and his buddy Chris, digging in Germany. (Photo courtesy of Leon)

Figure 88. Leon with metal detector and shovel. I eventually did go digging with Leon, but not for World War II relics. We went digging for Roman relics. With the assistance of maps and books, Leon knows areas where large Roman settlements were located and digs there. Unfortunately, it was summer and the farmers' fields where Leon had previously been successful were full of crops. Leon said "it wouldn't be nice to the farmer" to dig where their crops were. We dug around the adjacent fields and found some Roman roof shingles and various odd pieces of metal, but not much else.

1. Leon had the full names of the men he dug up, but we decided not to include them here. As Leon said, "The boys are dead so let them rest in peace."

GETTING IT OUT
OF YOUR SYSTEM

THROUGHOUT MY SEARCH, I SOMETIMES wondered why I was so interested in my grandfather's wartime experiences. If my grandfather had served abroad in the U.S. Symphony Orchestra instead of the U.S. Army, would I have been as interested in his experiences? Probably not. I think I have a healthy interest in and appreciation of history, but there is something about the history of war and war itself—human and social behavior at its extreme—that is particularly fascinating. My friend Eric, who went with me to visit Max Voron, describes his interest in reading WWII history as "a guilty pleasure" and said that "reading about art history is just so damn boring compared to reading about war." Thomas Hardy wrote, "My argument is that War makes rattling good history; but Peace is poor reading." Mark Twain said, "War talk by men who have been in a war is always interesting; whereas moon talk by a poet who has not been in the moon is likely to be dull." In a similar vein, several veterans I interviewed said they joined the infantry to be "where the action was."

Nobody reflected this attitude more than Leon. During my visits we talked about his fascination with war:

> Jeff, all my life, ever since I was a boy, I think, in my other life I'd be an American GI, or a soldat in a German Panzer division. But now I live in a peaceful time, at least in the Netherlands. So I talk to the people about the war.
>
> I talk to German soldaters, I talk to American GIs, I talk to Dutch underground, and they say, "Ok, you know a lot about the war. But you

have no experience. You don't know what it *feels* like to be there. So what do you really know? You don't know anything." And you know, Jeff, they are right. I don't really know anything.

I asked Leon if he could not just join the Dutch Army.

> Yes, I went to talk to them about that. At the time there was a lot of action happening in Lebanon, the U.N. was there. And I told them I wanted to go there. But they said no, they didn't need anybody for Lebanon. They said if I joined I would probably be sent to the Sinai. But there was nothing happening there. I didn't want to just sit in a hole in the desert. So I didn't join. Finally, I decided to go to Yugoslav.

> I was in Yugoslav two times. The first time was for about six months. We were digging foxholes. I didn't really see any action. Then we thought the war was going to be over and I went back home. Later, I saw a buddy of mine, and he said they were offering money for people to go back. I didn't really care about the money, I just wanted the experience. So I went back to Yugoslav a second time. For about six months again. This time we saw a lot of action. We were fighting in the town, house-to-house fighting, you know. We were fighting from the buildings. I used my gun a lot. Shot. Had people shooting at me. I was scared to death. So scared I shit in my pants one time. But I continue. Then the war ended and I had to come home.

> But you know, Jeff, I would go again. I would go for the experience.

I knew Leon had read enough serious literature, seen documentaries, and talked to enough people to know that war is ugly and that, even when people survived, they came back emotionally scarred. I thought back to a WWII documentary Leon and I watched together at his home. In one part, an elderly American GI sits in his chair in front of the camera sobbing and shaking while talking about his WWII experiences. I asked Leon how he felt about that aspect of the war.

> Yes, I knew that, but I not think of that at the time. [laughs] I just think of the experience. And when I was there, I hated it. I really hated it. Then I come back, and I am angry. I am pissed off at everything, angry all the time. People would say something to me and I'd just blow up at them.

After a while I get over that and I became less and less interested in the war. And I stopped most things. I sold all of my souvenirs and books and things. I gave away all my photos to you [Leon had sent me hundreds of original photos he'd collected]. And I stop digging. Now I just dig for Roman things.

Oscar Wilde said, "As long as war is regarded as wicked, it will always have its fascination. When it is looked upon as vulgar, it will cease to be popular." I do not know if Wilde was talking about political attitudes, personal attitudes, or something else. However, I did notice during my subsequent visits that Leon had really "cut back on the war," or at least the outward manifestation of it. His room was no longer filled with WWII souvenirs and memorabilia, and he seemed to now have other interests. He said he still enjoys a good war movie now and then, and still reads war books, but he seemed to more or less get it out of his system, realizing the ridiculousness of the entire venture. He said:

Figure 89. Leon, late at night at his home in Spekholzerheide.

Yes, I was obsessed. My whole life was World War II. I was obsessed. I go on holiday with my girlfriend, we don't go to museum or to beach or someplace nice, we go somewhere for war. I see a picture in a book, it is from the war. And I look at it and want to know more. Everything for me about the war.

But like the people said, I know a lot, but I really don't know anything. And they are right. So I go to fight in somebody else's war. [a laugh of resignation] But at least now I know.

MARIADORF REVISITED

IN JUNE 2005 I RECEIVED an e-mail from Ingo Schönhold, a researcher with a degree in library science living in Mariadorf, Germany. He had been doing research for Toni Andre, the town historian, and came across my Web page, which mentions Mariadorf and Mariagrube. Ingo said that, since the town was evacuated at the height of the war, they did not know much about this period. He was hoping I might provide some information.

I sent him what information I had. Three months later I had a business trip to Hannover, Germany, and made a trip down to Mariadorf. Ingo and I arranged to meet at Andre's house. In Andre's kitchen, with Ingo acting as a translator, Andre, seventy-nine, told me about Mariadorf during the war:

> There were about 15,000 people in the village. In September of 1944 the town was evacuated; almost everybody was forced by the Nazis to leave. I was born in 1930, and I was evacuated too. Maybe 300 or so people stayed, people who didn't want to leave. The coal mine was not working. The people who remained hid in bunkers that were dug during the previous years. One baby was born during that time.
>
> It was harvesting season, so there was food. The farmers provided food for the people in the bunkers. Some people had some cattle, some chickens, etc. And the coalmining philosophy was that everybody should have a little garden, so people also had food stored in the bunkers. Then the Americans came, and people came out of the bunkers. When the Americans were there, some of the Germans in

Mariadorf worked for the Americans, and the Americans paid them in flour. So they had flour too.

I showed Andre the map of Mariadorf with the location of the tunnel as described to me by Farran Helmick. He already knew about it. With grand visions of digging up the entrance and crawling down inside to find the dead Germans in their bunks, I asked him if he knew what had happened to the tunnel. He said:

> All the shafts of the coal mine were filled with concrete after the war, including all the bunkers. The dead people were brought out to a memorial site in Bardenberg. The English, American, German soldiers, they were all brought there. The dead civilians were taken to their local town, wherever they were from, and buried there.

Andre mentioned that his childhood friend, Josef Meisenberg, owned a bakery across the street from the tunnel, on Eschweilerstraße, the main street running along the coal mine. He telephoned Josef, and we arranged a visit for 2 p.m., when the bakery closed.

We drove over to the bakery and were met by an energetic man with lively blue eyes. He was wearing his "tooling around the garden" clothes—a raggedy old T-shirt he had obviously used previously for painting, a beat-up pair of soccer shorts, and tennis shoes. He sat down and talked to us in his kitchen. He was quite animated and enthusiastic when he spoke. Ingo translated:

> My grandfather started the bakery, in the same location it is now, in 1895. I was about ten years old during the war, born in 1932. I helped dig the tunnel. The entrance was just across the street from where we are now, under what is now the tennis hall. All the young men from Mariagrube were away for the war, and the women too. Only the older people and children were left in the town. The older people were digging the bunker to hide us from airplane attacks and artillery. My father was with them. They'd dig out the material in the bunker, bring it to the top, and then the children helping would take away the dirt. We had little wagons we used. It took maybe two to three months to build it.
>
> We slept there at night. In the bunker were bunks, maybe twenty or so in a line and about three high. And there were benches. The bunker had supports to hold it up. It was built by coal miners.

The tunnel was about two to three meters wide, maybe two meters high. The entrance went down at an angle, and there were tracks for the wagons and wooden beams for the tracks. There were no stairs, and it was steep. But the wooden beams formed a kind of stairs we could use to walk down. From the entrance, it went straight, then turned right, then left.

I asked Meisenberg to draw a picture. He showed the tunnel in relation to the main street, Eschweilerstraße, where the secondary entrance was, and the side street, where the main entrance was located. He placed the main entrance in the exact location described by Farran Helmick.

When the alarm came because of air attacks, the neighbors would run the one hundred meters or so to the tunnel. If it was night, then we slept there. The bunker could hold about fifty or sixty people. We slept there maybe twenty times, with neighbors, all the family, mother, father, sister. Most of it [the incoming fire] was from American artillery. They'd shoot at anything that moved. When they did, they'd push us children into the bunker.

When the Americans got closer, to Liebigstraße, then I was evacuated to Bremen. I think the first of October. In mid-November the Americans took Mariadorf, it took that long. I heard it took the Americans six to eight weeks of fighting to take Mariadorf. I never saw the Americans personally.

I returned in August 1945. When my family came back, the bakery was almost totally destroyed. The roof was gone, the ceiling gone, most of the walls, maybe one wall was standing. In the basement we found dead soldiers, not sure if American or German. The undertaker came and took them away. We built another bakery, in the same spot, using the foundation and maybe one of the walls. In our backyard we had seventy shell holes.

I was in the Hitler Youth, and when I was around ten or so, they taught us how to shoot at tanks with antitank bazookas. But one time a young kid burned his face during the training. After that accident we were ordered to stop. No more training.

I asked Meisenberg if he had any photos or souvenirs from the war.

No, I don't have anything. I left Mariadorf in September/October 1944, and I returned in August 1945. I had a camera but didn't have any film. The only thing I have is a hammer. When I came back there were six American tanks in the field behind my house, behind the bakery. All were destroyed. In one of the tanks I found a hammer. It was a very good hammer, very good quality. I still have it and I use it. I use it all the time.

I asked Meisenberg if I could see the hammer. He went to the garage and quickly retrieved it. The hammer had its original wooden handle. Written on the hammer was "Fairmount."

We then walked over to where the two entrances of the tunnel were located. Not surprisingly, there was nothing to see, just some bushes at the entrance of the tennis hall. Then we walked over to the railway line, which was in a ditch about thirty feet below the street. We stood on the bridge looking down, and Meisenberg told us more:

> The Germans, they had a good defense. They had a trench already built, the railway line, which was maybe already five or ten meters below the ground. They'd stay down there and shoot artillery over at the Americans, on Liebigstraße. When I was a kid during the war we would play down there. The train would come up, and because we didn't have air-conditioning then, it was hot. So the train would come by with the windows down. My friends and I, we'd catch frogs, and when the train would slow down approaching Mariadorf, we'd throw the frogs through the windows of the train. [laughs] What were they going to do, stop the train and come chasing after us?

Later, I asked if I could use this information in my book.

> Of course, sure. These are memories from my childhood. Nobody else is asking me for these things.

I asked Meisenberg if he knew anybody else who might know something about the tunnel. He said that his childhood friend, Albert Esten, probably would. We gave him a call. He agreed to talk to us, and we walked over to his house.

Like Meisenberg, Esten spoke matter-of-factly about his experiences in the war, seemingly without any outward regret or hard feelings, and sometimes with enthusiasm:

> Josef and I were good friends. We were the same age. No, he is thirteen days younger than I. [laughs] We were evacuated at the end

of September 1944. When we were evacuated we were told that we would be coming back in two weeks, that the Americans would be pushed back then. We came back September 1945.

There was bombing in Mariagrube since 1940. When the Americans were closer, there was artillery. As soon as the Americans saw people leaving the tunnel, they started shooting over artillery.

At first we hid in the basement, but that was not enough protection. So we decided to build a tunnel. We were coal miners, so we were experts. All the neighbors were helping build the bunker. I was twelve years old.

Esten drew a map of the tunnel that was almost identical to Meisenberg's.

When the alarm went off, we all went to the tunnel. It was almost every night. I spent maybe 150 nights a year in the tunnel. When I was there, there were only wooden benches. I don't remember any beds or bunks.

I asked what he did when he was in the tunnel.

There was only a little light. We slept. We read the newspaper every day; that was our only contact with the world. We were mainly chatting down there. The rule was that if the alarm was over before 1:00 a.m., then we had to go to school early. If it was over after 1:00 a.m., then we got to go to school an hour later. That was the biggest subject. When the men outside were shouting that it was over [the bombing or artillery], we were wondering what time it was. If before 1:00, then, oh scheisse, we have to wake up early.

When we slept down there we brought whatever we could. Clothes. Blankets. Every family had a little bag ready—with bank certificates, birth certificates, that stuff—which was taken to the tunnel. So if we came back and our home was destroyed, we had the important documents.

I asked if he had good memories, bad memories, or other feelings about those times.

Bad memories were at night. In the tunnel, it was wet, it was cold. You could feel the cold from the ground. It was big fun building the tunnel. Although it was hard work, it was big fun. It took maybe half a year to build it. I had a brother in Stalingrad, another sister who was away working. Both came back. The war, it was a big event for us as children.

There was no real bombing here; that was mostly in Aachen, Köln, Jülich. It started in 1942. When they did the big bombing in Aachen and Köln, they sometimes dropped a bomb in this area. But the artillery was much worse, more dangerous. Sometimes it was five minutes, sometimes all day. We could hear everything within twenty kilometers. At that time there was no school; [we] could hear it all day, [but we] only went to the tunnel if there was a big danger.

The elderly people said most of the bombs, the big bombs, were from when they went to Aachen and Köln and didn't drop them all. They didn't want to go back to England with the bombs, so they dropped them here. That's what they assumed. We could hear them dropping in Jülich. As children, we weren't allowed to climb on the slag

Figures 90 and 91. The Meisenberg bakery, prewar, above, with Josef's grandfather peering out the door (photo courtesy of Josef Meisenburg) and in 2005, with Toni Andre, Lisbeth Meisenberg, Ingo Schönhold, and Josef Meisenburg, holding the American hammer.

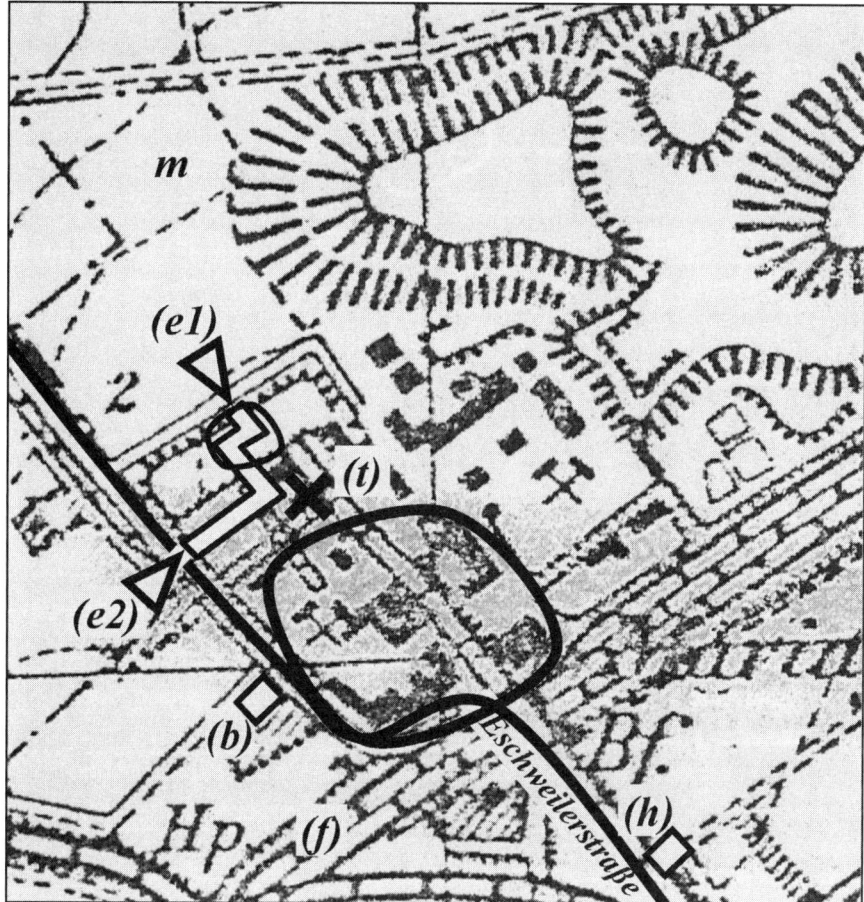

Figure 92. Map of Mariadorf with additional annotations after visit.

(e1)	**main** entrance to tunnel, as drawn by Meisenberg and Esten
(e2)	**secondary** entrance to tunnel, as drawn by Meisenberg and Esten
(t)	**location** of Sherman tank where Meisenberg found the hammer
(b)	**bakery**
(h)	**pockmarked** house in photo
(f)	**location** of German artillery and the frog incident

pile, but sometimes we did. Here we could see all the way to Köln, to the big cathedral, and see the smoke.

Esten mentioned the Germans in the recessed railway line firing artillery at the Americans. I asked him if he ever threw frogs through windows of trains. He just smiled.

Frogs in the windows? Yeah, maybe we did. [laughs]

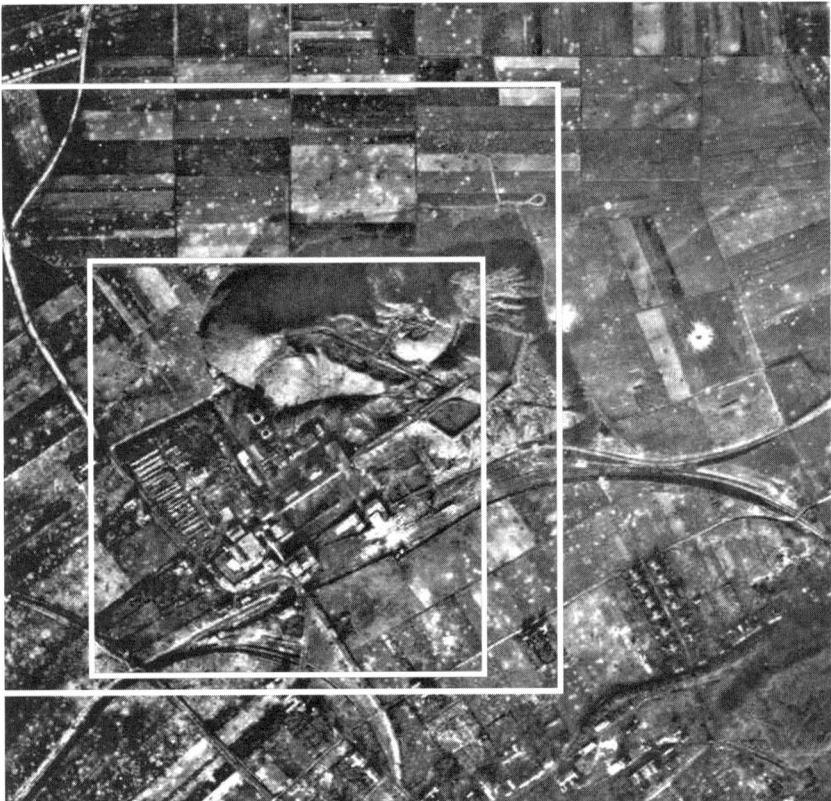

Figure 93. Mariadorf after the war. Notice pockmarks from bombs and artillery. White boxes show boundaries of previous maps. (Photo courtesy of Toni Andre)

————————

Ingo plays the accordion in a local band called De Pöngele. The band members dress up in traditional coal-miner costumes and play coal-miner music. One evening during my visit to Mariadorf, Andre and I went out to one of Ingo's gigs. We arrived and sat down in a long hall filled with about two hundred or so middle-aged and elderly men and woman drinking beer. From what I could gather, it was a get-together of some kind of traditional shooting society. I did not see any signs of guns or posters depicting shooting, and nobody was dressed in traditional shooting costume. They were just drinking and singing. One man, who spoke limited English, told me it was a society whose members get together regularly for shooting competitions and occasionally to drink. As the night wore on, I got the impression that it was

Figure 94. Mariagrube, 1953. (Photo courtesy of Toni Andre)

a society whose members get together occasionally to shoot and regularly for drinking competitions.

In any case, the night went on and, since I do not speak German, there was little to do but keep on drinking. The locals wanted to be polite, but since we did not share a common language, the only way they could be polite was to smile and keep buying me drinks. The only way I could be polite was to smile and keep accepting their drinks. They made an announcement in German saying, from what I understood, that I was over from America and that my grandfather had been in Mariadorf during the war. I got lots of smiles and polite nods—and more drinks arrived at the table. The pilsner kept coming, and I joined in the singing the best I could.

As the night progressed, I went over to the bar and started chatting with the locals, who were younger than the crowd in the hall. Nobody could speak English, except for a middle-aged woman who spoke a little. She kept asking me, incredulously, "Why are you in Mariadorf? Why not Berlin or Munich or Hamburg? Why Mariadorf?" I tried to explain about my grandfather and the 978th, but she did not understand, or feigned not to understand. A crowd gathered round.

By this time Ingo and his band had finished playing and joined us at the bar. I tried to explain again to the woman, but to no avail. I was not sure if she really did not know enough English to understand me or if it was her way of coming on to me. But the conversation was fun. Ingo, seeming to enjoy my efforts and the conversation, did not bother to translate, but kept warning me to stay away from this woman. "We have better looking girls in Mariadorf," he kept repeating. "Stay away."

She asked again, "Why in the hell you come to Mariadorf?"

Finally, the pilsner getting to my head, I took a napkin and drew a picture of a man with a short mustache and his arm raised in the air and said, "As you know, we Americans, we're not so good at history. But there was some man some years ago, I can't remember his name, Hilberg or Hilton or something. Germans are nice people. Jerry Schröder. Chancellor Helmut. Colonel Klink. Nice guys. But this guy, Hilton, he was not a nice guy." Next to him I drew a picture of another man with a rifle. "Mein opa. Krieg. Deutschland. Mariadorf Über Alles," I kept saying, the few words I knew in German. I then took another napkin and drew the two of them fighting hand-to-hand next to the slag pile. The woman said that now she understood.

The crowd gathered around and thought that it was the funniest thing going. Some chanted "Heil Hilton! Mariadorf Über Alles." One guy asked if he could keep the napkin and insisted the bartender keep the pilsner coming. Although I was a bit hesitant about "mentioning the war" and blurting out mangled Nazi slogans, it was the pilsner speaking. I also knew that I was in the company of a younger generation of Germans. They seemed to have a sense of humor about the whole thing. It was a fun evening.

We spent the rest of the night singing traditional Irish drinking songs, which Ingo and his band said they liked better than the German ones. Finally, we staggered back to Ingo's house.

––––––––

Early in the evening, Ingo and I had promised Toni Andre that we would meet him at 10:00 a.m. Obviously, this had been a mistake, but it was a promise we felt obligated to keep. We picked him up and drove to the Mariadorf cemetery. In one small section are the graves of the German soldiers who died in the Mariadorf area and civilians from Mariadorf who died in the war. I noticed the graves of several soldiers who died in 1944 and wondered if they possibly could be the men from inside the tunnel. But the gravestones gave only the year of death, so there was no way to tell for sure. We found the grave of an entire family—father, mother, son, and daughter—who were killed in 1942 when a bomb fell on their house. We also found the grave of one of Andre's childhood friends who, in 1945, stepped on a mine in a minefield near his house. He was Erwin Mommertz, 1932–1945.

And that concluded my second visit to Mariadorf. This visit was much more interesting than the first—which wasn't surprising. As I discovered time and time again, for the journey to be successful, you have to find the right people, like Ingo or Leon.

After having a lunch of schnitzel, cooked carrots, and French fries with Ingo, his parents, and brother, I said goodbye to Ingo. He joked that perhaps someday, sixty years from now, our grandchildren would get together to examine the time when Ingo and Jeff met in Mariadorf. I said that it was possible, but our meeting was just not nearly as interesting as the encounters in our grandfathers' generation. They were trying to kill each other; we were drinking together.

But then again, I doubt my grandfather ever imagined that his grandson would be hanging out in Spekholzerheide and Mariadorf. So who knows?

Figure 95. Ingo, top right, in bandana, with members of De Pöngele and various members of the shooting society.

Figure 96. Jülich, Germany, 1944. (Photo courtesy of William Musiker)

Figure 97. The Witches Tower, Jülich, Germany, 2005.

JÜLICH

AFTER SAYING GOODBYE TO INGO, I made the fifteen-minute drive down a small, two-lane road to the town of Jülich, the location of the Roer River crossing. This was the only road from Mariadorf to Jülich and, presumably, the same road my grandfather and Marvin Mangham drove down on their way to repair the crane. Before the war, Jülich had a population of 12,000 people.[1] When I visited, its population was 34,000. It is not a large city; it can be walked from one end to the other in about fifteen minutes.

As I entered the city I was greeted by a sight I recognized immediately from a photo from William Musiker: the Hexenturm, or "Witches Tower." A hotel is now built around the tower, and I got a room there. I then walked across the street, where a Turkish woman was selling fruits and vegetables. She let me take her picture.

Jülich was 97 percent destroyed during the war.[1] Marvin Mangham wrote that when the 978th crossed the Roer River in Jülich, "there was not a building left standing that was more than 4 feet tall." Consequently, after rebuilding, it is now a modern-looking city.

Jülich is divided down the middle by the Roer River, running from south to north. My mental picture of the town was divided into the "German side," where American assault boats had touched down, affixed the cables for the bridges, and started routing out Germans, and the "American side," where the Americans were assembling bridges. The next morning I walked along the banks of the "German side." Not surprisingly, there was not much to see. The terrain of grass, dirt, and trees presumably had changed little since 1945, although in February 1945 the river was flooded and the landscape would have appeared more sparse, as the trees would have lacked any foliage in winter and many of them would have been cut down by artillery.

Figure 98. September 2005, looking south from the current bridge to the location of the bridge-building sites at Site 2, where the foot-, heavy-pontoon, and treadway bridges were constructed.

I then crossed the current bridge, located at Bailey Bridge Site 2, to the "American side" of the river. I headed south along the bank, where the foot-, treadway, and heavy-pontoon bridges were constructed. I presumably walked past the location where my grandfather and Marvin Mangham repaired the crane. Several yards from the bank of the river was a road, with residential houses running along its western side. I was able to match up one of these houses with the shell of a house from the photos of the river crossing across the footbridge that was published in *LIFE* magazine in 1945.

Looking for more information, I walked to the Citadel, a large medieval fortress with high earthen walls topped with layers of thick bricks, ramparts, and bastions. During the river crossings, the Germans were holed up in the Citadel, using it as cover and shooting artillery at the bridge sites. The woman at the Citadel museum directed me to the Rathaus back in town. There I met two young men and an older man who study the history of Jülich. The older man said he was a veteran of the Eastern Front. They were very happy to share information, but they didn't have any more information about the crossings than I did. They had several official unit histories of American units involved in the crossing and the same poster that my grandfather had, showing the location of the crossing sites. They also had the same U.S. Signal Corps film footage of the crossing that I had already seen.

Figures 99 and 100. ` photo from March 12, 1945, issue of *LIFE* magazine of footbridge over Roer. Bottom photo, same house on eastern bank of Roer near location of footbridge crossing site, 2005. (Figure 99 © Time & Life Pictures/Getty Images)

My time was running out and I had a flight to catch from Cologne later that afternoon. I was tempted to change it to the next day, as I thought of poking around some more, perhaps even knocking on the door of the house I located in the *LIFE* photo. But I did not. I felt I had exhausted all there was to do in Jülich—or, at least, I probably had gotten all the "easy" information. Of course, I could spend weeks in Jülich, trying to track down people and more information. But there comes a time when you have to say "enough is enough." It was time to move on. My trip to Jülich was not as successful as my trips to Spekholzerheide and Mariadorf, perhaps because there just wasn't as much to find, or perhaps because I didn't find the right people.

1. Source: www.wikipedia.com

LEO PACKER

THE 978TH'S THREE HIGHEST RANKING officers were Captain Harry Ingraham, Captain Roy Krueger (who replaced Ingraham in Europe), and 1st Lieutenant Leo Pecker. Captain Ingraham was said to be a full-blooded American Indian, the son of a tribal leader in California, and a college graduate. He was highly respected in the unit. The GIs referred to him as a "man's man," "a natural leader," and "a tough-looking son-of-a-gun, thin legs, high cheekbones, all Indian." Several GIs said the Captain, who was trained as an infantry officer, felt constrained in an engineering unit and asked to be transferred out. Rumor was that, when the 978th was close to the combat zone in Germany, Ingraham and his driver would take their jeep up to the front in the middle of the night to "check things out" and "get a little action." He was said to be needlessly reckless and to have a death wish. During the Battle of the Bulge, Captain Ingraham's request was granted and he left the 978th. Krueger replaced him and was almost unanimously disliked by the men. Unfortunately, when I checked the Social Security Death Index, I found a listing that was most likely for Captain Ingraham. I did not put much effort into finding Krueger. His name was too common, and he was much older during the war, making the likelihood of him still being alive much smaller.

I also tried to find Pecker. Searching for Leo Pecker on Switchboard.com did not yield any matches. However, neither did the Social Security Death Index. Several years into my project, I still did not have any information or leads on him. If Pecker was alive, it looked like I was not going to find him.

Figure 101. Captain Harry Ingraham and 1st Lt. Leo Pecker at Camp McCoy, Wisconsin.

In 1946, when the 978th was in Japan, Pecker wrote the company history. One interesting episode he included was a description of the officers meeting a French family that lived close to the 978th's camp in the village of Les Pieux, Normandy. Pecker wrote:

> On the highway not far from the bivouac area, there was a farm house inhabited by a family called Laurent, father, mother and seven attractive children. A few days after the 978th arrived, several soldiers of the company stopped on the road and made friends with Monsieur Laurent and his family. From then on, his home was open to all our men, offering the modest but gracious hospitality of the family. The father loved to talk about his World War I experiences as an engineer soldier, proudly showed his helmet, service record, and medal, and in turn he always admired the American Army, its efficiency, weapons,

and its men. When a soldier visitor arrived, he was ceremoniously placed at the head of the table. Cognac and Cider were brought out and courtesies were exchanged while the children stood awed and respectful at a distance. Upon request, the children sang French patriotic songs, showed their English textbooks, imitated German military pomposity, and forgetting themselves chattered away happily in French. They loved Yanks.

One of the officers who spoke French invited Monsieur Laurent to visit the bivouac area on a Sunday afternoon. This was a special occasion, so he put on his best Sunday clothes, polished up his ancient bicycle until it was radiant, and pedaled sedately down the road. He brought with him a small straw basket filled with fresh eggs, which he explained was a token of esteem for his liberators. He was shown the vehicles, wreckers, shop trucks and equipment, all of which brought forth dignified expressions of amazement. He then concluded that the American Army had no equal and spoke his opinion (as an old military man) that we would knock the stuffing out of the Germans.

The night before the company left, the Laurent family invited several soldiers for supper. They brought out their fine heirloom tableware, decorated the dining room, poured ancient wines they had hoarded for years and served mutton and rabbit with sauces only the French can concoct. When the convoy moved out at 4 in the morning Monsieur Laurent and his entire family lined up by the road to wave goodbye to the Americans.

Other than this short account, I did not have much information about the Laurent family or the visit. None of the GIs I interviewed remembered a Laurent family. During my first trip to Normandy, in June 2002, I drove around Les Pieux, wondering if the Laurent family might be nearby. But without more details, I did not try to locate them.

A year or so went by and I tried again to find something on Pecker but did not have any luck. Switchboard.com still did not list a single Leo Pecker, and a broader Internet search also yielded nothing. Meanwhile, Pecker's name did come up in my interviews. Overall, the GIs liked and respected Pecker, describing him as a "sophisticate," a "braniac," a "very smart guy," "a good officer, but an egghead," and "a real nice guy, but reminded me of an absent-minded professor." Another GI mentioned the time when Pecker took a bunch of men on leave to Paris. He was astonished that, while the other GIs spent their time at the bars and brothels of Paris, Pecker spent his few days' leave visiting museums and cultural sights.

Later, while reviewing my old interview notes, I found a scribbled note about Pecker. One veteran had heard that Pecker changed his name to Packer after the war. I tried Switchboard.com again, this time searching for *Leo Packer*. Ten matches came up. That was more than I wanted to call, not knowing if I even had the right name.

But one address caught my attention. It was in Cambridge, Massachusetts, home of Harvard and MIT. Considering how the GIs described Pecker, if there was one phone number to call, this would be it.

I called the number and a polite, elderly woman with an East Coast accent answered. I explained who I was and that I was looking for a Leo Packer who served in the 978th in WWII.

"Well, I'll let you ask him yourself," she said. I did, and sure enough, he was the right guy.

Packer was more than happy to talk to me. We spoke on the telephone several times and exchanged e-mails. As the GIs said, he was a very intelligent man. He had received his master's and Ph.D. degrees from Harvard and Cornell in engineering sciences and had worked in Washington for the Johnson administration as Assistant Postmaster General for Research and Engineering. He also worked in the State Department as director of Technology Policy and Space Affairs, where he met both LBJ and Henry Kissinger. He worked in Egypt for three years as director of the U.S.-Egypt Science and Research Cooperation and in Paris for sixteen years as science counselor at the American embassy (Packer spoke frequently and enthusiastically about his fluency in French). He also had a considerable career in R&D management in private industry. His wife of fifty-eight years, Dorothy, is an accomplished musician and has a Ph.D. in musicology from Boston University. She is currently writing a book on prehistoric art and music.

Packer mentioned that his parents were born in eastern Europe and came to the United States in the early part of the twentieth century. In an effort to assimilate better into American society, they Anglicized their name to Pecker—not a good idea, Packer joked. Later, their daughter, Leo's sister, applied to have the family name changed to Packer. They did, but it did not go through until Leo was already in the Army.

Packer's tone was more formal and official than that of the other men, his words more measured and carefully chosen. His vocabulary and elocution were those of an educated man. Although my conversations with him were very interesting, I occasionally felt frustrated by them. I was not getting any "gritty details" or interesting stories. He always emphasized the positive and seemed protective of the men in his unit—as if they were still "his men"—and he would speak no ill of them or their work in the 978th. He spoke proudly about the "resourcefulness and initiative" of the men in the unit, using the same words as William Musiker. My questions were always answered with a very official-sounding reply that sounded like it came from a statesman—or perhaps an officer. It seemed that Packer still considered himself an officer of the 978th. Not even my questions about the looting seemed to tarnish his memory of the men of the 978th:

> Well, Jeff, everybody did it. You could discourage it to some extent. But in every war soldiers look for souvenirs: a Nazi flag, weapons, Nazi propaganda and such. Those are legitimate, and, for the most part, the officers turn a blind eye. But there's looting and there's looting. When it came to German prisoners of war—lining them up, taking

Figure 102. Both Thomas Orton and Leo Packer had a copy of this photo and sent it to me. The caption on Orton's photo read: "Dave Jensen, Luther Crisp, Walter J. Wright. Camp McCoy. July 1944." Packer's caption read: "Competent welders were very essential later in Europe."

wristwatches, fountain pens, and such, some people were robbing dead bodies—well, that's a different story.

I told Packer the story I heard about the GIs breaking into a bank and how they used a welding torch to burn a hole in the vault door.

> Well, I never heard that. [laughs] I was an officer, so of course I wouldn't hear about such a thing.

Then there was a short pause, and he continued, his voice filling with pride:

> But you know, Jeff, that doesn't surprise me one bit. Our people were highly trained and had lots of good tools. Even more importantly, they were extremely resourceful and always showed a lot of initiative.

Packer sent me hundreds of photographs he had taken in the war. Among them were several of the Laurent family. His memory was still vivid, and he also told me the story of his visit to the farmhouse, which did not differ much from the version he told in the unit history.

Figure 103. The Laurent family, Les Pieux, October 1944. (Photo courtesy of Leo Packer)

A few months after finding Packer, I had another business trip to Paris and was able to arrange it around the festivities in Normandy celebrating the sixtieth anniversary of D-Day. I assumed hotel space would be tight and expensive, so I stayed with a local French family. Although Packer had lived in Paris for many years, he had never returned to Normandy. However, he said he did not mind if I tried to track down the Laurent family. Before I arrived, I told my host family about my quest to find them, along with the name of their ancestral farm, Belle Etoile, and the names of their two youngest children, Andrée and Michel.

Upon my arrival, my host family had already done some searching and had found several Laurents in the area, including a Michel Laurent who lived at Belle Etoile. They next day we drove to the farm, and I recognized the farmhouse from the photo Packer had sent. We had coffee and Calvados in the same room Packer had been in sixty years earlier. Michel still lives in the house and, although only four years old at the time, did remember a "Monsieur Pooker or Booker" who came to visit.

Once I found the Laurent family, however, there really was not much more to do. Having been only four years old at the time, Michel did not remember much. Nevertheless, I was reminded that, as often was the case in my search, it was the journey and not the destination that mattered. The thrill of the hunt, the enthusiasm of the locals who took up my search, the nice family who took me in, and the interesting people I met along the way are what made it a more personal and fulfilling experience than it otherwise might have been.

My visit to Normandy prompted Packer to revisit his wartime friends. A few months after my visit, he made his annual trip to Paris, where he maintains an apartment. Michel came down from Normandy with his wife and his sister, Andrée, who lives in Alsace in eastern France. They had lunch with Packer and his wife, Dorothy. "Unintended happy consequences" was the heading of an e-mail he sent me after their trip, in which Packer spoke effusively about their meeting; the bread, cheeses, and wines they enjoyed; the gifts they exchanged; and their reminiscences of the evening at the farmhouse in 1944.

During a trip to Boston, I visited Leo and Dorothy Packer at their home. They live in the heart of Cambridge on the top floor of a 150-year-old

Figure 104. Leo and Dorothy Packer at their home in Cambridge, MA, 2004.

Victorian house that has been converted into apartments. Leo, as he insisted I call him, gave me a tour. I felt like I was in a museum, and there was an air of activity about their home. Thousands of books about a variety of subjects were stacked on numerous bookshelves and in corners of rooms. Down the length of a long window were various exotic plants. Art from around the world adorned the walls, and tucked away here and there were various sculptures and other odds and ends from the Packers' travels, including an odd-looking medieval French musical instrument with both strings and piano keys. A desk with a computer, academic articles, and scattered papers stood in the corner of another room. This was where Dorothy Packer does her work on Mesopotamian art and music. Now in their eighties, the Packers are still busy with living and learning.

Over coffee in his living room, Leo spoke of his previous involvement in scientific and engineering professional organizations, but said he now has little interest and believes that "retirement is a time to dip into new exposures." He currently teaches classes at Harvard, his most recent being the cultural history of Americans in Paris, the writings of political journalist Thomas Friedman, and the energy crisis and the hydrogen economy.

Leo and I then walked down to the main drag in Cambridge for lunch. We stopped at one of Leo's favorite haunts, a crowded restaurant/bar full of students, and got on the waiting list for a table. It was a bit too loud and rambunctious for me, and I suggested we find a place where we could talk. We settled on a trendy Indian place near Harvard Square. It was filled with students and, at thirty-three, I felt a bit old. But Leo seemed very much at home.

Packer was one of the most eloquent and intelligent men I interviewed, and certainly the most educated. In spite of this, I never got a feel for what his experience in the war meant to him. Perhaps it was the officer in him presenting a formal, positive picture of his unit. Or perhaps it was that Packer's life was still very much in the present. Still, I found it fascinating and inspiring to be with a man whose experiences spanned decades, wars, and continents, a man who could feel at home in a 1944 French farmhouse during wartime or, as an elderly man sixty years later, at a student bar in Cambridge talking about his latest undertakings.

"THE NICEST TIME I HAD IN MY LIFE"

AMONG THE PHOTOGRAPHS LEO PACKER sent me was one of a young woman in Spekholzerheide, along with a card that read name "Anny van Zandvoort." Packer met the van Zandvoort family when the 978th was in Spek, and they had several friendly encounters. During my second visit to Spek, Leon and I tried to find Anny. Leon made several phone calls to various van Zandvoorts in the phone book and quickly tracked down Anny's brother, Emile van Zandvoort. When Emile heard about the photo and my contact with Leo Packer, he insisted that we come over that evening.

We arrived at Emile's house and were greeted by a well-dressed, dignified, fit-looking man who had just returned from a wedding with his family. Emile spoke English fluently. He remembered Leo Pecker and the 978th's time in Spekholzerheide very well. I had coffee and schnapps with Emile, his wife, his son, and his son's fiancée in the family's three-hundred-year-old farmhouse. Emile spoke enthusiastically about the days and months just after Spek's liberation:

> For one year before the liberation, we couldn't go to school, couldn't study. Everything was bombed. Then the Americans came. I was twelve years old.
>
> Leo's unit was in Spekholzerheide, and Leo had an office set up there in a building. I managed to get into the office. I couldn't speak English. I don't know how I communicated with them. But I got a job helping them. Leo was the officer and had to censor the letters the men wrote home. So my job was to open all the envelopes, take out the

Figure 105. Emile van Zandvoort, far left, top, with siblings shortly after liberation. (Photo courtesy of Emile van Zandvoort)

letters, and set them out for Leo to read. Then Leo would read them, stamp them "censored," and then sign them. Afterwards, I put them back in and sealed them up to be sent.

The 978th was in Spekholzerheide for almost three weeks, waiting for a break in the German lines to occur. Emile remembered it differently:

> Leo was there about six months. Every day I would go to the office. And I helped him the entire time, opening the envelopes, taking out the letters, and then sealing them again. It was an important job. [laughs]
>
> The families were all so eager and proud to meet the Americans. We all wanted them to come to our houses. I was twelve. I had a younger brother, Theo, who was six. He was a charming guy. He would go to them and say, "Kom. Kom you mir home. Mijn papa. Schnapps." And they came to our house. And they'd bring chocolates. Oh, the chocolates. Wonderful.
>
> Theo had a friend from school who complained, "The Americans never come to my house." The friend had one sister, who was eight years old. So my brother goes to the Americans and says, "Kom. Kom. Mijn papa. Schnapps." And, "I have zusters." The Americans asked: "How old are they?" And my brother says: "One is eight jaars old, and, um, and the others, they are eighteen and twentig jaars." Then he takes the Americans to his friend's house, not our house, and says, "Oh, only the eight year old is home." [laughs] But they stayed anyway. And they gave him chocolates.

Figure 106. Emile and Marlies van Zandvoort, June 2004.

After Pecker left, then came the black soldiers. Wow! I'd never seen such a person in my life. Down the street from us a German V-2 landed in a house. A little girl was hit. A black doctor came and tried to help. But the girl was already dead when he arrived. A real gentleman he was. A few days later I met them, and when I went home that evening I told my father, "Papa, I met a black guy today." And he says, "Oh, lucky you, I wish I could meet such a guy." That was amazing for us. We'd never met such a person in our life! [laughs]

Emile's wife, Marlies, also remembered that time:

I was only five or six. And I was on the Americans' shoulders. They give me chocolates. And every day we see them and we say, "The Americans are coming." We loved the Americans.

Emile was almost giddy with excitement as he talked about this time in his life. First he offered us coffee and cakes, then came schnapps, then port wine, and then more schnapps. Emile had a very sincere interest in hearing about Leo Packer—where he lived, what his house looked like, the type of life he had, his wife and children. I could see Leo had made a strong impact on him. Emile spoke about their last contact:

> A few months later [after Leo left Spekholzerheide], he is in Japan. Leo sends me pictures of himself in Japan and of these Japanese children. [Emile's wife, Marlies, leaves the room and returns a few minutes later with the photos.] And that was the last I heard from him. I tried to send a letter to the address he gave in Brooklyn, New York, but it was returned. Many years later, maybe twenty-five years after the war, when I worked in Den Haag, I was at the American embassy and tried to find him. And they said, "No. There is no Leo Packer. There's a Leo Packer who is Postmaster General in Washington, D.C. But no Leo Packer." So I gave up. I never thought it could be the right guy.
>
> That time in the war, I have all good memories. It was the nicest time I had in my life.[1]

---

1. When I told Leo Packer about my visit, he said that he only vaguely remembered Emile. It was interesting to see the impact that he had on Emile without realizing it.

"MAGNIFICENCE MEN!!"

EMILE WAS NOT THE ONLY person whose memories of men from the 978th were still strong. Several months after I created my Web page about my search, I received an e-mail from John Borghouts, a seventy-two-year-old Dutch man from Spekholzerheide. He found my page while searching for information about Spekholzerheide and WWII. We corresponded by e-mail.

Borghouts was thirteen years old when the Americans came to Spek. In his e-mails he described in great detail the events in Spekholzerheide and his experiences during the war. He included photos of the coal mine, of himself shortly after the liberation, and of his family on their bicycles in front of Margratan Cemetery after the war, where they had adopted the grave of an American GI. His e-mails sometimes rambled on, but were filled with enthusiasm and a sense of urgency.

Most important to Borghouts was his meeting with two American GIs during the war. Shortly after Spek was liberated, two GIs came to visit the Borghouts family—John, his mother and father, and John's eleven-year-old sister. The GIs visited again several times. Borghouts wrote:

> They make both a very strong impression on our family and me. We were now a free land. We thank them on this way for coming to Europe. My age was thirteen years by the liberation from the Germans occupation and I can remember both US soldiers. They where very charming and civility. Magnificence men!! I remember them.

Before they left for Germany, the two GIs wrote in John's sister's diary:

Spekholzerheide   November 24, 1944
Best Wishes & Many Happy Returns of the Day from Two
Americans who will always be your very good friends in Peace or War.
Brooke Stanford   Joseph Andrews
East Long Lake Road   9323 Evans Ave
Bloomfield Hills, Michigan, USA   Chicago, Illinois USA

After the war, the Borghouts family corresponded with Joseph Andrews for several years and exchanged photographs. Around 1950, Andrews moved and they lost contact. Borghouts e-mailed me copies of the photos—of Andrews, his wife, and their infant son, Bobby, taken in front of their new house in 1947.

Borghouts asked me for help finding these two men, particularly Andrews. The 978th's roster listed both of them, a coincidence considering the number of GIs who passed through Spek. I checked the Social Security Death Index and found listings for both men that matched their age range and hometowns. It appeared likely that both these men were dead. I e-mailed Borghouts with the sad news.

But Borghouts was persistent. He asked if I could track down the family members:

Dear mister Jeffrey…But how is it with the others members of both families? Perhaps the little boy on the picture I sent. What have you reached in search of those families? Is it possible to make a search with the newspapers? Or perhaps in a radioprogramm?

Considering Borghouts' perseverance, I began to wonder if there was more to the story, that perhaps Andrews or Stanford had fathered a child in Spek. I asked Borghouts outright if this was the case. He said that it was not and added that it was so important to him that "you could compare it to" looking for your father.

Considering the sincerity and earnestness of Borghouts's letter, I felt obliged to at least try. The son's name was Bobby. Searching for *Robert*, *Bob*, or *Bobby Andrews* in Chicago yielded quite a few phone numbers. I then narrowed the choices down by searching by age on another site and came up with a few possibilities. I called them. None of them was the right guy.

A year later I made another trip to Spekholzerheide. Borghouts and I met at Leon's sister's house, and he told me his story:

The visit from the Americans was very important to my father. He was a technical man, an engineer. And we worked in the coal mine. After the war, the Germans kidnapped everything with them to Germany, all the big machines needed to run the mine. So after the war, there was no equipment to explore the mine. My father, he thought the Americans will bring material to restart the mine. Then the Americans come with all their new technical apparatus. And the men from the coal mine were very interesting in those things. But the new technical apparatus were first used for repair of the weapons of war. Not to repair the coal mines! That was my father's mistake. The Americans only used the mine for bathing. The Americans were there to fight the war, not to run the mine. [laughs]

I was thirteen. I wasn't in school. There was no school at that time. The school stopped during the war. Around July, August 1944, the planes were shooting. I was at school one day, the next day no school. We slept on the bottom floor, too dangerous to sleep on the top floor. Then came the American planes shooting German troops. We spent our days looking out to the street waiting for the Germans to leave. And they always looking in the window, with their machine guns. For five years, every day, they drill us [pokes his finger into my arm and turns it like a drill]. Five years. We were afraid during the entire war.

There was nothing to do. No school. Not until September '45 when the first school reopened close-by in Heerlen. We had to walk through the ammunition dump to get there. Then Sunday, 17th September at 11 a.m. the Americans came, in their khaki uniforms, rubber boots—not spiked boots like the Germans!—cigarettes and chewing gum. Chewing gum! Wow! That was magnificence. The next day, we were on the street, heard machine gun. Tat-tat-tat. Everybody run back into house. And I see a German screaming [becomes very animated, makes a frightened and foolish look on his face] "Ahhh, Ahhhh. The Americans. The Americans are coming." [laughs] The Americans come walking down the street, talking on their big radios. They stopped. And we shake hands. The first words we learned in English, the only words we knew, were "Goodbye." We got it wrong.

My mother later told me we should say, "Hello boys, how are you?" But it was all we knew. So when the Americans arrived we kept saying, "Goodbye, Goodbye!" [laughs] And the boys come in a big line and passed the street and we shake hands with every soldier.

My father hangs out Dutch flag. But at seven in the evening the Dutch government comes out and says, "All flags down!" And the Americans go back. They were just recon troops. Then we were afraid. Germans coming back, that the S.S. division were going to take Spekholzerheide back. The Americans saw the S.S. troops and went back. They were getting more munitions, more troops, more benzine [gasoline]. Then there was some fighting on the railroads. But the next day, Monday, the Germans left. And they didn't come back.

Andrews came in October '44. I was at home. And my father said, "On this evening there will be coming two American soldiers." My mother, she was in a panic, said, "Oh, no. What had to do and what must we serve both soldiers." We hadn't anything to offer. But my mother find a solution. On 10 May 1940, at the beginning of the occupation, the Germans banned several things, including tea and coffee. During the whole wartime, on Sunday, we got only one cup of tea, from India, which my mother had hidden. And when the U.S. troops liberated my town, my mother opened immediately the last package of tea. The next time the Americans came back they brought tea. I think they stole it in Germany. [laughs] A great surprise. It was in a great nice box. My sister has the box now.

One visit my father made pancakes. He was baking with a special type of oil for pancakes. And the Americans asked, what type of pancakes. And my father say, "with oil." And they think, oh, oil for motorcar. And they are giving us funny looks, oil for motorcar? And we tell them, "No, not for motorcar. For pancakes." [laughs]

They came ten to twelve times. Every day my father meet them at the coal mine and he makes the next appointment. And then they ring the bell and my sister and I run to the door and open the front door and there were our friends again. We learned many things from them. I was thirteen, my sister eleven. I couldn't speak English. We talked with our hands. Had an English wordbook. Looked up the words in the book. Lovely time. They come with their guns. [laughs] Not every day they came. When there was a day they didn't come we missed them. It was a lost evening for us.

Figure 107. Joseph Andrews and his son, Bobby; approx. 1947.
(Photo courtesy of John Borghouts)

It's very important to me to find these men. They made such a strong impression on the people of Spekholzerheide. We are always thinking about this, about this time. Or, if they are dead, to find Andrews' children to return the photos to them. My wife and I are alone, no children. I am seventy-three years old and my sister seventy-one. There is coming a time when we leave the world and the pictures go on. And that is a pity. Then God send me Jeffrey. And I think, this is my chance—the chance is small, but maybe we find them—to send the pictures back. It is very important to me. I can't explain it.

———

I never found Andrews or his son. I also searched the Social Security Death Index, but found nothing, probably owing to the common name. Perhaps with the publication of this book someone will come forward and Borghouts can finally bring the photos home. But for Borghouts, I don't think it was about returning the photos. It was something more. It was something

Figure 108. John Borghouts, with photos of Joseph Andrews and family, at Leon's sister's house in Spekholzerheide, June 2004.

about reconnecting with an important part of his life. More than sixty years have passed since the men of the 978th passed through Spekholzerheide. For most of them it left fond memories during a difficult time. For the people of Spek, the impact was much greater.

PERSPECTIVES

WORDS OF
ENCOURAGEMENT

I DECIDED TO WRITE THIS book in the fall of 2000. I started interviewing veterans more in-depth and also put more effort into finding more men of the 978th. I had just moved to Söderfors, Sweden, a tiny village far from any big city. Swedish autumns are dark, rainy, dreary, and depressing. There was not much to do in my free time, and I threw myself into this book, writing relentlessly in the evenings and on weekends. After a few months I was worn out and needed some encouragement. I knew that talking to Ski would give me a boost, and I gave him a call. As always, he was lively and encouraging.

Hello, Mr. Powasnik, it's Jeff Badger. How are you?

Jeff, how are you doing? Where you calling from this time, the moon?

The moon, Mr. Powasnik?

Yeah, every time I talk to you you're livin' somewhere different. I figured this time you might be calling from the moon.

Oh, I'm living in Sweden at the moment.

Sweden! Alright, pal. What do you say you send over some of those Swedish girls. You just send them over to my house in Bayonne, you know the address. Maybe four or five, I'm not asking for a lot. OK? So you just send 'em over. Thank you very much.

Sounds reasonable, Mr. Powasnik. Maybe you can give them some consultation from your experience at Maidenform.

[laughs] Not a bad idea. I learned a thing or two there. Oh, that reminds me. I better get down to the pharmacy to refill my prescription for Viagra. Extra strength this time.

You don't need any of that, Mr. Powasnik. You're a young man.

Of course I don't. It's not for me. It's for those Swedish girls you're sending over. So they can keep up with me. So you're writing a book? That's great. You're going to be famous.

Well, I don't know about that, Mr. Powasnik. But if so, we're both going to be famous. You know which photo I'm going to use on the cover? You know the one, Mr. Powasnik.

Of course. The one with me and the Swedish girls. That book's gonna sell millions!

I think it would. But I was thinking of the one with you and my grandfather.

Of course, I know the one, Jeff. Me and Leo in Marseilles. I suppose that one would be fine also. Either way, you'll be famous. I'll be looking for you on the TV.

Well, if so, who would you rather be on? Leno or Letterman?

Ah, both those guys are ok. It doesn't matter. As long as it's not that Geraldo guy. I can't stand him.

Yeah, I know what you mean. I only get Letterman here.

Yeah, I watch him occasionally. He's pretty good. But not Geraldo. No way I'm going on that guy's show.
But hey, you know who I really like? Old Rush.

Rush Limbaugh?

Oh yeah. You like Rush?

He's OK.

Rush is my hero. I listen to him every day. If you wanna know what's going on, tune into ol' Rush. My buddy. But Jeff, I gotta go. My grandkids are here, and I gotta go wrestle with 'em. Goodbye and have a great weekend. But, Jeff, Geraldo? Why'd you even mention that guy?

Figure 109. John "Ski" Powasnik and I at his home in Bayonne, New Jersey.

THERON SNELL

THROUGHOUT MY SEARCH, IN ADDITION to my interviews I did a lot of reading, first out of interest and later, as I got further into my book, to gain maturity in my thinking. I also rented numerous movies, mostly American but quite a few German, including ones from the 1950s and 1960s. Leon was a good source for recommendations.

Through all this I believe that my perspective of the war and the people who took part it in gradually evolved. I also became far more selective in my tastes in books and movies. Like Leon, my tastes shifted away from grand historical documentaries of battle plans and politics toward the small stories and details of the individual men and women. Those stories were what made up almost 100 percent of my interviews. In fact, I grew weary of historians' accounts of grand battles. I much preferred Bill Mauldin's recounting the monotony of the war, the mud and the blisters and how the war affected him; or Studs Terkel letting his interviewees speak for themselves. He realized right away that they had more to say than he did, and he let them do the talking.

There was no doubt much bravery by American GIs during the war, but for every act of bravery there were a thousand acts of day-to-day work and mundane tasks. During my interviews with men of the 978th, I never heard a single story of bravery or life-saving heroics (save for my grandfather's with George Patrias at the cathouse and coconut-shell bar). I heard about the day-to-day work they did. Granted, they were not a fighting unit, but even my interview with Merlin Clark, who saw serious action, yielded lots of interesting anecdotes of life away from the battle.

Yet the bravery is what makes up a large portion of the literature and movies. And news reports of WWII anniversaries like D-Day focus overwhelmingly on the victory for the Allies. Leo Packer wrote me in an e-mail regarding the sixtieth anniversary of D-Day: "I thought it was overdone as usual with too much hoopla and media coverage and political grandstanding. War memories are a private, personal matter and should be handled with modesty and dignity. That is one reason why I have never been interested in participating in the several veterans organizations."

I think this gradually maturing of perspective is typical. I was first exposed to it by Theron Snell. Theron's father, Richard "Gus" Snell, served in the 978th, and Theron and I corresponded a great deal over the years and shared our general experiences of interviewing GIs. I also visited Theron several times in Racine. Theron's views were a bit more acute than mine, perhaps because he was a product of the Vietnam generation, or perhaps just because he was a different individual.

Theron is an academic advisor and teaches as an adjunct instructor in the university's international studies program. Both responsibilities, according to Theron, "involve looking at culture, primarily the U.S. culture, in an international setting." I respect Theron's grounding in history and culture in general and his extensive knowledge of WWII. In his home he has a library of hundreds of books on WWII.

When we first met, I mentioned to Theron some of the books I had read on WWII, the most recent being Stephen Ambrose's *Citizen Soldiers*. He recommended some others, and over the years I read several of them. Through our discussions I became familiar with Theron's perspective on the popular histories of WWII and the image that WWII has assumed in the collective American memory. This was something he seemed to feel very strongly about and, given his extensive background in history and his having interviewed many of the same men of the 978th, I was interested in what he had to say. During our last meeting Theron spoke about his views:

> I'm not a big fan of Ambrose. He plagiarized big time. But more
> than that. It's hard to articulate, but I'd say it's because he's a rah-rah
> boy, flag waving, one dimensional, America rose up to fight fascism.
> He emphasizes certain traits, such as camaraderie, etc., and leaves out

about 80 percent of the rest. His books read like cardboard novels. He is superficial, too glossy.

There are so many better books. Ernie Pyle's *Brave Men*, Bill Mauldin's *Up Front*. They stand in opposition to the rah-rah and heroic that you'll get from Ambrose and lots of other authors. Other good ones are Robert Rush's *Hell in Hurtgren Forest;* Roger Shinn's *Wars and Rumors of War;* Charles MacDonald's *Company Commander;* Critchell's *Four Stars of Hell*, about the 101st Airborne; both volumes of Samuel Stoeffer's *The American Soldier;* Studs Terkel's *The Good War*. Or the division histories, like on the 30th, *Workhorse of the Western Front.*

Ambrose pushes a partial view. That in itself is fine, *if* people read more than just that. I tell my students that if they read Ambrose, they also need to read Paul Fussell's *Wartime.*

Fussell's book is the perfect antidote to Ambrose, the perfect corrective. In *Wartime*, Fussell is really reacting to the glamorization of WWII that's taken hold in the past ten years. He's saying, in my opinion, do not glamorize it to the point of forgetting that it was horrific, brutal. We may have been in the right, but we did brutal, awful things. Then we say that, when we did these things, it was an anomaly. It wasn't. And we need to look that in the face.

I read Fussell's book. In the preface he writes, "For the past fifty years the Allied war has been sanitized and romanticized almost beyond recognition by the sentimental, the loony patriotic, the ignorant, and the bloodthirsty. I have tried to balance the scales."

I had mixed feelings about Fussell's book. Although I understood and agreed with his premise, I found him somewhat supercilious and chronically negative on all sides. I mentioned this to Theron:

> He's negative, but his negativity comes from his reacting so vehemently against the glorification of the war, and how the awful part of the war has sort of melted away in the past ten to fifteen years from the histories and popular consciousness. He's reacting against the glorification of the evil we committed in the name of good. We tend to forget that.
>
> I can't say it's the best book in the world. But he was angry. He wrote it to be a cage-rattler. He wrote it to piss people off. ... If I'm not mistaken, I think he says this in his book; he says, "I'm reacting against

these things." Both have something to tell you, that's the thing. But in all the interviews I've had with combat vets, I tend to find more honesty in Fussell than in Ambrose.

In reading those books [other books, like Ambrose's], do you hear about friendly fire? Do you hear about the guys getting burned alive? Do you hear about the ten thousand Americans AWOL in Paris in 1944? It's not stuff they kept secret, you know. It was in the papers, in *Stars & Stripes*.

Every culture takes something from the war. I've always wanted to do a paper on combat art and advertising art. In combat art, Robert Capa and George Silk [we were looking at the *LIFE* magazine pictorial of the Roer River crossing, which had been taken by Silk], there's a huge list of dynamic photographers, you see the dirt and the fear and the self-doubt. That's published in *LIFE* and *Fortune* and *Colliers*. Now compare that with artwork in advertising, in the same issue of *LIFE* magazine. There's a woman sitting there, knowing that she can't buy Oneida silverware until her husband gets back from the war. Then, on the next page [in Silk's pictorial] there's the blood and guts.

And what's the collective memory of the United States? It's not the blood and guts. It's the Oneida ad, not the George Silk photographs. Maybe it's a natural progression in any culture, but in my opinion—*opinion*, what else could it be?—we as a nation, we've internalized the advertising; we have not internalized the combat photography.

I said to Theron that I think most people in the U.S. do not have illusions that war is heroic and that some more recent movies, such as *Saving Private Ryan*, have performed an important service in trying to show us how ugly combat really is.

Well, maybe. But a common complaint from vets [from his readings and interviews] about combat photography is that they do not show the reality. People were burned alive. They had their legs blown off. And in *LIFE*, what do they show? A dead American body. Sure he was dead, and that was a big deal at the time. But he was not face up. They'd show Germans' faces but not Americans. But even that is not that graphic. The vets know that.

I asked Theron if that was so bad, as people will inevitably focus on the positive.

Figure 110. Theron Snell at his home in Racine, Wisconsin.

Well, as a cultural historian, it concerns me that the vision of the war has come to be Stephen Ambrose and not Paul Fussell or Studs Terkel. You get a sense of heroism and all that too when you read Terkel, and yes there was that, but you also get a perspective of the fear and anger and self-doubt.

I asked if the books by the authors he named were more realistic.

It's not an issue of being realistic. It's what the culture makes of it, the collective memory we've created; and even a lot of veterans have accepted it. Read Studs Terkel. There was a lot of anger. Now, in WWII, when you look at the options, there were not any. We [the United States] said, we have to do this. We have no choice. It has to be done. It makes us dirty. But we have to fight evil with evil. It has to be done. But Ambrose says it's a heroic thing, war, that it's heroic.

It was noble not because they rose up as one to fight the enemy— there was a lot of fear and self-doubt and unhappiness. It's noble because they did what they did *in spite of* the fear and the doubt and the unhappiness. We had our doubts in Korea and Vietnam—and also in WWII up to December 7, 1941. But the collective memory does not reflect that.

The covers of many WWII books show brave, confident men looking forward, ready to engage the enemy. The cover of Fussell's book shows a soldier lying on the ground with his rifle, curled up in the fetal position, covering his face, seemingly afraid and trying to make his body as small as possible, perhaps to protect himself from a mortar or artillery attack. I think Fussell's choice for the cover photograph was to show the emasculated, undignified position of the soldier.

The younger generations owe a huge debt of gratitude to those who fought in World War II, and from my experience younger people overwhelmingly have a huge amount of respect for them and what they accomplished. They are our heroes, and rightly so. And it's inevitable that we romanticize them to some degree—as I had done, and still do, with my grandfather. But I think Fussell and Theron's main point is that, if we glorify and honor what they accomplished, we have to be careful not to glorify and honor war itself. And we need to balance the heroism and bravery and camaraderie with the blood and dirt and death and pain that are inevitable parts of the process.

FRANCIS MULDERRIG

FRANCIS MULDERRIG OF NEW JERSEY was probably the most optimistic, positive, and enthusiastic man with whom I spoke. He was originally in the 419th Combat Engineers, a unit that landed at Normandy three days after D-Day. He was transferred to the 978th a few months later. He was very candid in his communications with me, and he readily revealed personal details about his time in the service and his life in general. A devout Catholic, he seemed grateful for just about every experience in his life, both good and bad. Early in our first conversation, he told me that he used to be an alcoholic, a subject he brought up often and spoke of in detail:

> I was in the combat engineers, but never saw combat. Nothing hairy. We built roads, Bailey bridges, and stuff. Never saw any real action. I was a welder. Worked as a burner in the shipyards before going into the service.
>
> I wasn't a bad soldier. But I was a G.F.U., you know. I won't say the middle word, but a general blank up. I was a rebel; I just couldn't take authority. Couldn't take orders from some of these ninety-day wonders. I dug and filled in more six-by-sixes than I can remember. [laughs] You know, six feet wide, six feet long, by six feet deep. I didn't mind, just dug them and filled them in as I was told, smiled and laughed and called the noncoms names who were guarding me. It's the Irish personality.
>
> The one thing the Army taught me was how to drink. I didn't drink before I entered the service. That's were I learned. My problem is that if somebody calls me a chicken, I'll jump off the Brooklyn Bridge. And in the Army there wasn't a lot else to do, and there was a lot of

peer pressure. The first time I drank I got rip-roarin' drunk and got thrown in the stockade. [laughs] And that started it all.

If there was booze, I'd find it. I was an alcoholic. Not any longer though. Well, you know, once an alcoholic always an alcoholic. Before I got transferred into the 978th, I went to infantry training in France, outside Reims, up on the plateau. That's champagne country. We found the pure alcohol they make from white beets. We'd do anything to get a drink. In Münster, in Germany, we took over a brewery. We were shooting holes in the kegs and filling up our helmets. We'd shoot them up high, and if nothing came out we'd keep shooting lower and lower. That way it wouldn't get wasted. Alcoholics are con artists, take the gold out of your teeth.

One time four of us were sent on an assignment. We weren't in convoy, just sent out on this assignment in a six-by-six [truck] to fill up a whole bunch of gas containers and bring them back. This was in Germany. Well, we learned right away that the houses that didn't have snow on their roofs, that they were making booze. You know, the heat from the fermentation would rise and melt the snow. So, after we filled up the cans with gas and were heading back, we noticed this farmhouse with no snow on the roof. So we went there and bartered with 'em. You know, when in Rome, learn Roman. I could talk to anybody over there, learned enough of the languages to always get a drink.

We took two of the five-gallon gas cans, emptied them out at the farmhouse into this big container they had, and then filled them up with the wine. The gas was payment for the wine.

Then, on the way home my buddy and I were riding on the back of the truck, sitting on the gas cans drinking the wine. And he was sitting on top of these gas cans smoking, smoking a cigarette while we were surrounded by hundreds of these cans full of gasoline. [laughs] He was from West Virginia. Those guys from West Virginia and Kentucky and Tennessee were absolutely crazy.

Well, we were drunk on that wine, and I guess we must have gotten into a scuffle, and he knocked me off of the truck. Didn't bother to tell the driver.

I asked him if the other GI had noticed that he had fallen off the truck, and if so why he didn't tell the driver.

What do you expect? The guy's from West Virginia. [laughs]

Those guys are nuts. I had no hard feeling against him though. I'm just not that type. I'm the easiest guy in the world to get along with.

I woke up the next morning in a ditch, with no clothes on. I guess I decided I was going to bed in the ditch and hung my clothes up on a tree. [laughs] You do crazy things when you're drunk. So that morning I got dressed and managed to get back to the top of the road and started walking back. Went the right way too. Figured if we were driving on the right and I ended up in a ditch on the right, then I'd just go to the top of the road and turn right. I was cut and all bruised up, had a big strawberry on my knee with leaves stuck to it, and a big patch on my uniform. But I found my way back to the Army base. They didn't want to have anything to do with me, I must have looked that bad. And I found my unit again. I drank myself through the war.

I asked if he did that to cope with the pressures.

No. Not at all. Every individual is different. I've had a lot of hard knocks in life, so it takes a lot to make me cry. I didn't see any combat, and the war wasn't that hard on me as it was for some guys. The alcoholism, it's hereditary. My family, they were Irish and were all alcoholic. My father's nine brothers. It's ingrained. It's an awful thing. Truly awful. Been clean since 1970. She [his wife] made me stop drinking. One day she packed up my bags and put them at the bottom of the stairs. And she said, "You either pick up those bags and leave or pick up the phone and call A.A." I called A.A. That was 1970.

Mulderrig was a joy to speak with. At eighty-two years old he exuded a positive energy that was contagious. He seemed to be one of the more reflective and thoughtful men I spoke with. He took the time to listen intently to my questions and explore his answers in detail. He also seemed to be very charitable, something I gathered from what he said about his volunteer work. "Better to console than be consoled" was a phrase he used often in our conversations. He spoke frequently and candidly about his alcoholism and insisted that I write about it. He also spoke about his wife:

That woman was the light of my life. She got Alzheimer's, had it for fifteen years. I took care of her. I'm a Catholic. Not a great Catholic, but a good one. Better to console than be consoled, you know, St. Francis. The last eleven days I slept on three chairs with my hand on her shoulder. I was there when she went, on the side of the bed, telling her I loved her, 'cause they say the hearing's the last thing to go. And she went. But I had trouble with her eyes. They kept popping open. I brushed them closed but they bounced back up. [laughs] I closed them again and they bounced back up again. I guess she just wanted to get one last look at me.

These things aren't a coincidence. All these things that happen in your life, they're not coincidences. The man upstairs is keeping track of you.

Mulderrig's final words stuck with me for a while. It was something that I had thought about occasionally in my search—every time I found a new GI or a person in Holland and every time I was able to arrange a visit with one of my grandfather's war buddies—that there was more than just effort and good luck on my side.

When I began my search, all I had was a handful of photographs and the name of a unit. I did not have a single name of a person or hometown. Even my grandfather's photos had only vague captions. Yet somehow I managed to find many men who had served in my grandfather's unit and every single one of his buddies. Considering the ages of these men, I was lucky not only that they were still alive but also that they were still lucid and willing to talk to me. On top of that, I was fortunate that all of his buddies had sufficiently uncommon names that they could be found in the White Pages.

When I look back, I am awed by the series of fortunate coincidences that enabled me to find Ski. His name was not listed in the phone book, and he did not even have a *ski*-suffixed surname. But right when I had given up, along came Howard Cushing, the man who gave me Ski's address. Then, by chance, I had a layover in Newark, New Jersey, and was able to visit Ski at his home.

I did not find all the veterans at once—that would have been more than I could have handled. Rather, they seemed to come one at a time, with each new one coming just as I was beginning to get discouraged or think there was nothing else to do. I managed to find Marvin Mangham and Max Voron—and even Jack Cooper, in spite of an extremely common name. For each veteran, I had just enough time to get his story down, and then the next one came along. I found Thomas Orton at a perfect time, right when he was healthy enough to be able to speak to me and also when I had the time to spend with him. I made a business trip to Detroit and was able at last to meet the infamous George Patrias, just as his health was failing him. And all the people in Les Pieux, Spekholzerheide, and Mariadorf. And Leon—who better to help me with my search in Spek? Was it just coincidence that one of the only places I e-mailed in Limburg was the museum where Leon worked?

The window of opportunity—the time between the Internet becoming available and the veterans passing away in old age—was a small one. But it presented itself at a time in my life when I had the time to take advantage of it.

In the fall of 1999, my mom and I took a trip to Ireland and England. We saw an advertisement in the hotel for a psychic and, on a whim, paid her a visit. Neither of us place much stock in these things, but we thought it would be a bit of fun. The psychic brought up things about my mother's past and my childhood that were quite incredible, details that seemed too accurate to be attributed to mere intuitive skills or guesswork. Later, not knowing anything about my search or even that my grandfather was no longer alive, the last thing she told my mom was "not to worry about your son. Your father—I know he's been dead for a long time—he has a very strong tie with your son; he's the youngest one, I know. And your father is looking out for him."

Francis Mulderrig told me that the man upstairs is keeping track of me. Perhaps there is another man upstairs keeping track of me too.

"BUT I'M GRATEFUL I'M ALIVE"

EARLY IN MY SEARCH I received an e-mail from Coleen Seim, the daughter of a deceased veteran of the 978th, Warren Neaderhiser. She wrote:

> My father taught us more about the war than any history book could possibly do. I am sorry you did not have the privilege of knowing your grandfather. The men who served in the war had a different outlook on life and a great appreciation for life's little pleasures.

William Musiker's daughter told me something similar:

> Last year, when I was reminiscing about my childhood with my mother, I mentioned how boring growing up was. There was no "drama" in our family. Only then did my mother share with me that my father spent three years in the army and witnessed unbelievable horrors during that time. When he came home from work, he just wanted to have peace and quiet and a nice meal.

A question people sometimes ask after hearing about my search is, "What did you learn about your grandfather?" As my search and interviews progressed, my focus shifted away from learning about my grandfather toward learning about the history of the 978th and the veterans' experiences. Only when I got close to finishing the book did my focus shift back to my grandfather, trying to learn more about him and the way the war shaped his life. After all, it was one of the things that got me started on my quest. And in the end it proved to be my most difficult task.

My mother adored her father and described him as compassionate, sensitive, caring, and a good listener. His friends from the war, however, described him differently: "a hellraiser," "bullish," "a tough, no-nonsense guy," "a daredevil," "afraid of nothin'," "willing to do anything on a dare," "a good soldier," and "a good buddy." They were describing a pretty normal guy, and I was not surprised that I did not get the same feel for him from his war buddies that I got from my mom.

Of course, the Leo Kavanaugh as a twenty-five-year-old soldier in a war zone would be a very different man than the Leo Kavanaugh as a forty-year-old father at home. The kind-hearted personality my mother knew would not have served my grandfather well at war. As Thomas Orton told me:

> During the war you put on a certain front in order to protect yourself. Everybody handled things differently. I tried to stay busy. When you're active and have something to do, you don't get as stressed as the guys who are just waiting. There were people who were afraid to take a step. There was this one hillbilly kid from Montana. He could play any stringed instrument he put his hands on, but he couldn't read or write. And people picked on him because of that. He was scared to death. Some guys were cut-ups. Some seemed happy-go-lucky. Others acted tough, but you knew they weren't as tough as they acted. You develop a certain mindset to help you cope and stick with it. It's a coping mechanism.
>
> It was a situation that, well, you just don't think about it, or you'd cry every day if you did. Some guys handled it better than others. George [Patrias], I never saw him stressed out. I think George was able to handle it. Ski was one tough little bugger. He got a lot of ribbin' because of his civilian employment [in the bra factory], but he could handle himself. Leo, your grandfather, he was genuinely rock-solid. He was tough, but I can imagine that softer side you mentioned, even if I never saw it openly. He was in the construction business. And in that line of work you can't show weakness.

The difference between the Leo Kavanaugh my mother knew and the Leo Kavanaugh his war buddies knew is certainly due to the different environments of war and home. But I also think there is something else. I think that the war helped make him into the man my mom remembers, giving him a softer, more appreciative perspective on life. Several years after I began my search, my grandfather's sister died. Among the belongings we received after her death was a letter that my grandfather wrote to her when he was in Manila. By this time the war was over and he was waiting to be sent home. He wrote:

> We got paid Monday, after almost three months. The drunks were raising cane for a couple of days but are rather quiet now. The night before last, I had to lick a couple of them to make them quiet...
>
> I have been all over Luzon [an island in the Philippines] since I've been here. We have no work to do and we are allowed to go anywhere we want for recreation, as long as we have at least 5 men in the truck. I go most anywhere or at any time anyone wants to go as I haven't anything to do and the time passes faster...

I could not help thinking of my grandfather's "recreation" with George Patrias and the knife-wielding Filipinos. The most interesting part of the letter was toward the end:

> Well kid, I've really been around this damn world since the war started. A fellow really learns a lot too. I mean in a thousand different ways. I wouldn't trade my experiences for a million dollars, but I wouldn't give 10¢ to do it over again either.

Like Musiker and Neaderhiser, I think my grandfather took with him the lessons he learned from the war and carried them throughout his life, making him more gentle and patient.

That is not to say that life was all roses after the war. My grandfather probably drank too much and gambled too much. According to my mom, he seldom spoke about the war, so I can't know his true feelings about it. But if his feelings were similar to those of the men in the 978th I interviewed, he didn't speak about it because it troubled him. If that's the case, the war appeared to leave a lingering open wound that both nagged at him and made him more appreciative throughout his life.

During one of my last conversations with Ski, I asked him about his overall impression of his time in the war. Sixty years later, the perspective of my grandfather's best friend did not seem so different from the perspective I think my grandfather had. Ski said:

> *You know, Jeff, you ask me about that war. What can I tell you? It was sometimes tragic, sometimes sickening, sometimes happy, sometimes sorrowful. I didn't know if I was going to make it.*

Figures 111 and 112. Ski, then and now.

Some guys in the Army were happy-go-lucky, others were solemn.
Orton had his own little truck, his own machine shop. Didn't have to go out
on bivouacs. He had a good deal. Mangham had it tougher. He was sort of
a sour guy.

> Thomas Orton remembered Mangham as a
> happy-go-lucky kid.

Well, everybody was happy-go-lucky sometimes, sour other times. We had
good days, other days were miserable. That's the U.S. Army.

> Well, Mr. Powasnik, I've never been in the Army.

Well, Jeff, you can thank God for that.

I always had the idea that the German soldier was like me. Taken into the army to serve his country. I told you about that tunnel we went into. I mean, I didn't feel sorry for 'em, 'cause we were at war. But just for that little while it reminded me of home.

You know, especially at the holidays. We got a little turkey in our rations, and we thought about family. What are they doing? Are they enjoying it back home? I had a brother and sister and my parents back home. And I used to write to 'em.

But we were glad that we were alive. I have different memories. Sometimes it puts a tear in your eye, even today, even now. But even today, every day I get up, maybe I hear gunfire, maybe I hear something else, but I'm grateful I'm alive.

LEO KAVANAUGH AND HIS GENERATION

AS I GOT FURTHER ALONG in preparing this book, I talked to my mom about her father again. Now in adulthood, our conversations gave me a different and more complex portrait of my grandfather. Coupled with what I had learned from his war buddies, they also provided insight into the values of his generation. My mom said:

> My father, as I remember him, was very handsome and rough and tough. But at the same time he was gentle and fun to be around. Growing up, he did most of the cooking. His Irish stew left a lot to be desired [laughs], but the jokes and laughter made up for the stew. My sisters and I were all able to talk to him about anything.

> My father grew up during the Depression. His dad suddenly got sick, and his mom went to work scrubbing floors at Chicago City Hall to support the family. But that wasn't enough to support five kids, so my dad was forced to quit school to find work. He always valued education, and I think he was frustrated at not getting the chance to have more.

> He married my mom and, shortly after I was born, left for the war. My mother worked in a war plant to support us, so I was raised by a wonderful Polish woman, who I called Aunt Jennie, and her husband, Teco. My mom would visit on weekends. My dad came home from the war when I was about three and a half, and I still have vague memories of the day he and my mom came to take me home, a tall man in a uniform standing in Aunt Jennie's hallway.

We lived at 425 W. 74th Street, in a huge apartment complex with a dirt backyard. The apartment was 2 1/2 rooms. My parents didn't have their own room. They slept on a bed that folded out from the closet. My dad worked in construction, mostly running large cranes. Once in a while he'd take me to work with him, and I was so enamored by him, sitting with him on the huge crane. I truly believed that if your dad worked in a bank it had to be a boring job.

I remember him getting up early in the morning to dress for work in the bitter Chicago winter. I can still picture him, with his wool cap and earmuffs. It became a ritual watching him dress; it took so long to put on all the layers of clothes. He was always looking for extra work. When a sewer line would break in the middle of the night, he would get up and go out to repair the broken line. Now as an adult I wonder how he ever endured the freezing cold in the middle of the night. But he welcomed the calls, as this meant overtime. He also did a lot of work for our neighbors to earn more money. I think he put up every cyclone fence in our neighborhood. But he always found time for us; in the evenings he took us to Hamilton Park to play softball.

He worked overtime and extra jobs to earn extra money to save and buy a house, on 81st and Pulaski. And also so he could send my sisters and me to private school. We went to St. Carthage Grammar School, the best around. We were taught by Adrian Dominican nuns, who my father had lots of respect for. Never mind my side of the story; whatever Sister said was gospel truth. [laughs] We attended Mass most Sundays, and afterward we'd go to the local tavern for beer and socializing. So much of our social life centered around the tavern. It was the age of martinis and Manhattans. Everybody smoked and drank. A lot of them drank too much, and it caught up with many of them and hurt families. My mom's family was Irish and so was my dad's. I had an uncle who was a priest and head of the history department at Notre Dame. My dad was always a staunch Democrat. What else could an Irish Catholic from South Side Chicago be?

When I was a teenager and started to date, he would stand up and greet my date at the door and give him one of his looks and say, "Have her home by midnight." They always brought me home early. One fellow told me, "I don't want any problems with your dad." [laughs]

There was so much prejudice in Chicago. But even as a teenager, I realized there was something terribly wrong, that people hated blacks so much. When I was a teenager, I volunteered my time to work with young black girls. And my work was in a bad neighborhood. My dad was upset. Here I was, eighteen years old, white, a woman, venturing all by myself into a poor, all-black neighborhood. My dad would tell me I was going to get killed. Of course, being his daughter, I stood my ground and did what I thought was right. He let me go. He let me use his car because it was more reliable than mine. And what happens when I was there? The window of his car gets smashed, and I call him, hysterical. But he didn't say anything. He just told me to come home and we'll fix it. He and I discussed racism and values. I learned a lot from the children I worked with, just how bad it was. At the end of the year there was a dance for the girls in the class. I will never forget it. I went, and the priest and I were the only white people in the gym. Later on in the evening I look over and see my dad there talking to the priest. A look of pride came over his face as he talked to the priest, and he gave me a look that seemed to say, "I support what you're doing." He stayed for the whole dance and walked me to the car and told me he was proud of me.

When Steve [her first son, my brother] was born, Chuck [my dad] left for the reserves the next day. I was on my own. My dad stayed with us and would get up in the middle of the night to feed Steve so I could sleep. He'd change his diapers and burp him. When Steve was older he and my dad would go to the tavern for a beer and soda pop and to play shuffleboard.

My dad worked for various companies doing construction. He belonged to the union. But work wasn't always steady or guaranteed. My dad and his brothers, growing up in the Depression, were all worried about not having consistent work, so after a while he changed jobs and started working for the city of Chicago, which gave him a steady job. But he still stayed a member of his union, the Hoisting Engineers Union, Local 150, even though he didn't need to when he was working for the city. He was proud. He always wore a 150 button on his cap.

My dad was something of a fighter. He was always fighting for a cause. Maybe that's why I became a social worker. When his union became corrupt, my dad ran for office and stood up to them, spoke out against them, and said that some had criminal records. My mom was always worried he'd end up at the bottom of Lake Michigan, something like Jimmy Hoffa. He didn't think they could hurt him because he worked for the city now. The union couldn't fire him because he now worked for the city, but they had connections. After he started speaking out against the union, the city demoted him from the highest paying job to the lowest paying job. He was shocked and angry. Then he was late one month paying his dues, which was not unusual for my dad, and they used this as an excuse to kick him out of the union. The message I got as a young adult was that, no matter how strong and protective we all thought our dad was, and no matter how righteous he may have thought he was, there were those who were more powerful. Whenever I see a Local 150 button I still get choked up. He really did love his union.

My dad got a blood clot in 1970. We were all shocked because we never saw our dad ill. I flew to Chicago to see him in the hospital, and he said, "What the hell are you doing here? You should be home with the boys. I'm just fine." The next day we got a call to come in. As I walked to his room I saw one of the nurses in the hallway crying. I went into his room and took his hand, and I suddenly realized he was dead.

My sisters and I adored him. I truly thought I was his favorite daughter. One day, years after his death, my sister said to me matter-of-factly, "Well, you both know I was Dad's favorite." Then my other sister said she was the favored one. And I sincerely thought I was the favored one. [laughs] What a wonderful dad that each of his daughters thought she was his favorite.

I know I romanticize him a little. But only a little. He died before I was old enough to realize he wasn't perfect. I was twenty-eight. [laughs]

Based on the image I formed from my interviews, I think my grandfather was probably a better father than he was a soldier. That is not to say he was a bad soldier. Like most of the guys in the 978th, he was a good soldier, but not an extraordinary one—a good soldier in extraordinary times. So part of the difficulty I encountered in coming to know my grandfather as a young soldier was my need to deal with my own romanticized image of him, the one I developed during my childhood. The image I formed of him from his war buddies' recollections could never match the one I had pieced together from a trunk full of photographs and family recollections. But that was my fault, not his, and was inevitable. It wasn't disappointing. In fact, seeing him as an average guy in a war was more meaningful to me than the ideal picture I had

Figure 113. My parents, Charles and Judy Badger (far left and far right), and my grandparents, Leo and Virginia Kavanaugh, in the late 1960s.

painted as a kid. After all, it's better for our heroes to be ordinary people. It gives us something to strive for.

In addition to having a romanticized image of my grandfather, like many people I had a similar, idealized image of his generation. After all, it was the generation that struggled through the Depression, saved the world from tyranny, and returned to build a strong America. In some respects, meeting the veterans and seeing that they too were ordinary guys somewhat tempered this perception. But that is OK too. When we dig deeper into the personality of any figure that we idolize, we come to see them as a person and not as an icon. Looking at it from a mature perspective, it is better to know them as they really were than as we would like to imagine them. Looking at a hero through rose-colored glasses and putting them on a pedestal is not as meaningful an experience as seeing your heroes with all their faults and ordinariness—and then looking at what they accomplished and marveling at it.

What is true of my grandfather is also true for the entire WWII generation. That these men and women were ordinary is what makes them special. I don't think we need to deify them in order to respect their accomplishments. For if the time comes when this country and her allies have to rise up again, it would not be to our advantage to have a false standard of perfection that we, when looking for inner strength and finding our own deficiencies and mediocrity, feel we could never attain.

Through my interviews, I got a feel for the men and women of this generation. That sense goes beyond the simplistic "they were heroes," "they had strong principles," "they had a strong work ethic," or "they were patriotic." They were patriotic, but not blindly so. In fact, a better word than *patriotic* might be *grateful*. I found that, without exception, every veteran had an intense gratitude for having been born into a country that had a high standard of living, offered opportunity, and had respect for human rights. Many of the men came from immigrant parents, mostly from eastern Europe. Although predominantly white and Christian, they were still a diverse group: one GI was allegedly a millionaire, another an illiterate; many were first-generation immigrants; one was a mechanic; another was an East Coast intellectual. They had diverse opinions, ranging across the spectrum from left to right, which were anything but monolithic as they are sometimes described.

Tom Brokaw asserted in his book that my grandfather and my war buddies were part of "The Greatest Generation." Most readers agreed. Some disagreed, commenting on the racism and selfishness of that generation. As I learned for myself, some were bigots, some were alcoholics, some were good soldiers but also bank robbers. As I got to know the men of the 978th—and through them and their memories, my grandfather—I grew to love them. And I do think they were the greatest generation, but not because they were extraordinary. Rather, it is precisely that they were ordinary that makes them and their accomplishments so remarkable. It is hard to image any generation since then that has made the same sacrifice.

EPILOGUE

MY SEARCH FOR MY GRANDDAD'S war story and war buddies has been a wonderful and rewarding experience, filled with interesting people, trips to places I would never otherwise have visited, and a sense of adventure and discovery. When I first started this project in 1998, I had no idea that I would take it as far as I did—or that it would take me as far as it has.

When I look back, there were a few surprises. I was surprised at how the veterans reacted to and remembered the war. When I made contact with the first veterans, I took great care to respect their feelings, assuming that they would have strong, negative, and painful memories of the war. Some did. But others did not and considered the war the great adventure of their lives; some even became nostalgic about it.

Of course, for most of the men I interviewed, their war was in a maintenance company—an "easy war" compared to what a lot of guys faced—and this certainly had an impact on how they remembered it. As a general rule, the men I interviewed who were in combat units before being placed in the 978th had tougher wars and were more likely to have more painful memories.

But to say a harder war translates into more painful memories is not always accurate. Some of the men who were in combat units spoke of the war enthusiastically and did not seem traumatized by it. Or at least they had been able to get over the traumatic aspects to some extent. In contrast, some of the men in the 978th who never saw combat got choked up about the war, and it left permanent scars. It seemed that the dominant factor affecting how each man remembered the war was simply his personality and his ability to cope with negative emotions.

When I first read the history of the 978th, I was surprised to learn that my grandfather had served in a maintenance unit. With no evidence to the contrary, I had assumed that he was in a combat infantry unit, presumably because that is the image of soldiers that I had been exposed to in mainstream books, documentaries, and movies. In retrospect, I am glad it turned out that he was in a maintenance company. Not enough attention is given to the 90 percent of GIs who served in support roles. Yet their contributions were essential to the success of the war effort, even if their experiences were not as dramatic as those of combat infantrymen and aviators.

I also learned that the vast majority of time spent in war is mundane and boring—waiting days for orders, camping out in a muddy field in France for a month because of a clerical error, or walking guard duty all night. In many respects, the mundane became one of the most interesting aspects of the war for me: how GIs washed their clothes, where they slept, how they kept clean, what they ate and how they prepared it, what they did in their free time, and how they got along with each other. The subjects my war buddies chose to bring up and talk about were also interesting—looting and drinking runs, I discovered, were the most popular topics.

One of the most rewarding aspects of my search was to hear the veterans' stories firsthand. And through this, I felt I was discovering something. And in some respects I was, for the veterans and the people in Europe were usually telling their stories for the first time, and the stories would have been lost if nobody had asked the questions before they died. In addition, there is a difference between reading facts in a book and getting a more holistic feel for the men and their situation by talking to them face to face. This is something that cannot be conveyed through writing. It is something that cannot be conveyed in this book.

Finally, in writing this book and reflecting on everything I learned from my interviews with the GIs and my visits to Europe, I realized that the experiences of the veterans were so varied that no book could address them all. Often, we feel compelled to sum up the entire war in a few phrases that simplify and mythologize it. But to simplify and mythologize the largest war in history is to belittle its vastness and complexity. I have tried to reflect that here and to avoid any sweeping conclusions. To study the war is not to say "this is what happened" and "this is what it means," but rather to begin with the basics: these are the men who were there, this is what each one remembers, this is what it meant to him. Beyond that, any extracted meaning or grand conclusions are solely the reader's.

In that sense, I never felt satisfied constructing a single thesis, either for my project or for the information that I collected. I touched on numerous topics in this book: the work of a maintenance company, the memories of Jewish GIs versus those of their antagonists, the way veterans remember the war and even the same event in different ways, how some finally made peace with the war while others did not, and America's collective memory of the war. Each of these topics could be a book in and of itself. But I felt that focusing on a single subject would ignore the complexity of the war and the range of individual experiences. A history professor once told me that many historians feel pressure to address a new aspect of history or construct a perspective on history that is different from the perspectives of their predecessors. I was not required to have a thesis and therefore was not going to concoct one. So I wrote a book that was, for the most part, a collection of anecdotes from the people I met, all linked together by the story of my search for information.

When I first made contact with the veterans, by and large, they were flattered and a little dumbfounded that somebody would take an interest in what they did. But once we got going, they recounted their life stories with pride. For some of the men our conversations served to exorcise demons. Thomas Orton said that talking to me was "a challenge" that he "wanted to take up" and later told me that it helped "heal the wounds." When Merlin Clark got my letter, he decided he was finally going to talk about the war, and doing so "brought an end to the whole thing" for him.

As I have mentioned, fortunately for me the timing was right. If I had interviewed the men in the 1960s or 1970s, I do not think they would have been as forthcoming. And, being an outsider, a male, and about the same age the veterans were during their war also helped.

My introductory letter prompted several children of veterans to sit down with their fathers and do their own interviews. One daughter of a veteran told me, "You know, we got your letter and I thought to myself, 'This complete stranger comes along and wants to know about my dad. And he's *my* dad. Why haven't I asked him these things myself?'" In France, the Netherlands, and Germany, everybody was enthusiastic about talking to me. Many said the war was "the biggest event" in their lives and were proud to recount their experiences. Some were giddy. In many interviews, family members sat quietly and listened, both enthralled by the story and perhaps a little embarrassed that I was asking questions they had never asked.

As my search progressed, I felt a sense of obligation to record all of the stories and photos of the 978th in one place, to establish a historical record of the unit. I collected almost a thousand original photos from the 978th. I did not want them to end up in twenty years as discarded photos one finds in the "instant ancestors" box of antique stores. Such photos are priceless if the context is known. But when they end up generations later as unknown faces in unknown places, they are meaningless. I did not want my war buddies' photos to suffer the same fate. They are now displayed in my house in several large frames, assembled into a sort of collage, and take up nearly half a room. They're a heck of a conversation piece, and they're a record of our history.

When I was close to being finished with this book, I telephoned several of my closest war buddies. Marvin Mangham is doing well, as are Farran Helmick, Max Voron, and a few others. Ski called me in March 2006. He had just celebrated his ninetieth birthday. His family was worried about him driving, so he gave his car to charity and now rides the bus. As always, he was friendly, positive, and enthusiastic and said he "wakes up every morning and hears the birds, sees the cats come up to his porch looking for something to eat. And, well, you feel as good as you wanna feel. And I feel pretty good."

But inevitably, my war buddies are fading away. One GI, who a year earlier was filled with enthusiasm and bravado, told me, "I'm nearing the end. It's all behind me now. I have nothing to look forward to. In another six months I'll be dead. I can feel it coming." I called him again a few months later; his telephone had been disconnected.

I called George Patrias. I could tell as soon as he answered that our conversation was going to be different this time. His speech was slow. He did not remember our previous conversation and could only vaguely remember my grandfather. But a bit of the old George Patrias was still there. He said:

Well, I'm eighty-four years old. I had lung cancer a few years back, and they took out half my lung. I need a nursing home, I guess. But they can stick that nursing home where the sun doesn't shine. There's no way I'm going to a nursing home.

I do all right around the house. I don't feel too bad, just feel worthless. I'm eighty-four. Not doin' nothin'. I tell ya, it's another way of life. You can't imagine it. I cut the grass. But it takes me about two hours. And then I've had it for a couple of days. I guess I'm just, well, just waiting to die.

It was just a short time after our conversation that I had that business trip to Detroit and was honored to finally meet the infamous George Patrias at his home. He died two weeks after our visit.

Thomas Orton contracted cancer again, for the fourth time. He told his wife, "I've beaten it every other time. But this time I think it's finally going to beat me." He died in January 2005. I received an e-mail from Merlin Clark's son on April 12, 2006, telling me that his father had died the day before.

Eventually they will all be gone. My grandfather died before I met him, so I never mourned his death. But in some way I feel I am mourning his death by witnessing the fading away of his buddies. It has not been easy for me. It is the end of an era for a group of guys who helped to shape the world we live in today, and I admired, respected, and grew to love them. I am grateful that I had the opportunity to find them before it was too late and grateful for all they taught me.

I think that, as each generation grows old, the younger generation has an obligation to ask their parents and grandparents about their lives. It does not have to be an elaborate process; it is just a matter of spending a few evenings sitting down with a tape recorder or video camera, asking questions, and listening to what they say. We learn from doing this, and we have a permanent record. So that we have answers when, someday, somebody asks, "My great-great-grandfather was an infantryman in Vietnam, I wonder what he experienced?" or "My great-grandmother was a Mexican peasant who emigrated to Texas in a cattle car, I wonder what her experiences were like?" With modern technology, obtaining that narrative and hearing it will be just a click away. So I hope that if somebody takes only one insight from this book, it is that they should record the stories of their loved ones' lives for themselves and their children before it is too late.

So I leave it at that, mostly just the words of all the people I met, and if there is a story here, it is the story of the journey of my search. If you ever get the chance to go on a similar journey, even if it is just a day-trip to the National Archives to read about your grandfather's WWII unit, a weekend trip to meet the Belgian family who let your grandfather hide from the Nazis in their farmhouse, or to Vietnam to retrace your dad's footsteps, be sure to seize that opportunity. It is a journey you will never forget.

PART TWO

SOME COMMENTS ON METHODS

IN WRITING THIS BOOK, I tried to achieve a balance between making it accessible to the average reader, the non-historian, while still being responsible in terms of quoting my sources.

In the sections of this book that deal with individuals or specific subjects, general information that appears in the narrative refers to my sources in the third person. The quotes from interviewees, however, are all taken directly from my detailed notes or other primary documents. I have tried to reproduce these conversations word for word, but occasionally I did find it necessary to paraphrase and to replace missing words to complete a thought, make a point, or effect a transition. Immediately prior to completing the manuscript for this book, I sent all quoted material to its respective author, or the author's family in the case of deceased informants, for verification and approval.

I did not record or videotape the conversations. I took detailed notes during each meeting, and, when the interview was over, I annotated my notes by filling in previously unrecorded details while they were still fresh in my mind. I think that this casual but attentive approach resulted in greater comfort and candor on the part of the interviewee. This method worked well during my early interviews, and I decided to continue using it even after I committed myself to the idea of writing a book, even as some of the later interviews became much more in-depth. The amount of information that I obtained from my sources varied considerably—some provided comparatively little, others offered a lot. For one veteran with whom I developed a very close relationship, I have over two hundred pages of handwritten notes.

When quoting from letters I have retained the original integrity of the letter, complete with typos, misspellings, and other mistakes.

FINDING YOUR OWN FAMILY MEMBER'S WAR STORY ON THE INTERNET

INTRODUCTION

I HAVE ALWAYS HAD A strange connection and fascination with vestiges of the past. When I was in high school my family lived in a small town in south Texas. I would find a copy of an old ordinance survey map and note the locations of crosses, which signified graveyards. Then I would drag my girlfriend out to some ranch in the middle of nowhere in the Texas hill country, searching for some long-abandoned graveyards. We'd identify the approximate location off of the main highway, hop the barbed-wire fence, steer clear of any bulls and snakes, and traipse into the countryside in search of some family burial plot that had been abandoned eighty years ago. We'd eventually find them, four or five graves dating from the late 1800s to the last burial in the early 1900s, usually sitting miles from the nearest house, now overgrown with oak and mesquite trees, the tombstones sometimes split in half by a large tree trunk. I figured that we were perhaps the first people to visit these graves in fifty-some years, and I felt exhilarated when we found them. At first my girlfriend thought I was crazy, but she would straggle along, and eventually she came to enjoy our trips.

When I lived in Ireland I visited renovated castles, but they just never intrigued me. Instead, I again found an ordinance survey map, looked for the little red dots that marked some historic ruin on the outskirts of Dublin, and rode my bicycle out to the site. Whatever it was—an old graveyard, a standing stone, a small, dilapidated castle—it was usually off in a farmer's field. I would talk to the farmer, and he would direct me to a half-destroyed castle that nobody paid any attention to; it was certainly not on any historical society's renovation list. The farmer could never understand my interest; it was just the place where he kept his tractor.

In Poland, I visited grand cathedrals but preferred wandering around the buildings still lying in ruins from the war. In Guatemala, I was fascinated by the overgrown remnants of the cathedrals destroyed in the 1773 earthquake. In Israel, I visited the holy sites but enjoyed even more snorkeling in the Mediterranean near an old Arab village looking for shards of pottery.

Perhaps it was my father who planted this seed. For the first six years of my life, my family lived in Dublin, California. In Dublin there is a dilapidated, old wooden church that was built by the area's first pioneers in the mid-1800s. My dad and I would walk around the overgrown tombstones in the church graveyard. I got the feeling we were discovering something—that the graveyard at old St. Raymond's Church was somehow ours. It certainly had an impact on me, as this is one of my earliest and most vivid memories.

So when the opportunity came along to search for my grandfather's war buddies, maybe it was inevitable that I would get so involved with it. Also, a series of fortunate circumstances involving timing in my life made it possible: I had become mature enough to carry the project out successfully, the Internet had been developed, I was single and had free time to devote to the project, and I had a job that frequently took me close to the parts of the world where the 978th had served.

Some people argue that there are no more great discoveries to be made. Tutankhamen's tomb has been found, the isolated tribes in the Brazilian rainforest already studied, the South Pole and Mount Everest conquered. On a more pedestrian level, people complain that Venice is overrun with tourists. Prague was "discovered" by Westerners when it opened up in the late 1980s and is now a fashionable destination. In Guatemala I met "travelers" arriving in small, indigenous-Maya villages who seemed disappointed to find other Westerners already there.

But I think there are still discoveries to be made; they are just smaller and more personal. I have had the good fortune of seeing a lot of the world. I spent eight years abroad and currently half my work is overseas. Yet for all of the interesting places I have been, the destinations that have been the most personally rewarding to me are Les Pieux, Spekholzerheide, Mariadorf, and Jülich, towns that never appear on any tourist maps. I feel they are somehow mine, perhaps because during my visits to these places I was not a passive observer but a participant, and usually on a mission to find a particular person or place: Leon and I on a scavenger hunt from house to house trying to track down a person in a sixty-year-old photo, Ingo and I searching for somebody who knew something about a tunnel, Leon and I drinking in the beer hall asking the old-timers about the war.

These, too, are "discoveries," and in a way they are my discoveries and nobody else's. They belong to me. And that is why I cherish my search, the people I met, and all of these places.

In the pages that follow, I provide information and instructions on how to research the war story of a family member or other person, to make your own "discoveries." The information presented here reflects my own experience researching my grandfather's story and relies significantly on resources available on or through the Internet. I am most familiar with WWII-era places, events, and records, so I use these resources to illustrate the procedures and resources that I discuss, but these same general procedures can be used when researching the war story of veterans of any modern war. Beyond the Internet and conventional library and archival research, however, are the many opportunities for carrying out interactive research directly with the veterans and the people, places, artifacts, or institutions that were and are part of their military experience.

Many readers of this book will, I believe, be interested in following some or many of the steps that I took in my search, but such extensive commitment is not required. Even a limited effort can provide satisfying results. If, for example, you are not interested in or capable of tracking down people, there is a wealth of information available that can be very personally rewarding. If your great-uncle died at Normandy, you might be able to locate a history of his unit and learn what type of action he was involved in and the details of his death. That is just what Brian Kueker did (you'll find his story at the end of part 2). Or, if your grandfather's war medals have been lost, you can easily order replacements over the Internet. If your dad had a fiery romance with a French woman in 1944 and all you have is a photo of the two of them together, you might be able to find her or, if she is deceased, her children. If your grandfather hid out from the Nazis in a Belgian farmhouse, you might be able to locate the family that gave him shelter, find their address and contact information, and arrange to visit them. They have probably heard the same story passed down through the generations of their families and would love to meet you. Perhaps you have a photo of your great-aunt, who worked as a nurse during the war, sitting at an outdoor café in Paris in 1945. On your next trip to Paris, skip the Eiffel Tower, take the photo with you, and spend the day wandering around trying to find the same street and café where she was photographed. Ask the locals if they know where it is. Maybe you will find it, maybe you won't—but you will definitely have an enjoyable experience and meet lots of interesting people along the way.

Figure 114. A café in Paris, 1945. (Photo courtesy of George Patrias)

ARE YOU SURE YOU WANT TO DO THIS?

MANY OF US HAVE GROWN up with romantic images of World War II: the exotic lands, the battles, the heroism, the liberation, the camaraderie. As we grew older, however, the romantic images were often tempered by what we learned about the uglier sides of the war: the horrors, the death, the destruction, the suffering, the fear, the devastated lives and psychological scars of the survivors. All of these images are valid; they are generalizations made up of a diverse and complex assortment of truths, and they can be applied to wars other than WWII.

Anybody who sets out to gather truths surrounding a war must be aware that there are many "truths" and many facts, and they range from being good, admirable, and sources of pride and respect to being bad, shameful, and sources of pain and regret. So be prepared at the outset to uncover information that might well be new to you. We like to look at veterans in general as ordinary people who did extraordinary things in times of war, so we should not overlook the fact that they were just that, ordinary people—a sample, a cross-section, drawn from the entire U.S. population.

In my research, I found some veterans who were noble and admirable and others who hated one another, shirked their duty, and were considered cowards or incompetents by their comrades. I heard countless stories of looting, both the "acceptable" looting of war paraphernalia and the "unacceptable" looting of personal property. I heard rumors about one officer in the unit "going around raping the local German women." In addition, the stresses and chaos of war and the uncertainty of survival often translated into a dual set of mores among many men who otherwise behaved quite differently in civilian life.

Be aware of these realities in your search. If you go digging into the past, you might—and you might not—like what you find. We have all read heart-warming clips in newspapers about personal fulfillment: a Dutch woman who successfully tracked down her American GI father, old war buddies reunited after fifty years apart, a young woman presented with her deceased father's war medals. What we typically do not hear about are the searches that end in disappointment—or even worse, the searches that end up ugly.

A person searching for GIs from his dad's unit may find out that a lot of his fellow soldiers didn't like him, that his buddies thought he was an incompetent soldier, or that he deserted his unit instead of going back to the front. A Dutch woman who has heard for her entire life that her grandfather was an American GI who had a passionate love affair with the woman's grandmother may discover that the relationship was really a drunken, one-night fling. Or she might even find that the story her grandmother painted is only a fabrication intended to cover up something else. Prostitution was common when survival was first priority, and rape was not unheard of. If you obtain medical records, you might be surprised to find that your grandfather, married to your grandmother while he was overseas during the war, was treated three times for syphilis.

While hopefully you will find no uncomfortable information, you do need to be prepared for whatever you might find.

A woman who was conducting a search similar to mine contacted me after I put up my website. Her father had died in the Pacific during the war, and she had located some of his war buddies. She learned that he had not died heroically in battle, as the Army had told the family, but instead had been shot by a fellow soldier in a fit of rage during a mutiny. Another woman in London contacted me for help in finding her American GI father. We learned that he was deceased but that he had family living in the U.S. But as she dug deeper, the story her mother had told began to fall apart. She had formed a romanticized image of her father and was now running the risk of having this image shattered by the truth. She was having second thoughts about following through. One man who obtained his grandfather's military records discovered that he had not died immediately after sustaining an injury, as the Army reported to the family, but had lingered on in the hospital for two weeks before he finally passed away.

Although she never said it outright, I always thought that my mother was a bit nervous about what I might dig up—and understandably so. This was her father, a person she loved deeply. She told me several times, "I probably romanticized him because of his early death. He died before I could realize that he wasn't perfect." Fortunately, I did not find anything negative about him, and, in light of the circumstances, the stories of his escapades with George Patrias and Ski were more entertaining then denigrating.

Finally, if you interview or merely talk with veterans about their wartime experiences, you might be asking them to recall memories that evoke a wide range of emotions, some of which could be fond recollections or sources of deep personal pride and others that could be painful or otherwise unpleasant. Whatever emotions are stirred up, this process may go well, or it may not. Whatever you do, be sensitive to your veteran's feelings and personal history, be prepared for a potentially wide range of responses, and be responsible for your actions and how they might affect others.

Figure 115 and 116. Front and back sides of German propaganda thrown behind British lines by Nazis. (Courtesy of Leo Packer)

DAD'S WAR

THE BEST AND MOST COMPREHENSIVE website for finding a broad array of information and links to useful sites on the Internet to get you started on your search is *Dad's War*, located at:

members.aol.com/dadswar

Dad's War was created by Wesley Johnston, whose father, Walter G. Johnston Jr., served in Europe in WWII. This comprehensive site contains guidelines for researching a WWII veteran's war story, extensive information about WWII, war stories completed by family members and friends of veterans, and links to numerous other useful sites. *Dad's War* both illustrates the breadth and depth of information that is available on the Internet for those preparing to delve into researching a war story and presents examples of war stories that have been completed. Bookmark this site; you will want to consult it often.

Please keep in mind that Mr. Johnston receives countless e-mails from people asking for help. Out of respect for him and his efforts in creating and maintaining this site, please read through the site carefully, purchase his useful book *Dad's War: A Workshop on Finding and Telling Your Father's World*

Figure 117. "Jap kids are really cute. Isn't this a silly pose?"
(Photo and caption courtesy of Leo Packer, left)

War II Story, and exhaust all other possibilities before contacting him with a personal research question.

Figure 118. "The little Jap guide, who guided us thru the Nikko Shrines. He spoke a very queer English full of stilted, archaic phrases learned at Tokyo Imperial University many years ago." (Photo and caption courtesy of Leo Packer, right)

GETTING STARTED

THE FIRST STEP IN FINDING someone's war story is to get as much information as you can about that person's time in the military. How you approach this depends significantly on whether the veteran is alive or deceased. If the person is still alive and willing to talk with you, sit down together and explore the subject. Prepare a series of questions to ask your veteran before your first meeting. Even if your questions seem rather vague, they will help start a dialogue and will spark memories of other events. Some basic information that you should collect includes the dates that he was in the military, what kind of work he did, where he was based, and the name of his unit. Photographs are always helpful for stimulating recollections. Take extensive notes, and remember that no detail is too trivial. If you have access to a video camera or a tape recorder, ask your veteran if you may record the conversation. Many GIs say they don't remember much. But once they start talking, their memories will be jogged and they may not be able to stop talking. If your veteran is agreeable and able, continue to talk with him now and again; other events and people will come to his mind, and you will possibly have acquired additional information, and additional questions, from other sources in the meantime that might help encourage more conversation.

If your veteran is no longer alive or is not available to speak with you directly, consider talking with the people who knew that person best—wife, children, brothers, sisters, friends, nieces and nephews. Here too you will want to have some questions prepared and photos handy. These sources might tell you that they "just don't remember much," but don't despair when that is the initial response. They often remember more than they think they do but just need something to jog their memory or to have a clear understanding that what they consider unimportant might be a useful part of the story you are researching. So when your Great-aunt Georgina says that she just does not remember anything relevant to your story, be prepared to prompt her with whatever morsel of pertinent information you might have—a photo, a name, a vague memory. For example, asking her, "Didn't Dad have a best buddy in Vietnam from Texas?" might just be enough to jog her memory. "Well, I do remember your dad had a buddy from Texas.

They called him Kamowto or Kamodo or something. He was a short, stout, Hispanic guy. I think he lived in a place called Batesville or something like that. Komoetee or something. Camote. That's it. Camote."

Armed with this new information, you can call the local VFW or town hall in Batesville, Texas, and ask if anybody knows of a Vietnam veteran from the area with the nickname Camote.

Once you have talked to everybody who knew your veteran, you'll need to start looking for facts about his or her time in the war. If you do not already have it, begin with a unit name and/or serial number. This information could be located in any number of places: on a gravestone, discharge paper stuck away in a box in the attic, the inside cover of the family Bible, or a death certificate. If you cannot locate this information from readily accessible records, you may request it from the National Archives. You'll find instructions on how to do this in the next section.

MILITARY RECORDS AND REPORTS OF SEPARATION

THE NEXT STEP IS TO get your veteran's military records. In July 1973 there was a catastrophic fire at the National Personnel Records Center that destroyed 80 percent of the records for Army personnel discharged from 1912 to 1960. There were no duplicate copies of these records and the files, and the information that they contained was permanently lost. So if you request a person's military records, you will most likely receive only discharge papers, a Report of Separation. This report will provide the name of the veteran's unit, the decorations and medals received, the date of entry and discharge from the service, the address at time of discharge, and other information. To request a Report of Separation, go to:

> vetrecs.archives.gov

The next of kin (a surviving spouse who has not remarried, father, mother, son, daughter, brother, or sister) may submit this request online. Simply click on the large, red "Request Military Records" button and follow the straightforward instructions that will quickly lead you through the short process. You can request records on benefits, employment, medical history, retirement, awards/decorations, a correction of awards, personal military history, or genealogy. When you have entered and reviewed the necessary information, you will be asked to print out, sign, and submit, by mail or fax, your declaration of next-of-kin status.

If you are not the next of kin, you will need to submit Standard Form 180 (SF 180). To obtain an SF-180, go to *vetrecs.archives.gov*, where you can print a copy or request that a copy be faxed or mailed to you. Once you have the form, it needs to be completed and faxed or mailed, as instructed.

You may also request a copy of SF-180 by writing to:

> National Personnel Records Center
> Military Personnel Records
> 9700 Page Blvd.
> St. Louis, MO 63132-5100

Once you have submitted your request, be prepared to wait. The *vetrecs.archives.gov* website claims that routine requests will require two to four weeks to complete, and those requiring reconstruction due to the fire will require twelve weeks, but I have heard of people waiting much longer to have their requests filled.

IF HE DIED IN THE WAR

IF YOUR VETERAN DIED DURING the war and you want to search for information related to the death or burial location, the following sources should be consulted, depending on the war your veteran participated in.

If your veteran died overseas, obtain a copy of his *Individual Deceased Personnel File* (IDPF). An Individual Decreased Personnel File from the U.S. Army Human Resources Command is an extremely valuable document that contains records about the GI's death: where and when he died, reports of the action involved, and sometimes testimony from the men who were with him when he died. It is the most important record for those who died overseas. The amount of information in each GI's file can vary greatly, ranging from extensive details to almost nothing.

To obtain a copy of your veteran's IDPF, send a letter to the U.S. Army Human Resources Command stating that you are willing to pay the Freedom of Information Act fees in exchange for a copy of the IDPF, although these fees probably will be waived if your veteran is a relative. You should include as much information in your request as possible: the veteran's full name, including middle initial; rank; and serial number. If some of this information is not available, provide other details that might help in locating the record, such as the date of death, place of death, place of burial, home state, etc. In some cases, the requested records might not be located on the first try. If your request is not filled, wait six months and then write back, stating that this is your second attempt. The address is

> U.S. Army Human Resources Command
> ATTN: AHRC-PAO (FOIA), Rm 7S65
> 200 Stovall St.
> Alexandria, VA 22331-0400
> (703) 325-9256

Please be aware that an IDPF may contain graphic information such as medical records and details of the GI's death. Be prepared for how this may affect you emotionally.

Vietnam Veterans

There are several websites that list records of military personnel who died during the Vietnam War. These sites can be found by searching the Internet for *Vietnam Wall*. Two of them are

> **www.thevirtualwall.org**—This website gives the individual's name, rank, date of birth, date of death, home city and home state, unit, panel and row on the wall, and sometimes the place of death.
> **thewall-usa.com**—This website provides the same information as above and also the GI's religion, marital status, race, gender, length of service, place of death, and the nature of the action during his death.

Both sites can be searched using hometown, age at death, rank, and other options when information is limited. Both sites also provide the opportunity for family members to post a photo and comments about the individual.

If your veteran died overseas and the body is still overseas or was never recovered, contact the American Battle Monuments Commission. If the veteran died during the war, he or she will either be buried or have a marker at an American cemetery. The American Battle Monuments Commission has a record for each death in WWI, WWII, Korea, and Vietnam. The Commission may be contacted at

American Battle Monuments Commission
Courthouse Plaza II
2300 Clarendon Blvd., Suite 500
Arlington, VA 22201
(703) 696-6897
www.abmc.gov

The Commission's website gives the full name, rank, branch of the military, serial number, unit, state from which the veteran entered the service, date of death, cemetery, and plot, row, and grave number for WWI, WWII, and Korean veterans. The site also has much other information about the cemeteries, activities, and services.

There are eight WWI cemeteries in Europe and England and fourteen WWII cemeteries in Europe, England, North Africa, and the Philippines (see Table 3). A white, marble cross marks most graves, except for those for soldiers of the Jewish faith, which are marked by a Star of David. Upon request of the next of kin, the ABMC will send free of charge a black-and-white photo of the headstone or inscription on the Wall of the Missing.

Table 3. WWI and WWII ABMC cemeteries in Europe, North Africa, and the Philippine Islands.

World War I

Cemetery	Location	Graves	Missing
Aisne-Marne	Belleau Woods, France	2,289	1,060
Brookwood	Brookwood, England	468	563
Flanders Field	Waregem, Belgium	368	43
Meuse-Argonne	Romagne-sous-Montfaucon, France	14,246	954
Oise-Aisne	Fère-en-Tardenois, France	6,012	241
St. Mihiel	Thiaucourt, France	4,153	284
Somme	Bony, France	1,844	333
Suresnes	Suresnes, France	1,541	974

World War II

Cemetery	Location	Graves	Missing
Ardennes	Neuville-en-Condroz, Belgium	5,329	462
Brittany	St. James, France	4,410	498
Cambridge	Cambridge, England	3,812	5,127
Epinal	Epinal, France	5,255	424
Florence	Florence, Italy	4,402	1,409
Henri-Chapelle	Aubel, Belgium	7,992	450
Lorraine	St. Avold, France	10,489	444
Luxembourg	Luxembourg City, Luxembourg	5,076	371
Manila	Manila, the Philippines	17,202	36,285
Netherlands	Margraten, the Netherlands	8,301	1,722
Normandy	St. Laurent-sur-Mer, France	9,387	1,557
North Africa	Carthage, Tunisia	2,841	3,724
Rhone	Draguignan, France	861	294
Sicily-Rome	Nettuno, Italy	7,861	3,095

The superintendents of the cemeteries are very helpful and typically do reply to e-mails. Addresses for each of the cemeteries can be found on their websites, which in turn can be accessed from www.abmc.gov.

UNIT HISTORIES AND OTHER DOCUMENTS

THE U.S. ARMY MILITARY HISTORY INSTITUTE (USAMHI), an institute of the U.S. Army Heritage and Education Center in Carlisle, Pennsylvania, maintains an extensive research center, much of it available online at:

www.carlisle.army.mil/ahec/MHI.htm

They also maintain an extensive collection of unit histories which, once identified via an online request form, can be viewed via interlibrary loan.

SEARCHING THE INTERNET

ONCE YOU HAVE ASSEMBLED AS much of the basic information as you will need to search your veteran's war story, you will be ready to extend your search in any of a number of possible directions, and the Internet is a good way to explore your options quickly, efficiently, and with very little cost.

You will search the Internet with the assistance of an *Internet search engine*. A search engine is a very fast computer or set of computers sitting somewhere in the world that spend every minute of every day opening up Web pages and recording into a huge database every word contained on those pages along with the location of the Web page. When you use a search engine, you will ask it which Web pages contain a certain keyword or phrase, and in response, it will provide you with a list of all of the Web pages that contain that keyword or phrase.

There are numerous search engines. Two of the best and most popular are

www.google.com
www.dogpile.com

Google is a single search engine; Dogpile is a website that searches several search engines at once and gives the results from all of them.

A good search engine will have visited billions of pages and will contain billions of keywords. For example, a recent search of Google.com for the word *war* yielded 1.5 billion hits. A similar search for *Normandy* yielded 17 million hits. It is easy to see that a search should be as narrow and specific as possible.

If you are searching for your veteran's unit, you will need to consider the relative size of the unit designation you search for. In order of size, from smallest to largest, the U.S. Army is organized as follows:

> Platoon
> Company
> Battalion
> Regiment
> Division
> Corps
> Army

Searching for "9th Army" will yield more results than you probably want. But searching for a specific platoon might yield nothing, as a platoon is a rather small entity.

Figure 119. Chow line, location unknown.
(Photo courtesy of William Musiker)

My grandfather was in the 978th Engineer Maintenance Company, which included about two hundred men at full strength. It was a part of the XIXth Corps of Engineers, which included several thousand men; and that was a part of the 9th Army, which encompassed even more. If I were looking for information about my grandfather or his immediate unit, therefore, I would search for the 978th Engineer Maintenance Company rather than the 9th Army.

As you search, remember to try all possible variations and spellings for the unit. For example, the 19th Corps of Engineers may be written as "XIX Corps," "XIXth Corps," "19 Corps," "19th Corps," or "Nineteenth Corps." You should search for every variation.

Boolean Searches

Boolean search operators allow you to both include many words and variations in your search and exclude other words. For example, while searching for my granddad's unit, I found out that there is a 978th Military Police unit, which is still active. To avoid finding all Web pages that reference that unit, I could try the following search:

> (978th OR 978) AND (engineer OR engineers or engineering or
> engr) AND NOT (police OR MP)

The search engine will handle this search by (1) finding all pages that contain either of the words "978th" or "978"; then (2) finding all the pages that contain "engineer," "engineers," "engineering" or "engr"; then (3) determining which of these pages contains keywords from both lists; and finally (4) it will exclude any pages that contain either "police" or "MP."

Boolean searches are presented in different ways on different search engines, but using them is usually rather easy to figure out.

Also, keep in mind that military units often go by variations of their name. For example, a search for

> 345th bombardment

won't be exhaustive, since many pages list this unit under the name

> 345th Bomb Group.

When searching for place-names, consider variations in spelling. Many foreign place-names have been Anglicized. William Musiker sent me photos with the caption "Juelich, Germany" written on the back.

Searching the net for

> Juelich AND war

didn't yield much, but searching for

> (Jülich OR Julich OR Juelich) AND (1944 OR 1945)

yielded a lot of information, including several pages on the Roer River crossing, which my grandfather and Marvin Mangham took part in.

An Example of an Internet Search

As an example of an Internet search, let's look for information on the 37th Combat Engineer Battalion, Merlin Clark's unit that landed at Normandy on D-Day. If we begin our search at

> www.google.com

and pull up

> **Google Advanced Search**

we get a menu that looks like the one below. Of course, the Internet is constantly changing, so the layout may be different, but the functionality is still the same.

Since we are looking for information on the 37th Combat Engineer Battalion, we could start with

> **Find results:**
>
> with **all** the words: 37th Combat Engineers
>
> with the **exact phrase**:   _____
>
> with **at least one** of the words: _____
>
> **without** the words: _____

This search yields a convoluted mess of over one hundred thousand pages, many of which have nothing to do with the 37th Combat Engineers or even WWII in general. So let's try

Find results:

with **all** the words:	_____
with the **exact phrase**:	37th Combat _____
with **at least one** of the words:	engineer, engineers, _____
	engineering, engr _____
without the words:	_____

This narrows the search. It yielded fifty-four hits.

However, some of the hits were for a unit that was in the Gulf War—not World War II. We can eliminate these with the **without the words** option, like this:

with **all** the words:	_____
with the **exact phrase**:	37th Combat _____
with **at least one** of the words:	engineer, engineers, _____
	engineering, engr _____
without the words:	Gulf, 1991, Iraq, Kuwait ___

This search reduces the number of hits to thirty-two. Sifting through the results, we find that some still are not relevant—one of them was a unit in Vietnam and two are contemporary units.

The ones that are left, however, are a goldmine:

- *www.vets.com* gives the name, address, and telephone number of the reunion organizer for the WWII-era 37th Combat Engineer Battalion.
- The *Lubbock On-line* website gives the date and location of the reunion for the 37th.
- A page giving a personal account of a soldier who landed on D-Day, where he mentions that he was on a landing craft with men from the 37th. This site includes photos of the men on the craft and, better yet, an e-mail address for somebody who might be able to provide helpful information.

- The history section of the U.S. Army Corps of Engineers, with personal testimony of a GI who, like Clark, was a bulldozer driver on Omaha Beach.
- On *www.vets.org* we find two postings from people searching for individual GIs who were in the 37th.
- A page put up by a man whose father was in Company B of the 37th, along with photos.

Not bad for ten minutes of work.

REUNION LISTINGS

REUNION RECORDS ARE EXCELLENT SOURCES of information about people and the military units in which they served, and they are easy to access. There are several sites on the Internet that give rather thorough listings of reunion associations.

The Ben Myers Associations and Alumni Database at

www.military-network.com/ben/Associationmenu.cfm

contains a huge listing of over 13,000 associations, organizations, and military alumni databases. Reunions are listed by unit type: infantry, engineers, armored, airborne, and so on. If you cannot find what you are looking for, the site has an e-mail link to Ben Myers, who can help you find it. This website gives the address and phone number of the contact person responsible for the reunion.

Reunion associations enjoy hearing from children, grandchildren, and family members of veterans. In 1961, Alma White's Uncle Roy of the 105th Combat Engineers called his twenty-three-year-old niece to his deathbed in Russellville, Kentucky. He pulled out an old, folded map that he had carried with him for years and said to her: "Alma, I want you to keep this and if anyone wants to know what I did in the war, this will tell them." Alma took great care of the map and, twenty years later, found her way to his reunion association, where she met many of the men that her uncle served with. The association also invited her to stand in for her uncle during a reunion.

MESSAGE BOARDS

THERE ARE SEVERAL WEBSITES ON the Internet where users can post messages stating that they are searching for a certain person or information about a specific unit, place, or event.

In terms of finding specific people, message boards are a long shot. Considering the millions of people who have served in the military, the chances that the person you are searching for, or even a friend or family member, will see your post are pretty slim.

But even if it is a long shot, it's worth doing for several reasons. First, even though the chances of finding the person you are looking for are remote, the chances of finding somebody who knows something about the unit are better. Second, assuming a search engine finds this site, there is a permanent marker on the Internet stating that you are looking for information about this specific person or unit. If somebody else searches the Internet for that information, it will direct him or her to the site that lists your name and e-mail address.

It is worth taking a quick look to see if there is anybody else looking for people from the same unit. But don't spend too much time browsing through all the posts. Go to the search feature on the site and search specifically for the unit or person you are looking for. Just be certain to search for all the possible variations of the unit name.

It is important to word your post for maximum exposure. Some of the sites require people to open up the message, so put the important information in the header. If your header reads, "Hey! I need help finding one of my uncle's war buddies!" very few people will open it to see your message. Instead, state specifically in the header who or what you are looking for—"Grady Koehl. 37th Combat Engineers, Co. C. Normandy, Carentan"—with additional details in the body of the message.

Figure 120. A bar in Marseilles, France, probably June or July, 1945. (Photo courtesy of William Musiker)

You never know who will help you out. The Internet is filled with helpful people who might have seen something about that unit before and will send you what they know. That is how I found Theron Snell. I left a post telling about my search for my granddad's unit. A nice guy in California named Paul, perhaps bored at work, took up my cause and searched the Internet for the 978th. He found the reference to Theron Snell and e-mailed me about it.

There are many forums and message boards for veterans and those interested in military history. Here are three:

ww2.vet.org
www.worldwar2history.info
www.ww2f.com

THE PHONE BOOK

THE INTERNET WHITE PAGES ARE a valuable and versatile resource. It is extremely unlikely that I would have been able to find my war buddies without them. At least the task would have been enormously more difficult than it turned out to be. The directory I used is *Switchboard.com*. It is basically a giant online phone directory containing everybody in the country who has a telephone listing. It is available at

www.switchboard.com

The site prompts you for first name, last name, and city and/or state. But be careful. Your skill with this site can determine whether or not you find the correct person. For example, when searching for a GI named Thomas D. Orton, I tried all of the following:

Thomas D Orton
Thomas Orton
Tom D Orton
Tom Orton
T Orton
T D Orton

I did this because people are often listed under shortened versions of their names, under their initials, or even under misspellings.

Also, keep in mind that you can search for an initial instead of a full first name. With uncommon names, this can be very useful. For example, searching for "T Orton" yielded

> Toddy Orton
> T J Orton
> Thomas Orton
> Thomas D Orton

If the person has a very common name that yields thousands of hits, try searching by home state if you know it. If you were looking for Terrance Harrison from Sturgis, South Dakota, you would get

T Harrison (in the entire U.S.)	yields 6,000 listings
Terrance Harrison (in the entire U.S.)	yields 550 listings
Terrance Harrison in South Dakota	yields 25 listings
Terrance Harrison in Sturgis, South Dakota	yields 2 listings

Narrowing your search might seem like common sense, but it is sometimes easy to forget. Put some thought into how you phrase your search.

If you hit a dead end, do not despair. Be creative in how you search for things. Let's say your search for Terrance Harrison in Sturgis, South Dakota, came up empty. Try searching by the last name only; people didn't move around as much fifty years ago as they do today. If searching for

First Name: _____   City: Sturgis_____
Last Name: Harrison_____   State: SD_____

yields only one listing with the same last name—Wendy Harrison—you may still be in luck. Give this person a call and tell her what you are doing. It might not be the Terrance Harrison you were looking for, but it may end up being his cousin or perhaps his ex-wife who tells you that Terrance retired to Florida. And even if Wendy doesn't know Terrance, if you show a little enthusiasm and a touch of despair, she might take up your cause. "Well, I don't know him. But I do know Mrs. Sherman. She's ninety-four years old, and she knows *everybody* in the town. I can go ask her if she knew a Terrance Harrison and then give you a call back."

In addition to *Switchboard.com*, some other Internet white pages sites include

www.ussearch.com

people.yahoo.com
www.whitepages.com

The first site, *www.ussearch.com*, has a feature for searching by age. However, there is a modest charge for information other than names and ages. The charge might be worth paying, but even if you choose not to pay for the additional information, it does not hurt to search so that you can find out which of the ten people you found on *Switchboard.com* are in the correct age range for your veteran.

The last site, *www.whitepages.com*, allows you to search by address. Even if your veteran moved out of the house fifty years ago, it might not hurt to call the telephone number of the house where he used to live. One woman I corresponded with found one of her father's war buddies this way. She wrote:

> I got stuck on a few names, and decided to take a chance. I looked up the old address without the name. I then made calls: "Hello, this is really odd, but I am looking for Mr. Andrew Murph, and he used to own your house…" If you tell folks you are looking for your father's buddies, they will do anything for you. In this instance, these folks knew nothing of the Murphs, but told me, "Call Katie down the block, she is 90 and knows everyone." I called Katie, and she knew Andrew's sister and gave me her number, and she put me in touch with his kids.

IS HE DECEASED?

IF YOUR SEARCH ON SWITCHBOARD.COM does not turn up any hits, you might want to determine if the person you are looking for is deceased.

The *Social Security Death Index* (SSDI) lists all deceased persons who had previously registered with the Social Security Administration. It gives the deceased person's name, date of birth, date of death, Social Security number, last known residence, and state where his or her Social Security number was issued. There are several websites that have this database; two of them are

ssdi.genealogy.rootsweb.com
www.ancestry.com

These sites also have advanced search options for searching by home state, date, or other criteria. Keep in mind, though, that the list contains sixty-six million names, so try to narrow down your search. And, don't write somebody off just because somebody with a similar name is listed there.

The Death Index can be useful for tracking down family members of deceased people. If you look up the name of the person based on home state, the index will give the place of death. You can then use this to search for family members in the area with the same name, and, if you are successful, you might enlist their help with the search for your veteran's war story.

TO PHONE OR TO WRITE

ONCE YOU HAVE FOUND THE name and address of a person you want to contact, you must decide whether to call or to write.

When I first found names and addresses of men who had served in the 978th, it took all my restraint to keep from calling them immediately. However, I knew that I needed to approach the matter carefully; my chances for a favorable reply would be better, I thought, if I took the time to think about how to approach them in a way that would bring about a favorable reply. In addition, you never get a second chance to make a first impression; if you manage to alienate your subject at the beginning, it can be difficult or impossible to rectify the situation later.

A well-thought-out letter will allow you to control your presentation in a nonthreatening way. It will also give your veteran or other source time to consider your request in a safe environment with less risk of misunderstanding. You can follow up with a phone call a few days later after the veteran has had time to digest the letter and fully understand what you are doing.

I made first contact with my grandfather's war buddies by sending a letter along with some photos. Although I insisted that they should not feel any obligation to reply, the overall response I received was very positive. Two years into my search, I did follow up with telephone calls to many of the people I had never heard from. In most of these cases, the addresses and telephone numbers were incorrect. However, several times the address had been correct but the GI said that either he had never received the letter or he was just too old to write—but nonetheless he was glad I called. And I regretted not having called sooner.

However, there are times when "cold calling" is necessary. If you have fifty names and addresses for a single person you are trying to locate, it would take a long time to send letters to each of them. In these cases, cold calling is the only option. However, you must be very careful how you approach the subject. Make it clear from the beginning who you are, what your possible relationship with the person is, and what you are trying to do. Never call and start asking questions without an introduction or explanation. It will raise suspicions. And in this age of telemarketers, people may hang up on you.

Also, keep in mind that widows can get nervous. Receiving a telephone call from a person asking for a husband who has been dead for thirty years can be a little disconcerting. When an elderly woman answered one of my cold calls, I gave her my name and quickly made it clear what my connection was and what I was looking for. I wanted her to know immediately that my call was legitimate and considerate. Once this woman and others knew that my intentions were genuine and honorable, most were very friendly and flattered that somebody was interested in their deceased loved one. Several of them sent me photos.

Whichever strategy you choose to make contact with sources, the most important thing to remember is to be respectful. You are looking to open delicate, complex, and often painful memories. Think about the most difficult time in your life and all the associated emotions involved. Would you really want some stranger poking around those feelings? Veterans often feel the same way about their time in the war. You might find, as I did, that these veterans are now more ready than ever to discuss their experiences. But if you do not have their trust, they will shut you out immediately—and you will never have a chance to get back in. Out of respect for these men—and in the best interests of your search—take the time to do things right.

THE CONTACT LETTER

WHEN MAKING CONTACT WITH A potential source, the contact letter is the most important part of your communication. How you word the letter will most likely play a large part in whether or not you get a reply.

Some points to keep in mind with respect to your letter:

- Keep it short, shorter than one page if possible.
- In the first paragraph identify who you are and what you want.
- Say where you got the person's address.
- Be honest.
- Speak from the heart.
- If you are planning on making a follow-up call, say so.
- Show genuine empathy for the person's situation and feelings, but do not say you know how they feel; you don't.
- Make sure your contact information is on the letter itself; attached papers and cards can get lost.

You might want to enclose copies of any relevant photos you have. I sent copies of the photos of my grandfather and his buddies. Quick-print photos are readily available and affordable, and you can fit quite a few on a single page. Also, enclosing a self-addressed stamped envelope increases your chances of a response.

FINDING PEOPLE OVERSEAS

FINDING PEOPLE OVERSEAS IS NOT as hard as you might think. Almost all small towns in Europe and many in Korea, Vietnam, and the Middle East have a Web page, and many of these pages have a guestbook. Make a post in the guestbook explaining what you are looking for, and send some e-mails to the city council members. People everywhere are fascinated by wartime history, and you are sure to find somebody who will know something or take up your cause and ask around. I made a posting on the Web page of the small town of Gedern in Germany, where Tommy Kulick was killed, asking if anybody might have some information on the memorial service the 978th held for him the morning after his death. My post was a long shot, as the 978th passed through Gedern quite quickly and did not have much contact with civilians. Nevertheless, I received e-mails from two people in Gedern who tried to help me. We did not have any luck finding a connection to the 978th's time there, but one of these people, Uwe Bergheimer, was nice enough to translate my homepage about my search into German, which I put on the Internet.

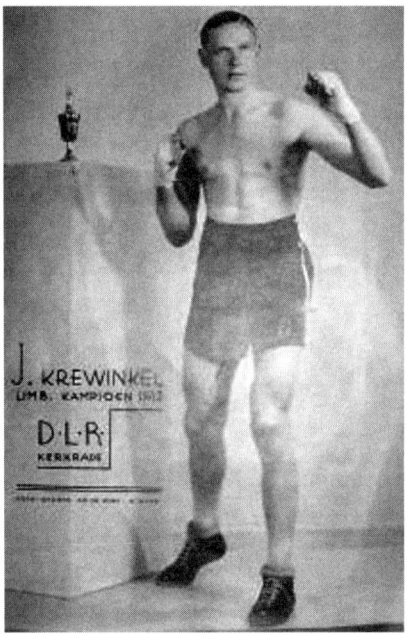

Figure 121. J. Krewinkel, the Dutch fighter who boxed my grandfather in Ski's exhibition boxing match at the beer hall.
(Photo courtesy of Leon, from his detective work)

MEDALS

VETERANS AND NEXT-OF-KIN FAMILY MEMBERS who want to order replacement medals can do so easily. Regardless of the branch of the military he or she served in, you will need to fill out Standard Form SF-180 and mail it in. The form can be downloaded at

www.archives.gov/veterans/military-service-records/replacement-medals.html

OTHER RESOURCES

IF YOU HIT A SNAG while using the search channels I have listed, or if you want to delve deeper into military records, you may want to consult one of the following books:

1. *Finding Your Father's War: A Practical Guide to Researching and Understanding Service in the World War II US Army*, by Jonathan Gawne. Recently published, probably the best book out there.

2. *How to Locate Anyone Who Is or Has Been in the Military*, by Lt. Col. Richard S. Johnson and Debra Johnson Knox. This is a somewhat dry but extremely thorough reference book for serious researchers and/or tough cases.

3. *World War II Military Records: A Family Historian's Guide*, by Debra Johnson Knox. This is a very thorough, Internet-focused guide to WWII records, with lots of information on different types of medals and how to obtain them.

4. *Touchstones: A Guide to Records, Rights and Resources for Families of American World War II Casualties*, by Ann Bennett Mix. Mrs. Mix, whose father was killed in Italy in 1945, is the founder of the American War Orphans Network (AWON). AWON is active in giving support to WWII orphans, which total an estimated 183,000 children in the U.S. If your father died in WWII, this book and this organization are definitely for you. This book is available from AWON at *www.awon.org*.

5. *Dad's War: A Workshop on Finding and Telling Your Father's World War II Story*, by W. Wesley Johnston, MA. This seventy-two-page booklet provides down-to-earth instructions on how to find and tell your veteran's war story, along with information on finding maps, books, and government records such as after-action reports. It is short on Internet resources but has lots information on traditional research routes. This book is available from the publisher at *members.aol.com/dadswar*.

6. *World War II Resources on the Internet*, by Roland H. Worth Jr. A comprehensive reference that lists the URLs for almost 3,000 WWII-related websites by subject matter. Good for finding sites related to a specific unit, campaign, or group.

7. *World War on the Web: A Guide to the Very Best Sites*, by J. Douglas Smith and Richard Jensen. A small, selective list of WWII-related sites. The authors actually visited these sites and have chosen them as being the best on the Internet. They provide a useful summary of each site, with ratings on content, aesthetics, and navigation. Good for finding interesting sites but not a strong source for research material.

Caveat

Always keep in mind that there are a few unethical and misdirected individuals and websites on the Internet. If you are contacted by somebody professing an interest in your research, take a minute to ask them some questions and feel them out. Do not stay in the homes of strangers you meet on the Internet. Not everybody is as kind, gentle, and genuine as Leon. I did not have a single bit of trouble in my search or my travels, but that doesn't mean I couldn't have. If you make contact with somebody and it just doesn't feel right, it probably isn't. Do not let the possibility of insincere or exploitive encounters inhibit you in carrying out your search, but do stay alert.

Also, beware of imposters (several prominent people have been exposed for lying about their Vietnam service) and extreme revisionist sites (for example, those that deny that the Holocaust happened). And finally, with the exception of fees for obtaining official government records through official channels, do not give anybody money for information that they might provide you. Everything I found was made possible through the goodwill of people I met.

SUCCESS STORIES

AFTER I PUT UP MY Internet page about my search, I received thousands of e-mails and corresponded with many people who also searched for information on a friend or family member's war story. I found two of them particularly interesting and have put them here as an example of the type of information that can be found, the methods used, and the ease of finding this information.

Finding Great-Uncle Kueker's Story at Normandy

Brian Kueker, forty-seven, is a real-estate investment manager in Dallas, Texas, and the father of three children. While reading about his family's genealogy in a notebook that he had received from a cousin, Kueker noticed that his grandfather's cousin, Arthur F. Kueker, had been killed in Normandy on June 14, 1944, and was buried at the Normandy American Cemetery. The notebook did not provide any more details about Arthur Kueker's death.

Kueker said, "I thought back to the opening and closing scenes in the cemetery in *Saving Private Ryan* and wondered if there might be something on the Internet." Going online, he quickly found the American Battle Monuments Commission website. Brian entered his uncle's name, and sure enough, up came his listing:

> Arthur F. Kueker Entered Service from Colorado
> Staff Sergeant, U.S. Army   Died: June 14, 1944
> 18070999   Buried at: Plot F Row 21 Grave 42
> 357th Infantry Regiment, 90th Infantry Division
> Normandy American Cemetery
> St. Laurent-sur-Mer, France
> Awards: Silver Star, Purple Heart

Brian was pleasantly surprised, "Wow! Look at this! Just like the family genealogy said!" The ABMC website said that the next of kin could order a photograph of the grave. Although he was not exactly next of kin, Brian figured that since he had the same last name, he would give it a try. He downloaded, completed, and submitted the application form.

Having no idea how long it would take to receive the photo, and now in possession of the additional details about his uncle's military experience from the ABMC site, Brian started looking on the Internet for information about the 90th Division and the 357th Regiment. He found the Center for Military History's text of the 90th Division History, which included a description of the 357th's action on June 14:

> The 357th Infantry, on the right flank of the 359th, also encountered difficulties. On 14 June it prepared to attack Gourbesville again, its objective being the Gourbesville-Beauvais line. An air mission arranged for 1400 was canceled for lack of proper marking smoke, and an artillery preparation was substituted at 1800. Because of poor coordination, a number of shells fell on American troops and the attack became disorganized. The concentration was fired again at 1930 and the 3d Battalion entered the village at 2230. It was unable, however, to clean out enemy resistance that night, and Gourbesville remained in enemy hands.

Brian thought that this must have been where Arthur was killed. The 90th Division history included maps that showed the regiment's location every twenty-four hours. Brian could not determine whether Arthur had died as a result of action on the 14th or action that actually occurred earlier. He just knew that this was the 90th's position on the day Arthur died.

A few months later, Brian received two eighteen-by-twenty-four-inch lithographs of the memorial at the cemetery with three-by-five photos of Arthur's grave overlaid in the lower-right-hand corner. Brian said, "They were magnificent and more than I ever expected."

These images were so impressive that Brian decided to see if anybody in Arthur's family in Colorado would want one. He checked the family genealogy again and discovered that Arthur had two sisters, Clara Marie and Esther. Using an Internet phone book, he found the name and address of the younger sister and sent her a letter explaining his entire venture.

A few days later he received a call from Clara, who said that she and her sister were the only ones left in the family and that they never knew any details about their brother's death. They said they would be delighted to receive the lithograph. Brian mailed it to them.

Clara also said that she and her sister almost fell out of their chairs when they saw the ABMC printout showing that Arthur had been awarded the Silver Star. They had never heard anything about it and wondered if it was a mistake. Brian said he would do some checking. In the meantime, Clara received the lithograph and proudly hung it up the same day.

Brian went to work trying to find out more about the medals. He told the story to a buddy, Ira, a fellow adult leader in his son's Boy Scout troop and retiree of the 101st Airborne. Ira said that it could have been a bureaucratic mistake or that the medal went to the parents. Or, since one of the stages of grief is anger, they may have discarded it. Ira took the liberty of contacting the 90th Division Association and discovered that it soon would be holding its annual reunion in Little Rock. In the meantime, Brian had confirmed that Arthur had indeed been awarded the Silver Star and arranged for the entire family, including Clara and Esther, to attend the reunion, where a replacement medal would be presented to them.

In the meantime, Brian contacted the U.S. Locator Service to try to find Arthur's military records. He was informed that they had been destroyed in the fire of 1973. He then tried the only other two places that might have something: the IDPF and the National Archives, Modern Military Records, in College Park, Maryland, which keeps regimental unit histories. He hoped to find Arthur's name on a Morning Report or an After Action Report.

The reunion was approaching and Brian wanted to have additional details about his uncle before the big event. He sent another letter to the National Archives, explaining the urgency of the situation. A few weeks later he received a reply, which included a copy of General Orders, No. 31, dated 31 July 1944. It was the Silver Star, awarded posthumously to Arthur, with details of his actions:

> S Sgt Arthur F. Kueker, 18070999, Inf, United States Army. On June 14, 1944, Sgt Kueker and one man advanced against a mortar and a machine gun position that were holding up their unit with intense fire. Sgt Kueker and his companion, without thought of personal safety, worked their way to a point from which they knocked out the mortars with hand grenades. Then, having no more hand grenades, they turned upon the machine gun position and assaulted it with their bayonets. In the ensuing action Sgt Kueker was killed. By his gallantry and aggressiveness, Sgt Kueker made possible the continued success of his unit.

Brian read the words in awe and said, "Now we know . . . 'having no more hand grenades, they turned upon the machine gun position and assaulted it with their bayonets.' I had to wonder what makes men do extraordinary things at times like these."

The 90th's reunion came, and Brian got to meet Clara and Esther. A large photo of Arthur hung on the stage as the Silver Star was awarded to the sisters. Later, Brian said:

> The most amazing thing about this last year is the way so many people have responded with information, referrals, stories, etc. People would send me little bits of information from websites, bulletin boards, family histories, research they had done. It was like a puzzle. Sometimes the meaning of a particular piece wasn't clear until it was in the context of other pieces. I would go back and reread things that I had been over before and something different would then make sense.
>
> The main thing though, after all is said and done, is that two sisters from Colorado, for whom I am sure their big brother was always a hero, now know that he was a hero to the rest of us too!

Figure 122. Photo and grave marker of Arthur F. Kueker. Normandy American Cemetery, St. Laurent-sur-Mer, France.

Kurt Stauffer and the Envelope

Another person I corresponded with after he found my Web page was Kurt Stauffer. He told me about his project over the phone and through e-mails.

> I've always been interested in WWII history. In grade school I began to read books about the war, and many of my book reports were about the subject. I also collected stamps and coins. As I grew older, my interest in WWII history combined with my collecting habits, and I grew into collecting and preserving WWII memorabilia. I'd buy a Purple Heart at a flea market and track down the story of the guy who received it. I'd get the IDPF [Individual Deceased Personnel File] and read the details about the action when he died. A medal's just a piece of metal unless you have a person and a story to go with it. One time I bought a Purple Heart on eBay, and just from the name on the medal I was able to track down a photo of this soldier. Another time I found a Purple Heart and an Air Medal of a VF-17 pilot [U.S. Navy Fighting Squadron 17] from a pawnshop in Reno. The pilot was killed in action and I tracked down some history concerning him written by a guy who served in the same unit. The guy said he was the worst pilot in the outfit and that it didn't surprise him that he was shot down. He said he was a "tail-end Charlie."
>
> Occasionally I track down family members of the soldier who had received the medal. Normally they are the people who sold it in the first place. One time a soldier's medals were stolen. I tracked down the soldier's son. He was elated to get them back. Sometimes I'm at a garage sale and some guy tells me he just threw away his grandfather's WWII photos, saying that nobody wanted them. Crazy. I've dug through dumpsters to get these things.
>
> In 1994 I attended a show in Seattle for stamp collectors. I don't collect stamps anymore. Instead I look for WWII prisoner-of-war letters and postcards. On this occasion I found postcards from an American POW, John J. Hummel, sent from the Zentsuji Prisoner of War Camp in Japan to his wife in Seattle. The first card was written on August 5, 1943. It was only a few words. The Japanese limited the number of words to fifty, and later to twenty-five. On the card he said the last piece of mail he'd received from home was in November of 1941. So he was without word from home for almost two years.

That piqued my interest not only because they were from my home state of Washington but also because they were sent to his wife: "Attention University of Washington Wind Tunnel." I knew a research project was in front of me and I purchased the cards.

This was in the days before the Internet was popular, so that weekend I visited the Seattle Public Library. I began a search for articles in the local Seattle papers that mentioned 2nd Lt. John J. Hummel. I knew from experience that the library kept a file of articles specifically about local solders and that they were sorted by year from WWII. I started with 1942, knowing that when Bataan fell, an article would have been printed announcing that Hummel was an MIA and then later a POW when they found that out.

I found two! I also looked through 1945, knowing there would be an article announcing when he was liberated. Sure enough, I found it. The articles detailed his service in Company D of the 194th Tank Battalion. John was a tank commander. His unit, composed mostly of National Guardsmen from Minnesota, was transferred to the Philippines in September 1941, where it was placed near Clark Field to protect it from attack. When the Japanese began their attack on the Philippines, the 194th left for the Bataan Peninsula. John's unit fought on Bataan for five months, until their surrender on April 9, 1942. John was later captured on Corregidor and survived the war as a POW in Japan.

The newspaper articles told about John's marriage to his college sweetheart, Nell, ten days before he left for the war. During the war, Nell, an aeronautical engineer, did research at the University of Washington Wind Tunnel for Boeing. She later got word that John was missing in action. She didn't learn of her husband's fate for another three months, when she learned that he was a POW in the Philippines. He stayed there for six months and was later sent to a POW camp in Japan. After one year he was able to send a photo of himself with other POWs. But that didn't arrive until a year later. He'd eventually spend almost three years in the POW camp in Japan, during which time his young wife received only three pieces of mail, although he mailed many more. They were finally reunited, right after their fourth anniversary.

After looking up all this information, I got to wondering: Is John still alive? I grabbed a copy of the local phone book and found a John J. Hummel in Arlington, just sixty miles north of me.

I called the number and John answered. I began to explain the purpose of my call. There was some hesitation in his voice and he passed the phone to his wife. I found out John was suffering from Alzheimer's but was still capable of discussing his experiences as a POW. I mentioned to his wife about the postcards and she put John back on the line. He got on the phone and said, "So you got my postcards, huh? It's amazing you found them." Then he said with a laugh, "I'm guessing my ***** ex-wife must've sold them after the divorce!"

We set up a time to meet. He said he didn't want the postcards back. He said that I could keep them but that he would like a copy of them. A few weeks later my wife and I drove up to Arlington to meet John and his wife, Caroline, for lunch at their house. John and Caroline were married after her first husband, who also had been a POW, passed away.

John proceeded to tell me about his experiences as a POW. He was a tank commander and had served throughout the Bataan campaign, earning a Silver Star and a Purple Heart. On December 27, 1941, John's tank was hit by Japanese machine-gun fire. He was seriously wounded and spent the next two weeks in an army hospital in San Fernando. He returned to his company, which was suffering an acute shortage of food. His commanding officer assigned John's company to furnish rations for the entire battalion, and John became, in his own words, "Chief Caribou Rustler." For several months he continued fighting the Japanese and scrounging for food until Bataan was surrendered by the Americans on April 9. When Bataan fell, John wanted to continue to fight, so he and his sergeant, Aaron Hopper, decided to try to make it across the water to Corregidor. They tied an empty five-gallon gas can to each end of a hospital stretcher to make a makeshift raft, entered the water two miles south of Cabcaben, and began swimming across Manila Bay. The odds of making it were slim, two miles through shark-infested waters with strong currents. John and Aaron were picked up by the water tender *Vega*, a small U.S. Navy ship, and were taken to the dock at Corregidor. John was assigned to an M.P. company and lost track of Aaron. Their trip across the water had earned John and Aaron a few weeks of freedom. But then the Americans at Corregidor were forced to surrender, and he was finally shipped to a POW comp, where he spent several years before being liberated in 1945. He never heard from Aaron again.

John told me, "I've always wondered what happened to Aaron. I don't even know if he survived the war." I told him, "Give me a few days and I'll find out."

A few years earlier I had received a copy of the WWII Repatriation List, which the National Archives maintains. It's now available online at *aad.archives.gov/aad*. I knew that if Aaron survived, he'd be on the list. Sure enough, there he was! The list also provided the state he had enlisted from. I figured if he was still alive, I could find out where he lived. This was before the days of the Internet, so I made another trip to the local library to use their microfiche phonebooks. I found Aaron, still living in the same general area where he'd enlisted fifty years earlier.

I called John's wife and gave her the number, telling her John would be happy to know his buddy survived. A few days later John called Aaron, closing a chapter on his life that had gnawed at him for years. What they discussed is known only to them.

John passed away in 1997 from the effects of Alzheimer's. Aaron passed away in 2000. I was very proud and honored to get to spend time with John while he was still able to talk about his experiences in the war. These men and women from "our greatest generation" are heroes, and I treasure every moment I can spend with them. Soon they all will be gone.

It's amazing that two seemingly insignificant postcards could start a journey that would reunite a pair of old soldiers who had no idea if the other survived and that would give me so much satisfaction in learning the story associated with them. To be able to help John and Aaron find each other after all those years is a small feat compared to the sacrifice they made during WWII. I felt it was my responsibility to do it.

Figure 121. The envelope that started the search.

WHERE TO FROM HERE?

THE INFORMATION I HAVE GIVEN here will get you started doing your own research on a family member's war story. If you don't find what you are looking for in these pages, keep looking. There is such a vast amount of information on the Internet, with new sites coming online every day, that creativity, curiosity, and perseverance will be your greatest tools.

Finding information about a family member's experiences in war can be an extremely rewarding experience. I wish you the best of luck in your search—and whatever surprises come your way, I hope they are pleasant ones. Please feel free to keep me posted on what you find.

Good luck!

Jeffrey A. Badger
Austin, Texas USA
www.jbadger.com
badgerjeffrey@hotmail.com

BIBLIOGRAPHY

Ambrose, Stephen E. *Citizen Soldiers: The U.S. Army from the Normandy Beaches to the Bulge to the Surrender of Germany*. New York: Simon & Schuster, 1997.

Brokaw, Tom. *The Greatest Generation*. New York: Random House, 1998.

Collins, Julia. *My Father's War*. New York: Four Walls Eight Windows, 2002.

Conquer, The Story of the Ninth Army. Washington, D.C.: Infantry Journal Press, 1947.

Critchell, Laurence. *Four Stars of Hell*. Nashville, TN: Battery Press, 1982.

D-Day in South Limburg: Diary of the Liberation. Maastricht, the Netherlands: Uitgeversmaatschappij De Limburger BV.

Fussell, Paul. *Doing Battle: The Making of a Skeptic*. New York: Little Brown & Co., 1996.

Fussell, Paul. *Wartime: Understanding and Behavior in the Second World War*. New York: Oxford University Press, 1989.

Gawne, Jonathan. *Finding Your Father's War: A Practical Guide to Researching and Understanding Service in the World War II US Army*. Drexel Hill, PA: Casemate, 2006.

Graves, Robert. *Good-Bye to All That: An Autobiography*. London: Penguin Books, 1960.

Gray, J. Glenn. *The Warriors: Reflections on Men in Battle*. Lincoln, NE: University of Nebraska Press, 1998.

Hedges, Chris. *War Is a Force That Gives Us Meaning*. New York: Public Affairs, 2002.

Hewitt, Robert T. *Workhorse of the Western Front: The Story of the 30th Infantry Division*. Nashville, TN: Battery Press, 1980.

Johnson, Richard S., and Debra Johnson Knox. *How to Locate Anyone Who Is or Has Been in the Military*. Spartanburg, SC: MIE Publishing. 1995.

Johnston, W. Wesley. *Dad's War: A Workshop on Finding and Telling your Father's World War II Story*. San Ramon, CA: author. Nd.

Knox, Debra Johnson. *World War II Military Records: A Family Historian's Guide.* Spartanburg, SC: MIE Publishing, 2003.

MacDonald, Charles B. *Company Commander: The Classic Infantry Memoir of World War II.* Washington, D.C: Infantry Journal Press, 1947.

Mauldin, Bill. *Up Front.* New York: Bantam Books, 1945.

Megellas, James. *All the Way to Berlin: A Paratrooper at War in Europe.* Novato, CA: Presidio Press, 2003.

Merrill, Sandra D. *Donald's Story.* Stockton, MD: Tebidine, 1996.

Mix, Ann Bennett. *Touchstones: A Guide to Records, Rights and Resources for Families of American World War II Casualties.* Bountiful, UT: Midmarch Arts Pr, 1996.

Moore, Deborah Dash. *GI Jews: How World War II Changed a Generation.* Cambridge, MA: Belknap Press, 2004.

Pamp, Captain Frederic E. *Normandy to the Elbe: XIX Corps.* Reproduced by 62d Engr Topo Co.

Pyle, Ernie. *Brave Men.* Lincoln, NE: University of Nebraska Press/Bison Books, 2001.

Richmond, Peter. *My Father's War.* New York: Simon & Schuster, 1996.

Rush, Robert S. *Hell in Hurtgen Forest: The Ordeal and Triumph of an American Infantry Regiment.* Lawrence: University Press of Kansas, 2001.

Shinn, Roger Lincoln. *Wars and Rumors of Wars.* Nashville, TN: Abingdon Press, 1972.

Smith, J. Douglass, and Richard Jensen. *World War on the Web: A Guide to the Very Best Sites.* Wilmington, DE: Scholarly Resources, 2002.

Snell, Theron P. Orphans in the Storm: A Collective Experience of War. The 978th Engineer Maintenance Company in World War II. Ph.D. dissertation. University of Minnesota, 1997. Available from University of Michigan Dissertation Services, 800-521-0600.

Terkel, Studs. The *Good War: An Oral History of World War II.* New York: Random House, 1985.

Torgovnick, Marianna. *The War Complex: World War II in Our Time.* Chicago: University of Chicago Press, 2005.

Worth, Roland H. Jr. *World War II Resources on the Internet.* Jefferson, NC: McFarland & Company, 2002.